Racial Tensions and National Identity

Proceedings of the Second Annual

Vanderbilt Sociology Conference

November 4-6, 1970

Vanderbilt University

Nashville, Tennessee

Racial Tensions and National Identity

Edited by

Ernest Q. Campbell

VANDERBILT UNIVERSITY PRESS
Nashville • 1972

Library of Congress Cataloguing-in-Publication Data
Vanderbilt Sociology Conference, 2d, Nashville, 1970.
    Racial tensions and national identity.
    Includes bibliographies.
    1. Race problems—Congresses. 2. Nationalism—Congresses. I. Campbell, Ernest
    Queener, ed. II. Title.
HT1505.V37   1970   301.45   70-185873
ISBN O-8265-1179-1

Printed in the United States of America by Western Publishing Co., Hannibal, Missouri

Acknowledgments

This conference was made possible by a grant to the Department of Sociology and Anthropology, Vanderbilt University, from the National Science Foundation.

Special contributions of Dr. Alice Withrow, of the National Science Foundation; Mrs. Robert L. Weaver, who served as conference secretary; and Professor Stanley Smith, who advised on conference participants and procedures are also gratefully acknowledged.

Contents

Preface

This book contains papers read at a conference on racial tensions and national identity held at Vanderbilt University on November 4-6, 1970, under financial aid of the National Science Foundation. The conference was sponsored by the Department of Sociology and Anthropology, Vanderbilt University, and I was its organizer.

In the conference format, two commentaries were scheduled following each paper, and in most instances those too are included in this volume; unfortunately, several were not made available to us in written form and could not be included.

The introduction, which follows, describes the purpose of the conference and certain issues and themes that emerged during and from it.

The chapters are presented here in a sequence somewhat different from the order in which they were read at the conference.

Nashville, Tennessee
April 1971

Ernest Q. Campbell

Racial Tensions and National Identity

Editor's Overview
and Introduction

THESE CHAPTERS aim collectively to contribute to a growing and needed literature on comparative race relations. Those preoccupied with issues of the here and now have much to learn, and needed perspective to gain, from studies that deal with the distribution of racial structures in time and space.

These papers, and the conference at which they were presented and discussed, are essentially case studies—although the "case" may be a rather large set of African countries (as in the chapter by Wallerstein) or such a city as Nottingham, England (see the chapter by Katznelson). They are not, individually, comparative; each author takes a racially significant political unit or contiguous units and analyzes segments of its race structure that seem to him significant. But in sum they inform the reader in analytical terms about important race-relevant structures and processes in some of the world's most crucial areas. This is not the only model that might be taken by a set of essays preoccupied with race relations in comparative perspective. Alternative styles could concern themselves with abstract theory and conceptual schemes, or with the task of specifying general empirical processes that operate whenever races are in significant contact. Each has its advantages, its distinctive contribution. A word of explanation as to our choice is in order.

The case method, followed here, allows a more intensive attention to a particular society at a particular time, and to particular historic processes, than is possible when one's purpose is to abstract the general processes that operate across sets of reality or to define and distinguish the conceptual apparatus that may prove useful in comprehending racial contact wherever it appears. As well, it seemed in planning the conference that we had an opportunity to involve

3

scholars whose prior work was not principally on race relations as such, rather whose careers and reputations focussed on area studies or on disciplines in which race was not a primary concept. I, often distressed because race as a subject of study has drawn the serious attention of far too few scholars, was immensely attracted by the prospect that experts whose prior work rested on other topics would bring their immense knowledge to bear on the subject of race. The task of eliminating redundancy among the authors, when planning had to be carried out at long distance and the participants could not meet with each other prior to the conference itself, seemed vastly simpler if each dealt with a separate segment of the globe. Finally, I must acknowledge my own belief that we have had in the social sciences, most of all in my own discipline of sociology, far too much searching for comprehensive explanatory schemes and far too little careful attention to the structure and dynamics of particular circumstances: relationships, families, issues, organizations, neighborhoods, communities, national states. From such considerations came the choice of a case approach.

It is customary for a conference to have a theme, and this one is no exception: the theme, as carried in the title of this volume, was racial tensions and national identity. It is altogether necessary, even when a general theme is set, to allow the conference content to reflect what the participating scholars are prepared to do; the risk is too great otherwise that the autonomy and hence the best creative insights of the author are lost. A theme, then, is a loose directive intended to point the way in a general manner and to raise certain topics which each writer may consider for possible coverage in his paper. So in the present instance: we identified some critical world areas of racial contact and asked the specialist for a given area to consider such topics as schism and conflict; the allocation of power, privilege, and other resources; forms and goals of protest, and modes of control and response; secession, independence, and relocation themes; host countries and migrant pressures; the definitional and labeling processes that determine who is considered to be what, racially speaking; identity and other preservative themes; styles of accommodation or absorption; emergent patterns and prospects for the future. Over-all, the preoccupying issue, so I intended, would be the effect of race structures on the capacity of a people to commit themselves psychologically, in the form of loyalty and obligation, to the nation-state in which they reside. Obviously, a host of variables makes one situation differ from another—England with its long history of white residence and the recent arrival of colored migrants in still relatively small pro-portions is quite different from South Africa with its native black majority and a government not empowered by nor acting to secure the loyalty of that majority—and no author would find all these topics equally provocative and appropriate. We expected, then, to achieve some common concerns across the papers but to avoid a sterile con-sistency by making each author the judge of what his paper should cover. Authors were advised that although comment on contemporary headlines would be appropriate, focus should be on historical pro-cesses and basic matters.

It remains for the reader to decide whether we achieved a desir-able coherence within diversity. Certainly the papers pursue different paths, and we cannot expect continuity and development of theme from one author to the next; thus, Wallerstein's concern with whether and for what analytical purposes the terms *race* and *racism* are even needed in conceptual social science, and Saunders's careful destruction of the myth that skin-color is irrelevant to the fate that awaits the resident of Brazil, are both distinctive contributions to our under-standing, but they are far from being mirror-images.

In what follows immediately below, I review certain themes and issues that were recurrent not only in the formal papers but as well in the informal commentary and discussions among participants. One adds his own preoccupations, his own sense of what's important, to what he hears, and I would not pretend that I am able to give, nor do I wish to give merely a stenographic rendition or an abstractor's digest of the proceedings. I want to discuss five recurrent issues.

Race: Essence or Epiphenomenon?

There is, first of all, and despite our relative disinterest in con-ceptual matters, the question of what race is, and how important it is, or has to be, in the affairs of man. There is, on the one hand, the view that race is an artificial construction forced upon the awareness of many by the colonial period in which West Europeans expanded their markets and their sources of raw materials. (Though, to be sure, race may perhaps be a basic social category not activated in our awareness until numerically and geographically extensive contact re-quires it to be so. That is, race might be *both* basic and often nascent.) Those who urge that we be color-blind, that we judge others by their performance or by other "relevant" criteria, seem to say of race that it not merely ought to be, but reasonably can be, a trivial epiphenome-non. Those fall into this category too who say that race and the emotions that accompany it are a kind of mythology, a false consciousness, whereas the true and critical relationships are between economic groups, i.e., those who relate in different ways to the means of production. There is the opposed, and equally vigorous, view that race is of the essence in the way man groups himself and where he places his loyalties. It is, that is to say, a primordial phenomenon, of which region and religion and language may be other such, operating as a primary source or magnet of loyalty and identification wherever men gather. Races, in terms used in Esman's chapter, are communal or solidary groupings, and we would expect boundary relationships to appear whenever those who can recognize themselves as physically different are in contact. Conceivably the relationships that evolve between racial groups will not be characterized by intense hostility and the subordination of one to the other (Hoetink, for instance, distinguishes vertical from horizontal stratification or segmentation), but race is nonetheless and always a primary loyalty and a basic universal source of human grouping and association.

It is transparently true that we are debating a critical matter, not simply playing with words. For example, if race is an irrational obsession or a passing fancy, the question of social strategy becomes one of how to persuade the public that we are, as it were, brothers under the skin. If, however, it is necessary to challenge a primordial identity to accomplish co-operation and an era of good feeling between Malay and Chinese in Malaysia or blacks and whites in the United States, if race is a basic schism or earth-fault that can be covered over, perhaps, but not removed, then the strategic question becomes that of discovering and publicizing what cohesions of similar fate, common experience, shared loyalties, and mutual goals can counter and compensate for the unavoidable adhesions of this primordial identity. Policies of assimilation versus policies of pluralism represent a less stark version of the same issue. How curiously appropriate to the issue is Booker T. Washington's oft-defiled proposal for proper race relations in the United States: As separate as the fingers, as together as the hand!

Simply put: Should a multiracial society aim for mutual dependence or for mutual deterrence?

Government: What Is Its Role?

As Katznelson comments, concerning the entry of race into the political process in England: "Competition for the allocation of scarce resources is a political process involving political decisions." So long as and wherever racial awareness accompanies racial contact, it must be expected that governments will institute policies that affect if they do not control distribution among the races of the facilities and perquisites of the society. It is sheer foolishness to contend that the government is either impotent or irrelevant; and where such claims are made, it is obvious that the government is aligned with the status quo. And as obviously, the control of the machinery of government will be one of the matters on which racial struggle and tension must invariably occur, and strategic decisions concerning how to appeal to and utilize the means of the state will require the attention of those who make protest against alleged racial injustice.

Empirically, we observe a large variety of practices and proposals concerning the role of government in dealing with the structure of race relations. Perhaps we will not do violence to the bewildering variety of real instances if we utilize a simple dichotomy: Governments engage in either rectifying racial inequality or in sustaining and creating specific privilege. In the latter case, they follow what may be called a "spoils of war" perspective, since essentially they operate as an arm or extension of whatever race is on top. In the former instance, government becomes an agent of forced change, a primary means of rectifying perceived injustices or inequalities. The matter of effectiveness is a different question altogether.

Both modes present us with immensely fascinating empirical instances. South Africa, analyzed in detail by Turk in this volume, is one of the most intriguing, and extreme, examples of the role of government in establishing, protecting, and extending privilege. Here, though the blacks constitute an overwhelming majority of those resident in the territory, they are hostages rather than clients of the national government, and this government does not act and is not committed to act either in their behalf or to secure their support; indeed, it intends to ignore rather than to reflect the wishes of this majority and exclusively to follow legislation and policy that protects and entrenches the favored position of the white minority. South Africa is unique in extent but not distinctive in direction among the nations of the world. (The use of government not to regulate contact and conduct when races already share the same territory, but to control and limit racial contact through restrictive immigration policy, is an interesting aspect of the issue, though not a subject for discussion in this volume.)

In the United States, the privileged race, which is accustomed historically to viewing the government as its own, is also the numerical majority. In South Africa, the privileged race, which continues to use the government as its own instrument, is distinctly a minority. There are other instances in which the majority race both controls the government and remains relatively unprivileged; these afford particularly interesting conceptions of the role of government in increasing privilege among those once dispossessed. Thus the Government of Kenya is engaged in removing Indians from the retail trade sector in order to extend the means of livelihood available to black citizens. And the Malays in Malaysia, Esman reports, contend that they must not be excluded from the modern sectors of the economy but that they cannot participate in this sector without vigorous government assistance because they are disadvantaged in training and experience. Of course, the theme of "treating us with special privilege in order to treat us equal" may appear even when the disadvantaged do not control the government and are not a numerical majority. Witness the present-day United States, where the demands of militant blacks for direct reparations, preferential treatment, open-admission colleges, etc., are articulated from the twin premises that past and present injustices must be rectified and that traditional, well-established criteria for appointment, admission, and advancement (such as grades, achievement tests, and the performance ratings of superiors) are themselves instruments that perpetuate inequality unjustly and unfairly.

In short, are we able even to imagine a government that deals fairly with all interests in a multiracial society?

Control: The Power to Label and Stereotype

Let us consider for a moment some of the ways in which two races, which preserve their identity over time, may relate to each other in the social system. Each may select its own leaders, or one may be able to confer leadership upon select representatives of the other. Each may feel proud of its (partly mythological) heritage and sustain views of the other that carry a negative valence, or A may persuade B of A's superiority and B's inferiority. One may create labels, images, myths, claims that are effectively parried by the other, or the labeling of both may be successfully accomplished by the one. And in those circumstances where it is evident that the one race possesses an excess of widely accepted virtues (e.g., more education, higher income), the other may emulate as fully and as quickly as possible or it may adopt alternate (not necessarily opposed) virtues of its own to emphasize.

In a word, there may be common acknowledgment that Race A is superior and in control, or the two may be in active competition for the same values, or the two may espouse and pursue somewhat different goals, sharing the same territory but sustaining reasonably distinctive social and cultural systems. Hoetink's distinction in this volume between vertical and horizontal pluralism catches much of this distinction.

Who (which race) imposes the labels—words and their valences? Who creates the stereotypes? Who selects the leaders? Katznelson points out that leaders in England's minority community are selected, or at least validated, by the white power structure, and are generally middle-class, nonrepresentative spokesmen who pursue an elite, consensual strategy that is inappropriate to the circumstances the minority faces. Kilson's essay makes the point that earlier black protest leaders in the United States sought economic gains for the bourgeois rather than political strength for all blacks, and that the new leaders reflect an ascendancy of lower-class (mass) criteria in legitimizing black leadership; even modern black intellectuals are sympathetic to a popular-based nationalist militancy that rejects the established intellectual style and is xenophobic to white society. Other authorities have noted that the earlier black leadership in the United States, at both national and community levels, required the endorsement of whites, and Kilson hints that this perhaps continues (more subtly, and attenuated) to be the case in that black radicals depend on white money to mount effective programs. At the more direct interpersonal level, we may note Saunders's observation that in Brazil the white does not select a black as friend and social companion. Perhaps an unavoidable tendency to see events from the perspective of whites sufficiently explains why subject and object are not reversed in his statement; i.e., a reversed statement would take the form, The black does not select the white as friend and social companion. Literally, both statements could be true. But in the total context of his analysis, it is far more likely that the right of the white to make friendship choices and the obligation of the black to acquiesce in these decisions without initiative of his own are fairly well established in the social system.

Such perquisites of choice are revealing clues to the system of race relations. Preference for the comforts and amenities of middle-class neighborhoods as against the slums, or for well-kept club facilities over dilapidated ones, may reasonably be regarded as natural and not to require explanation. But when it is the *company* of another that is considered, there are essential questions to be asked concerning who does the choosing, whether choices are reciprocated, whether choices are freely made, whether rejection occurs and is painful when it does occur, and what the actual patterns of interracial association are as to incidence and level of intimacy. Likewise, there are important questions as to whether races resident in the same nation-state share perceptual and value systems that impose labels and stereotypes, define the contours of interaction, and establish appropriate and accepted physical and social places for each race to occupy. And if such perceptual and value systems are shared, are they created and sustained by the free competition of both? Attention to these minutiae is essential to analyzing race relations in comparative perspective.

Loyalty: Commitment and Rootedness

It is in the interest of governments that those governed give positive commitment to the institutions, traditions, and practices of the constituted authority, and that the governed believe those who govern to be acting in their best interests. It is in the interest of the people that they believe themselves to be effective members of some larger whole, and that they have the satisfying experience of knowing their history, carrying on a tradition, and creating a shared future. Governments are threatened with revolt and revolution, passivity and impassivity, when those they govern willfully withhold or cannot willingly give their loyalty. People experience despair and anomia when they cannot take pride in heritage and do not anticipate a gratifying future. It is an unhappy moment for both the government and the people when there are residents who cannot obey the laws nor respect the symbols of the state. Defacement of national symbols such as flags and monuments, irreverent attitudes toward heroes and myths, forthright opposition to and reluctant compliance with duly enacted statutes, signify the inability of state officials to conduct the affairs of office in a way which allows the affected parties to give their loyalties and feel themselves a participating part.

The objection of oppressed races to the relationship between them and the territorial government is one of the most anguished cries of the twentieth century. Black exiles from South Africa write hauntingly of their loyalty to land and people but they defile as alien the constituted government of South Africa. Blacks in the United States, joined by many young whites, protest that the policies and practices of government defy their wish to be loyal and to participate. Asians and West Indians in England complain that a government so shrewdly indifferent to their interests deflects their natural impulses to be fully loyal and committed participants in the affairs of community and nation. Samkange's essay in this volume argues eloquently that a government of, by, and for the sons of the soil will eventually reign in Rhodesia (Zimbabwe) whereas now the policies of government incite rage and rebellion rather than loyalty and hope. Wallerstein in his paper makes clear that in a substantial set of African countries under native rule there are significant minorities, racially or tribally distinct, that regard the government as hostile to their interests and an alien body. Esman suggests that when Chinese in Malaysia do not hold political power even though they are an economically privileged segment, they have ambivalent attitudes toward the government and feel themselves strangers in an adopted land. Separatist blacks ask for a territory within the continental United States that can be theirs as a self-governed entity, since, they contend, a government established and run by whites lacks the capacity to be responsive to their needs and cannot command their loyalties nor gratify their need for commitment.

One widely used model of human social systems builds outwards from the individual to include ever larger units with which the individual identifies and to which he commits himself: friends and family, village and community, territory and region, tribe and nation. No model regards symmetry and harmony among all interests at these several levels as inevitable and total, but it is assumed that generally their interests are compatible and accreting, such that one's satisfactory involvement at one level makes more probable, not less, his involvement at another.

We see recurrent evidence that the multiracial state in the modern world has not solved the problem of articulating national awareness with racial awareness. Policies are not yet developed which allow the subject-citizens to experience loyalty to land, to government, and to race as mutually reinforcing emotions. It may well be true for some, for one dominant race which controls the land and the organs of state, but it is not generally true in the multiracial state that, whatever their race, its residents may experience the satisfying emotions of love of land, pride in nation, involvement, commitment, loyalty. How can this be accomplished? Where and to what will loyalty be given when it cannot reasonably be vested in established government? What are the longer-term consequences of the failure of government to secure the affection of blocs among the governed and of the inclination of the disaffected to say that this failure results from racist policies? What, if any, compromises and adaptations short of a utopian ideal may reasonably be expected of racial minorities when they do not share proportionately in the control of government? And what constraints on power can be exercised upon the governing race by those who are governed? It is obvious that the general form of these questions is important quite outside a racial context; the question of the proper articulation of mutual obligations between government and the governed is far more general and more historic. It happens, however, that in our time, in this century preoccupied by problems of color, race enters heavily into questions of where men can place their loyalties, and the policies of the nation are sensitively judged and responded to in terms of race. The search for rootedness, for permanent commitment to place and form, characterizes alike the powerful and the powerless, the possessor and the dispossessed, whether in Rhodesia or Harlem, Malaysia or London. The dispossessed or powerless prefer to say of wherever they are, This is my land, my place, my country; they would not freely choose to give allegiance to a distant place or an untried scheme, nor to withhold their loyalties altogether. Yet one dynamic base for repression and exploitation is precisely the fear among those who rule that, were this rule relaxed, they themselves would be the object of an excluding loyalty that contained reprisal and exploitation—especially when, as in South Africa, they are such a numerical minority.

Race: How Important Is It, Really?

We turn finally to discuss a question that is not easy to ask in the context of a set of essays devoted to emphasis on race as a real and powerful phenomenon in the modern world. Nor, quite aside from this, is the matter easily phrased so as to express its essence. We shall try to give the question a simple form and then expand upon it: Is race an important phenomenon in the affairs of man? Or may it be said that it is rather trivial, despite all the attention given it in this volume and in many other places?

Let it be emphasized, first, that the question is neither rhetorical nor regressive. It is worth more attention and debate than it has been given. It is beyond question that the United States is a racist society inasmuch as its people apply racial labels freely and divide the nation's goods most unequally by race. At least then for the sake of argument, and hopefully of edification, we may pose the question: For a representative black citizen of the United States, and a representative white, how significantly is what each experiences in his daily rounds affected by the fact of his race? Think of the minutiae, the everyday experiences that comprise his existence. He rides a bus, buys a cup of coffee, performs work routines, receives his mail, makes telephone calls, takes in a movie, asks street directions, gets his TV set repaired, strolls along a sidewalk, talks with his friends, applies for a bank loan, calls the police for assistance, complains about the plumber's bill, dreams about buying a boat, fixes Jello for the kids to eat after school. Or perhaps he quarrels with his wife, shoots heroin, visits the welfare office, robs a bank, sits idly on a stoop. The vital question is, Does anything happen to him during these experiences *because of his race?* Or better put, because of his race in connection with the race of those with whom he interacts? —Not because of his income; nor his education; nor his personality; nor the times he lives in: because of his race. The question does not imply negative answers. Waitresses may slop the coffee, work companions may be aloof, the police may be brusque or worse, the bank may require undue collateral—because of one's race. But could it not be well argued that of the uncounted thousands of separate events which make up his workaday life, rather few are seriously affected in either process or outcome by the fact of race? Certainly, the temptation is strong to attribute to race what is really due to class, or style, or religion, or happenstance, or the mood of another.

Some will say that we have posed the issue here in absolutely the wrong form. Perhaps we have. That is, it may be argued that the insignia of race is significant not to the minutiae of everyday life but to establishing the setting within which these routines occur. If an American black is slighted because he is poor but is poor because his race placed him in schools that trained him poorly, we play with words to say his slight is economic and not racial. A South African Bantu may live in the interior of the Transkei because he cannot get the work-permit and pass that give him exit; and, by virtue of where he lives, his daily routines will be almost totally free from any experience with whites; and thereby his race is relevant hardly at all in any direct sense; but it cannot meaningfully be said that race is irrelevant —indeed it is compellingly relevant—to how he lives and what happens to him.

This caution to our question is well taken. It is, nonetheless, essential to make the substantiality of race problematic, not assume it. What part of all the contacts between blacks and whites is conditioned by race? And of that portion so affected, what portion is affected negatively? Considering all instances in which antagonists —ruler and ruled, oppressor and oppressed, exploiter and exploited, or competitive equals—differ in race, there is an unknown proportion in which race is not the causal source nor even a significant factor, and the question of when it is and when it is not, and why it is in some cases but not others, must be taken as a continuing empirical question of critical theoretical importance.

Once we acknowledge, tacitly and explicitly, that not all instances of conflict-between-races are racially-inspired-conflict, that not all instances of personal abuse of a racially different person are racial in nature, we have extended the analytical significance (and complexity) of matters in which race is or may be involved.

We can, to show its importance, raise our question above the level of the individual in his workaday world: In the pantheon of evil, how great an evil is race? (For, most interestingly, race is always discussed in terms of evil. Why this is so, and whether it need necessarily be so, is itself worth our attention.) It is the custom of laymen and scholars alike to discuss matters of race within the general context of pathology; as we tend to see them, such matters reek of the inhumanity of man to man, and it is to this inhumanity that we attend.

We note in passing that this *is* a limiting perspective which denies us those understandings that come when race and race contact are approached as natural rather than diseased phenomena, and many of the essays in this collection, notably those by Hoetink and Wallerstein, demonstrate the value of a less common approach. But it is not the mission of my essay, nor of this collection of essays, to challenge such a perspective, except as we may do so by example. To return to the relative status of race among the problems of man: The spoils of office awarded to the winning party in politics is not unlike the use of government to give jobs particularistically to those of given race; the rape of land and people accompanying victorious campaigns in war bears similarity to the abject subjugation of one race to another; the myths of race and the myths of class are interchangeable; old-school-tie loyalties are comparable in nature to instances of race discrimination in the job market; etc. Within the total set of events marked by particularism, discrimination, favoritism, exploitation, and personal abuse, it is not at all clear, at least it must not be an unexamined assumption, that those occasioned by race occupy a very prominent spot, or are particularly virile and vile.

Only one of the essays in this collection deals with any explicitness with the matters raised here. The paper by Wallerstein takes explicit note of the confusing admixture of religion, region, tribe, and race in a large tier of newly independent African states; doing so, the author offers the engaging proposition that there exists a limited set of salient social groups in any social structure at any given time: class, status-group, and party are three different existential forms of the same essential reality; people exercise the *option* of grouping themselves racially; and we need the concept of "race" only because the nations are not discrete and separate and race is an international status-group, there being on the international scene a fundamental status division between white and nonwhite. But although no other chapter is explicitly concerned with disentangling the essence of race from its confederates, the issue can be discerned in several others. New experiences create new awareness, and it is in the context of what we experience that race enters our awareness as a (among many possible) category system. Thus Katznelson in his analysis of the entry of race into the political process in England is dealing with an underlying process (the allocation of scarce resources) that *surfaces* in the issue of race. And Saunders is definitive in his demonstration that chromatic differences are determinative of the life the Brazilian lives; he shows us beyond reasonable doubt that what the perceptive social analyst (especially one who has experienced the United States) sees to be race is important in the affairs of man in Brazil. But we may ask, *Is* it race, when it is neither known nor acknowledged to be such by those who experience it most intimately, and when sufficient explanations of the Brazilian experience are as obligated also to class, and region, and rural-urban differences, and family lineage, and traditional loyalties, and local histories?

There is, to be sure, no final answer. But if we are persuaded that a society in which race and racism were nonexistent might not thereby show appreciable gain in the positive virtues, might be as corrupt, oppressive, and deadly as one infested with racism, must we not give race and racism less uniqueness and regard them instead as particular manifestations in particular situations of general social processes?

This brings us naturally to raise the possibility that social science studies of the structure of race relations have focussed excessively on conflict, protest, and change—nowhere more so than in the United States in the past decade, although generally in the postwar period of the last quarter-century. It seems too obvious to mention, yet the fact that steady states are achieved in relations between races requires emphasis. Just as protest and conflict need not signify excesses of exploitation and oppression, adaptation and equilibrium occur when utopian states of justice and equality have not been reached. Peoples of different races do learn to coexist when the absence of conflict cannot be explained either by racial justice or lethargy. Various systems of exchange, various symbiotic ties, various patterns of mutual sustenance and unspoken understandings from which all participants receive portions they regard as acceptable, where both costs and rewards are commonly seen as falling within tolerable limits—these are far less spectacular than ghetto riots, preventive detention prisons, and undeclared civil wars, but they are a part of the picture and they are very important. Perhaps we are too prone to see only seething cauldrons whenever we have objective evidence of inequality associated with race. Some would argue in rebuttal that we have seen only the beginnings in the 1960s; older patterns are no longer acceptable anywhere and newly emerged racial sensitivities and pride will never again allow peaceable accommodation to patterns that rest on or imply anything less than full equality. The future will see more, not less, forceful protest, even race wars, and we are right to focus our attention now on violence and explosive action, since it is a foretaste of things to come. One judges that Turk, for example, would argue that such a preoccupation is appropriate in the case of South Africe, as would Samkange in the instance of Rhodesia. Such is an appropriate perspective in particular situations, but it is not sufficient for the panorama of race structures. We are well cautioned to remember that people develop stable, workable relationships within imperfect systems, and race is no exception. Even in times of turmoil and revolution, race riots and threatened wars, guerrilla fighters and rising expectations, a balanced perspective requires that we describe and analyze persistence in pattern and form and examine the patterns of psychic and material gain that underwrite accommodative race structures—if for no other reason than that we may, possibly, discover that the more things change, the more they remain the same.

1 H. HOETINK

National Identity, Culture, and Race in the Caribbean

ON ONE level of abstraction, it is not difficult to analyze in common terms the recent acts of collective violence in the Caribbean area—from the Dominican Revolution of 1965, via the riots in Jamaica in 1968 and in Curaçao in 1969, to the series of bombings in Puerto Rico and the massive disturbances in Trinidad in April 1970. On this same level of abstraction, we may classify these events as expressions of frustrating discontent with internal social structures and with externally imposed patterns of domination. Local governments can be looked upon as stooges for foreign capital and interests; the higher social strata can be viewed as collaborators and middlemen of large, often multinational, corporations. A premise of such an approach related to the theme of this conference would be that economic dependence is not only an obstacle to "real" political independence, but that the "colonial" self-contempt which accompanies such an economic and technological national client-role smothers the awakening, let alone the growth, of national identity.

From a different perspective, it is also possible and rewarding, à la Crane Brinton, to analyze the "anatomy" of these conflicts as sociological processes, by emphasizing a number of parallels: the role of local university members (or, where there is no university, of teachers and academics recently returned from metropolitan countries) as intellectual stimulators and, sometimes, organizers; the communication of

17

their ideas through special periodicals (*Abeng* in Jamaica, *Kambio* in Curaçao, *Tapia* in Trinidad, etc.); the alliance with some trade union leaders (as in Curaçao and Trinidad), with the dissatisfied military (as in Trinidad and Santo Domingo), or with student groups (as in Puerto Rico, Santo Domingo, and Jamaica); the phase of mass demonstrations; the first martyr; the confrontation; the role of outside intervention if any; and the aftermath of success or suppression, of absorption of ideas or personnel, or of continued tensions and struggle.

Again, it is also legitimate to stress historical continuity in these types of conflict. As Lloyd Best and other British West Indian economists maintain, there are indeed similarities between the old plantation economy and the new bauxite or oil economy: the interests of external ownership, the externally determined market conditions, the local management contracted elsewhere, the profits flowing elsewhere. One may even observe the fact that some of the complaints of twentieth-century Curaçaoans against the policies of Royal Dutch Shell or against the social behavior of its personnel curiously resemble the complaints of their eighteenth-century predecessors against the West Indian Company and its hirelings. In both cases, these criticisms result from the supremacy of a powerful economic organization, more backed than checked by the metropolitan power, in a small society whose own resources are too scanty to provide an adequate response.

These approaches have great appeal for the sociologist, for at least two reasons. First, the social categories used in these structural analyses are "universalistic": they can be applied to *all* societies where strong external economic and political influences have demonstrable repercussions on their internal economic structure and social stratification; thus, they respond to the sociologist's avid desire for wide generalization. Second, these approaches have ideological components, attractive to many: they support the idea of basic similarities in the external relationships and internal structure of all "Third World" societies, and they imply a structural remedy which, in principle, would be universally applicable.

I recognize the usefulness and academic legitimacy of these approaches. What is more, I am willing to accept several of their implications (and I refer here especially to the first and third approach) a priori, as given; they form, in my opinion, the broadest possible framework in which the greatest number of societies or even social groups subjected to "external domination" can be brought together in a methodological fashion that is still acceptable.

But this recognition also implies a severe limitation. For the high level of abstraction of these analyses makes it possible to find, say, Haiti and Indonesia, or Ghana and the black "internal colony" within the United States no more different than Tweedledum and Tweedledee, as far as their supposedly *essential* structural traits are concerned. This gives some works written in this vein the fascinating monotony of a broken record, while some of their practitioners are endowed with the apparent conviction that when you have seen one "Third World" country, you have seen them all—a conviction which, in more sophisticated form, may even be the justification for the "sociology of development" as a subdiscipline, and for the scholarly prestige of some of its representatives.

Those societies which, at the moment of their historical inceptions, were characterized by socially relevant racial and cultural diversity, lend themselves to a comparison of the ways in which their cultural and racial components have reacted to the external forces mentioned earlier. Those who attempt such an analysis must not shrink from concepts that deal with racial and cultural cohesion and with group alignments along "racial" and cultural lines, even if those concepts failed to receive much attention in "classical" sociology, based as it was on the study of more homogeneous societies.

Such comparative research will try to find answers to questions, some not even posed by the other types of approaches. Thus we may ask: Why is conflict in the Dominican Republic not being expressed in racial terms, even though this country, measured by a U.S. racial yardstick, has an overwhelming majority of "Negroes" and a tiny minority of powerful "whites"? Why do some Trinidadian radicals stress the "blackness" of their movement, while others hopefully emphasize the chances of interracial solidarity between Negroes and East Indians? Why is black militancy in Curaçao or Jamaica more ambivalent than in the United States?

All questions of this type are aspects of the larger question of the relationship between race, culture, and national identity with which this conference occupies itself. Let it be clear, at the outset, that whatever answers I may come forward with are of a speculative and impressionistic nature, as are most other statements in our academic field. In order to enlarge the field of comparison and thus enhance the chance for limited generalization, I should like to refer sometimes to multiracial societies of the Western Hemisphere, outside the Caribbean area. I shall first touch upon lower strata "emancipatory" movements, then upon changes in national symbolism, and finally upon national cultural and social identity, always with a view toward establishing correlations with cultural and socio-racial structure.

For good reasons, the historical origins of Africanism as a cultural movement are to be found in Haiti. This country, formally independent since the beginning of the nineteenth century, had a socio-racial structure comparable to the Indo-American Indio-Ladino dichotomy and in which, *grosso modo*, the lowest rank was occupied by Negroes, the highest by mulattoes. This meant that the *somatic* line of division between the two groups could not be rigid; there existed a socio-racial continuum. The castelike structure of which Leyburn writes (1941) found its legitimation not only in somatic preoccupations, but also in a drastic cultural separation: the mulatto bourgeoisie, French-oriented in life style, family organization, religion, and language; the black masses, Afro-Haitian in culture and organization. Hence, these parallels with Indo-American sovereignty, racial continuum, and cultural-social separation which produced the conditions under which an intellectual avant-garde would gain the insight that cultural and physical identification with a white Europe responded neither to their own nor to the national situation. After the late nineteenth-century works of Antenor Firmin (1885) and Hannibal Price (1900), came Jean Price-Mars's *Ainsi Parla l'Oncle* (1928) to affirm and to consolidate the trend definitely. Coulthard[1] comments on the great similarities between Price-Mars's work and that of the postrevolutionary Mexican indigenist writers:

The same ground is covered as in Gamio's *Forjando Patria* (1916): rejection of racial inferiority, acceptance of a native cultural past, and a suggestion that it should be incorporated into the mainstream of Haitian culture; an interpretation of Haitian religion, but not in comparison to Christianity . . .; an encouragement to writers and artists to look at the true (Afro-French) situation of Haiti; and finally, a criticism of the distortion of Haitian cultural life by the snobbish, prejudiced worship of European models.

In French Martinique, one found on the one hand a wider and more intense communication with France and French Africa, and on the other, a "colonial" social structure in which the colored intellectual suffered from the social prejudice of the white dominant group (instead of, as in Haiti, belonging to the dominant stratum). Here, in the

1. See his "Parallelisms and Divergencies between 'Négritude' and 'Indigenismo',"
(1968:31, 57, 49), from which article several of the following data are taken, though not their interpretation.

context of a less African-influenced folk culture than that of Haiti, Aimé Césaire and Frantz Fanon initiated at a somewhat later point a series of ideas which, though similar in intent and sentiment to those of the Haitian *"Africanistes,"* were more abstracted from the local situation, and more consciously addressed to a metropolitan audience. They pronounced strong indictments against European colonialism and Western civilization (Césaire, 1955), they analyzed "colonial" racism (Fanon, 1953), and proposed the mystical-racial idea of a general cultural *négritude* (Césaire, 1947). In this fashion their intellectual movement acquired an international flavor that *Indigenismo* lacked: via Leopold Senghor, French Black Africa bacame part of it. In his later years, Frantz Fanon came to reject the concept of *négritude*, in which he saw the danger of cultural exhibitionism, and, focusing on the global consequences of Western colonialism, he broadened the basis of his potential followers by addressing himself to all "Damnés de la Terre," whatever their color.

Not only is Fanon's life history—from psychiatrist in Martinique to participant in Algeria's struggle for independence—reflected in his works, but also in the two tendencies which commonly characterize every "emancipatory" movement: the emphasis on one's own cultural and psychic dignity, and the stress on the political and economic struggle which must lead to ultimate equality or even to a reversal of positions. Fanon's shift from the first to the second emphasis coincides roughly with the change in his personal role and position: from (in his case, near-desperate) objectively analyzing observer, member of the upper middle stratum in Martinique's socio-racial structure, to activist in a non-Black part of the Third World, identifying himself completely with the role and position of his subject.[2]

It would seem that there exists some relation between social position and the ideological (as distinguished from fashionable) preference for either the cultural or the political-economic aspects of emancipation. It could be that the cultural aspects are generally somewhat more heavily emphasized by those whose socio-economic position is relatively secure and who, as a group, are not bound to expect considerable advantages from radical economic changes; they generally belong neither culturally nor somatically to the group whose lot they describe and sympathize with. They invite comparison, *mutatis mutandis*, with the intellectual upper stratum avant-garde of the European

2. Similar stages in the development of colonized intellectuals were described by Fanon himself in his essay, "Sur la culture nationale" (1961).

labor movement in the nineteenth and early twentieth centuries. Their solidarity with the emancipatory movement—however far-reaching in its consequences—is academic and romanticizing, and it is supported rather by often highly personal discontent with their own immediate environment than by any social or cultural affinity with the milieu that receives their emotional preference. They are rarely able to bridge completely the distance between themselves and their subjects.

In this category—roughly hewn, to be sure—fall the early *Indigenismo* of members of the Mexican and Peruvian white and mestizo cultural elite, and the *"Africanisme"* of the Haitian bourgeois mulatto. This is the category, so to speak, of Frantz Fanon in his Martiniquan phase. Those who feel more committed to the political and economic aspects of an emancipatory movement would seem to be socially more closely linked to the subordinated group; the intellectuals amongst them are sometimes marginal men insofar as they or their families are concerned, precisely because their social origins prevented their acceptance as social equals in the higher (nonwhite) strata of society. The initially literary and subsequently political activities of the rural doctor François Duvalier in Haiti perhaps should be understood in this perspective: "un Noir au pouvoir" was the slogan of his friend Estimé in 1946. Also the life history and actions—especially those in Jamaica—of Marcus Garvey fall into this category; *qua* depth of identification and subjectivism, it reminds one of Fanon's Algerian phase.

There are at least two reasons why the political-economic emphasis on the Negro struggle was developed most strongly in the United States. First, in that country there exists no intermediate and socially separate category of "coloreds" to whom the social definition of Negro is not applicable (although *within* the "Negro" category there does exist a differentiation based on both objective and somatic criteria), so that the intellectual, of whatever nonwhite shade, *could* feel an existential involvement with the "Negro problem"; no aristocratic distance comparable to that of his Mexican and Haitian counterparts separated him from his object. Further, given his categorization as a Negro, he had no fears to entertain with regard to radical changes in the socio-racial structure; and finally, it was the same social definition of the Negro group which made legal discrimination possible in the U.S. on a scale unknown elsewhere in the hemisphere.

In several Caribbean societies, on the other hand, the success of *political* "black" movements has not been as great as one would expect in societies where the whites only form a small minority. The main reason seems to be that the colored groups (as opposed to the Negroes) are not eager to change their perception of the socio-racial structure, in which they traditionally have occupied an intermediate position, into one constructed along U.S. lines. The pamphlet literature in Curaçao in the wake of the riots of 1969 bears clear testimony to this reluctance, which can also be observed in Jamaica. The same phenomenon goes far to explain why, in the latter island, black activism has for a long period manifested itself in the escapist, messianistic Ras Tafari movement.[3]

The greatest chances for a closer social co-operation between coloreds and blacks are to be found in those Caribbean societies, such as Trinidad, Guyana, and Surinam, where roughly half of the population consists of descendants of indentured East Indian workers. The presence of such a large segment that is culturally, somatically, and in social organization, different from the old "Creole" population at least seems to have mitigated somewhat the latters' formerly incisive color and class differentiation. This incipient solidarity, based on common Euro-African descent and culture, is perhaps being challenged by still newer solidarities: in 1970, the black militants in Trinidad tried to involve the East Indian sugar workers in their protests against a third common and external adversary: the foreign-based corporation. In this way, the revolt, though it originated and became known as a black uprising against the "phony Afro-Saxon alliance" in government and economy, tried to include all "Damnés de la Terre" in Trinidad; the future success of these efforts cannot be predicted, but it seems doubtful.

Although in the non-Hispanic Caribbean the cultural differences between the white and colored elites, on the one hand, and the mass of the population, on the other, are generally more pronounced than in the Hispanic countries—one need only to think of linguistic and religious differences—they are not so easily reducible to a European-African cultural dichotomy as would *appear* to be the case in Haiti. The chances for a purely cultural "Africanism" (in its anthropological sense) is smaller, and, as I have suggested already, with regard to Martinique, the cultural notions of the black movement tend to be expressed in the less concrete, more mystical terms of *négritude*.

This is, of course, a fortiori the case in the United States where, comparatively speaking, the cultural-anthropological heritage of African origin, insofar as it is characteristic of *only* the Negro population,

3. Cf. Lowenthal (1968:302-349, 317). On the Ras Tafarians, generally see Barrett (1969).

is small and diffuse. In fact, the remarkable lack of cultural-anthropological diversity along white-black lines in the United States can only
be compared to some Hispanic Caribbean societies. Yet the latter have
no black movements to speak of, while the United States has. This
suggests that, by itself, the lack of pronounced cultural diversity along
racial lines is no impediment to the development of a black emancipatory movement, provided that, as in the U.S., (or, for that matter in
the non-Hispanic Caribbean) the socio-racial structure is discontinuous
instead of, as in the Hispanic Caribbean, continuous. The case of Haiti
(and Mexico) would seem to show that a socio-racial continuum can
produce a pro-black (or pro-Indigenous) movement, provided that
cultural differences between the upper and lower socio-racial strata are
very marked.

When we speak of "Afro-American" culture we cannot, of course,
limit ourselves to elements of distinctly African origin confined to the
Negro population (see also Mintz, 1970). At least two other cultures
of the Negro group have to be taken into consideration: one is the culture, in a sociological sense, as product of a long period of low status,
be it in slavery or in ghettoes; the other we might call the emancipatory culture, the creation of which serves the function of increasing
the recognizability and solidarity amongst the militant minority of the
Negro group: hairstyles, clothing, language forms, perform these
symbolic and communicative functions, which no emancipatory movement can do without. Such an emancipatory movement further needs,
as parts of its cultural apparatus, its own interpretation of history with
its own heroes and martyrs, and its own social art, to further foster
internal cohesion, to convert the brothers outside the movement, and
to undermine the self-assertiveness of the dominant adversary. The
parallels with other historical emancipation movements are obvious.
Yet in spite of these parallels, it may be useful to take a closer look at
the term *emancipatory movement* which we have been using rather
loosely so far, and to determine whether the black movement, especially in the United States, can be said to be really of an emancipatory
character.

Emancipation, it seems to me, aspires to a change in the position
and roles of the members of a minority. The change of the social system as a whole is an unavoidable concomitant or consequence of such
an emancipation. The point I should like to make here is that emancipation is directed toward and stands for successful *inclusion*; once the
goals have been reached, the movement loses its raison d'être. The rituals, groups language, uniforms or "Schiller-shirts," hairstyles, and

fanatical poems of the socialist movement of the twenties and thirties were abandoned after the struggle's successful conclusion which made "bourgeois" out of most West European workers. Is such a course of events to be expected with regard to the black movement in the United States? Talcott Parsons thinks it is. In his article *The Problem of Polarization on the Axis of Color* (1968:352) he defends the interesting thesis that "the race relations problem has a better prospect of resolution in the United States than in Brazil, partly *because* the line between white and Negro has been so rigidly drawn in the United States because the system has been sharply polarized," for "sharp polarization seems on the longer run to be more favorable to effective inclusion than is a complex grading of the differences between components, perhaps particularly where gradations are arranged on a superiority-inferiority hierarchy."

This bold and rather unexpected exercise in dialectics, whereby antithetical polarization leads to synthetical inclusion, deserves for a fair discussion and a satisfactory refutation more space than I have here.[4] Yet I think the topic too important for our purpose to leave it completely alone.

The basic error in Parsons's reasoning can, if I am not mistaken, be paraphrased as follows: "The great emancipatory movements in Western Europe (Reformation, Democratic Revolution, Labor Movement) were in their initial phases characterized by rigid polarization; they were successful and their success is demonstrated by the inclusion of the emancipating group and the subsequent mitigation, or even resolution, of the conflict. It follows that polarization *generally* is favorable, hence, the racial problem in the United States 'has a better prospect of resolution than in Brazil,' *quod erat demonstrandum*." It is one thing to argue, as I did earlier, that because of its bi-polar socioracial structure, the political-economic black struggle developed most strongly in the United States, which means that the polarity of the structure was and is reflected in the polarization of the struggle. It is a different matter altogether to predict, on the basis of such a polarization, that the "resolution" will be "favorable," that is, leading to inclusion.

As Parsons acknowledges (1968:352), "inclusion . . . presupposes some order of *common* value-commitment." An escapist movement like the Ras Tafarians is not emancipatory; neither is Zionism. A strug-

4. See Hoetink (forthcoming).

gle for civil rights, against discrimination, and for improvement of social conditions is emancipatory, a struggle for political independence or
even autonomy is not; the desire for *exclusion* implies a self-perception, so different from the dominant adversary, that the goal cannot be
equality with him, but only equivalence separate from him. In this
context the terminology of *internal colonialism* is interesting because
"real" anticolonial struggles are also aimed at self-determination, and
colonial peoples commonly have a different self-perception from their
colonizers, based on cultural and/or somatic factors. It seems clear
that emancipatory and exclusionist elements are both present among
black leaders in the United States, with the exclusionists gaining
ground in recent years, which might make one wonder whether increased polarization—at least in this case—does not *diminish* the chances
for inclusion.

Thinking of "the problems of national integration faced by those
Caribbean societies whose populations appear today to be seriously
divided by ethnic factors," Sidney W. Mintz (1967:153) opposes the
view that "national identity hinges upon some sort of total social
homogeneity of values . . . Societies characterized by marked heterogeneity can exhibit a high degree of national identity, as long as individuals are able to align themselves on different issues on bases other
than membership in particular ethnic or class groupings . . . Not the
number of groups, but the extent to which they interpenetrate in the
mainstream of communications and in the solution of national issues,
may be the critical factor."

The same concept of interpenetration, together with pluralization,
is being used by Parsons. The general idea behind his use of these
terms would seem to be that increasing socio-economic differentiation
tends to build a series of new solidarities (occupational, associational)
which cross-cut and mitigate the older solidarities based on cultural or
socio-racial identity.

It appears to me that the effect of such socio-economic differentiation is not the same in all socio-racial systems. It is quite possible to
imagine a multiracial society in which such a differentiation, as far as
its sociological effects are concerned, is limited to its dominant racial
group, especially when the latter, as in the United States, forms a vast
numerical majority. Where, on the other hand, the dominant racial
group is very small in numbers, increased socio-economic differentiation does lead to a more complicated class-structure *within* the subordinated segments, but not necessarily to a greater interpenetration
among all segments.

A functional relationship between economic differentiation and the increase of interracial or intercultural solidarities may rather be expected in those societies where the dividing lines between the segments run *vertically;* in these societies, indeed, *all* horizontal solidarities—such as those based on economic position—foster intercommunication and may mitigate the existing cultural or racial antagonisms.

It is interesting that the modern societies which often are put forward as examples of reasonably well-functioning cultural heterogeneity, such as Belgium, Switzerland, Great Britain, and the Soviet Union, all have vertical cultural boundaries, to the point that their cultural segments even have territories of their own, with a certain degree of cultural and sometimes political autonomy. Although European history shows many cases of repression, expulsion or political elimination of such territorially limited cultural minorities, and although it would be naive to underestimate the still existing cultural and political tensions in countries like Belgium or Great Britain, it is correct to assume that a minimum of horizontal interpenetration and communication gives these systems certain viability (cf. Pool, 1970:86-102). Countries like Surinam, Guyana, and Trinidad, where the cultural and somatic divisory lines between the main population segments run vertically, seem therefore best fitted for a formal federative or quasi-federative collaboration among these groups, provided that a minimum of interpenetration can be maintained.[5] The question here is whether, due to differences in demographic growth, economic ethos and social mobility, one of these groups may, in the long run, not end up being dominant, so that the vertical lines of division thus become horizontal once again.

In most other multiracial societies of the Western Hemisphere, these lines always have been and mostly still are horizontal, or are conceived as such. In such societies, stimulation of solidarities based on economic or class position may have an aggravating effect on socioracial or cultural antagonisms.[6]

All governments attempt through the inculcation of nationalistic sentiments—in school, in the army and otherwise—to diminish intra-

5. "[Ethnic] partition and communal representation was actually suggested by some Hindu leaders in Trinidad on the eve of independence, but those suggestions provoked far more hilarity and derision than serious discussion among the majority of the Negro and Muslim populations" (Bell and Oxaal, 1964:36). More recently, similar suggestions have been made in Guyana and Trinidad, but without official party endorsement.

6. Except when there are two or more subordinated segments, in which case the polarization between the dominant group and all others will be promoted.

national divisiveness. Although it makes sense to distinguish—as Mintz also suggests—between *national identity* and (political) nationalism, there is some nexus between the two; an abundance of political nationalism often indicates a weakly developed sense of national identity. This is a logical correlation, for if we define national identity as the degree to which the historical experiences of the nation are perceived and transmitted as *common* experiences, then it is clear that acts of political nationalism in the past and the present may serve to strengthen this notion of commonness.

It is obvious that territorial chauvinism, using informal channels, can flourish without political independence. Many Caribbean islands attest to this; the insular sense of identity is nourished through comparison with neighboring islands, especially if these are in an equivalent but competitive position vis-à-vis the metropolitan patron-state— e.g., Jamaica-Trinidad, Aruba-Curaçao, Guadeloupe-Martinique—and further, through comparison with the metropolitan country itself and its local representatives, where the cultural differences are often marked.

In the same fashion, interterritorial or regional chauvinism may develop. In the Caribbean, one remembers the ideas of Hostos, Martí, Betances, Luperón and others about the common destiny of the Greater Antilles, especially the Spanish speaking of them, leading in the seventies and eighties of the last century to plans for a confederation of these islands. One may also think of the ideal of Caribbean integration —in the first instance, between the English-speaking countries—which is still considered by many present-day young intellectuals of the region, in spite of the failure of the attempt at Federation in the fifties. There are, finally, solidarities of an even wider scope, such as the Latin American awareness in Cuba, the Dominican Republic, and Puerto Rico; emotional and cultural bonds with Africa or India as in several other countries; a varying sense of pride and belonging in British, French, or Dutch (supranational) political frameworks; and, in a few groups, an incipient sense of solidarity—at least intellectually—with the Third World. But it is clear that formal sovereignty with its own national symbols, with its international representation and activities, but, above all, with its institutionalized mechanism for inculcation, increases and fortifies a territorial sense of identity. Seen in this perspective, the United States, Haiti, and the Latin American countries are at an advantage, *ceteris paribus*, compared to the recently created British Caribbean States, and even more to the French and Dutch areas, and Puerto Rico. *Ceteris paribus*, because there are, of course, other variables which determine the strength and extension of national[7] feelings of loyalty. First there are variables of an *objective* nature: the infrastructure of a country may be insufficient, and some population groups therefore so isolated that they hardly have any national consciousness at all: their perspective is limited to their own community or region, they are not nationally integrated in an objective sense. This phenomenon is well known in Central and South America, but less so in the Caribbean. Then there is the *subjective* variable: to what extent can the national experiences subjectively be accepted as common?

In the vertically segmented societies of Trinidad, Guyana, and Surinam, we may observe in action the process of designing a "national" mythology, in which heroes and memorable feats are carefully distributed over the cultural heritages of the two main groups.[8]

In the older, horizontally layered societies, we see in their *traditional* national mythologies a high place allotted to the king or president who signed the decree of the abolition of slavery; in colonies of monarchal mother countries, the royal family was always stressed as a loyalty symbol, often rationalized by certain historical actions of monarchs as wise arbiters in internal conflicts, or, even better, in conflicts between colonials and metropolitans. Generally, in these traditional mythologies, the "good" dignitaries from the dominant segment achieved the status of national symbol; the noble priest, the governor with sympathy for the poor—in short, those who would have a maximal acceptability for the subordinated segments.

Only in the Latin American countries whether independent or not, do we also find the holy priest from the *non*white stratum, even the dark-skinned saint; and further we encounter there the institution of the *national* patron saints. Also, in many Latin American republics during the turbulent nineteenth century, full of internal instability, one president or another of decidedly nonwhite origins came into power (Juarez in Mexico, Paez in Venezuela, Heureaux in the Dominican Republic). Thus we see Iberian Catholicism, both because of its national inclusiveness and through its creation of national-religious human symbols, exerting a favorable influence on the awareness of national identity in the Latin American countries, while at the same time the early independence of these countries—except Cuba and

7. In what follows, I mean by nation, the total society, whether politically independent or not.

8. For the problem of rewriting history in such societies, see Maingot (1969:67-86).

Puerto Rico—led to political mobility—however chaotic—which had the useful effect of increasing the sense of participation of the lower socio-racial strata in national politics.

In the United States, also early independent, the only comparable period is that of the Reconstruction after the Civil War, but here the phenomenon was not national but regional, and it included a strong retrograde reaction.

In many Latin American countries, furthermore, dark-skinned military men and intellectuals also played a sufficiently great role in the struggle for independence to be incorporated in the national pan-theon: one may think of Piar in Venezuela, Antonio Maceo and Máx-imo Gómez in Cuba, and Sánchez in the Dominican Republic, to name just a few. Or would it be preferable to say that this incorporation—which, significantly, did not always come about without protest and delay—was rather the reflection of an already existing and sufficient integration of the population groups, and not so much a consequence of an increase in such an integration as a result of their personal ac-tions? Both points of view are plausible and are not incompatible.

In any case, the contrast with the War of Independence in the United States has a near symbolic significance: in this country the Revolutionaries were initially reluctant to admit Negroes in their ranks, while the British were not. It was the colonial power, and not the na-tionalists, who promised freedom to the slaves; and it was with the evacuating British that thousands of Negroes fled. Yet, in spite of this, there were also "hundreds of Negroes whose exploits are remembered for exceptional bravery and allegiance to the cause of the Revolution," (Drimmer,1967:133) but none of these became incorporated in the neotraditional mythology of the new republic.

Where the achievement of formal independence was not accom-panied by a drastic change in socio-racial structure—and the latter was only the case in Haiti—the new national mythology preserved its "tra-ditional" traits as far as the recruitment of its heroes was concerned; only in Haiti were all of these dark-skinned; in the United States they were all white; and in Latin America they were predominantly white with, however, as we saw, in nearly every country at least one sig-nificant exception. It may be noted in passing that in the portrayed—that is, symbolic—countenances of these dark heroes there was a ten-dency to "whiten" them, even in Haiti,[9] for a long time to come.

9. Compare the same phenomenon in the portraits of the twentieth century Puerto Rican political leader and nationalist Albizu Campos.

The extent to which this traditional national symbolism subsequently came under attack and criticism, and to which alternative symbols were adopted or demanded, correlates rather clearly with what we have written earlier about variations in the emergence and success of *indigenismo, africanisme, négritude*. The Mexican Revolution, one century after the achievement of Independence, led to a new national mythology, proposed by an intellectual élite and accepted by the state, in which Indian symbols are preferred over European ones (which may have been, as we suggested earlier, rather the result of a *mestizo* affirmation, and not necessarily a truly *Indian* nationalism).

In Haiti, an *africaniste* ideology, strengthened within a predominantly mulatto avant-garde during the period of U.S. occupation in the twenties and thirties, achieved only in more recent decades the political backing which made it possible to place, though hesitantly and ambiguously, the Vodun religion and the Créole language on the altar of national dignity, some one hundred and sixty years after independence.

In the United States, characterized not by a cultural but by a social pluralism between black and white (cf. van den Berghe, 1967), the militant blacks now demand recognition of their own group symbols and culture, and some of them have begun to reject the traditional national symbols.

In the recently independent British Caribbean, as well as in the French and Dutch areas, a growing awareness of *négritude* asks for its recognition on a national level, but finds some resistance from the "two-tone" colored middle sectors and the white elite in the horizontally layered societies,[10] and from the Asian population groups in the

---

10. See Lewis (1968:176) about the return in 1964 of Marcus Garvey's ashes to Jamaica and his "elevation by the Jamaican government to the status of official hero" and the controversies this produced. "At the time of independence, some Jamaicans were reluctant to accept the growing emphasis upon African origins and slavery in the interpretation of Jamaica's past . . . Such resistance . . . reflected either the rejection of identity with the Negro racial stock . . . or the principle . . . that the symbols of the African origins and slavery were somehow degrading" (Bell and Oxaal, 1964:63). It is interesting to note that these authors express themselves forcefully against "the story of the rise of the enslaved black man from Africa" becoming "*the* history of Jamaica" because "some Jamaicans, perhaps all those who are not fairly dark-skinned Negroes, might be excluded from sharing in the new Jamaican history, perhaps from the new Jamaican society itself" (Bell and Oxaal, 64). The authors praise Eric Williams, premier of Trinidad-Tobago, for the emphasis in his *History of the People of Trinidad and Tobago*, issued on the first day of national independence, "on the common history of exploitation" of the two main population groups (65). In Curaçao, the demands of some young intellectuals in 1967 to have streets in Willemstad renamed after leaders of the 1795 slave revolt met with sufficiently strong public opposition to be refused.

vertically structured societies, the latter insisting on equal representation on the national symbolic level.

It would seem that *only* in the Afro-Latin societies has the traditional national symbolism (as far as it is relevant to interracial relations) remained reasonably free of observable tensions.

A word must be said here about Cuba. Though this country underwent a profound economic-political revolution, which, as far as can be ascertained, had some favorable consequences for the *character* of race relations, it did not undergo a drastic change in its socioracial *structure;* movements to foster exclusively Negro-oriented cultural or social goals do not seem to have been stimulated,[11] and some foreign black militants may be disappointed in the limited ideological usefulness of the Cuban Revolution for purposes of *négritude.* On the other hand, the revolution was, of course, the creator of powerful symbols—Fidel, Che—for the struggle of Fanon's "Damnés de la Terre" against the capitalist exploiters, who are only accidentally white in their majority, just as the Cuban cabinet is. In Cuba itself, the concurrent use of older national symbols—José Martí—serves to stress the historical continuity with the national past.

Within horizontally layered multiracial or multicultural societies, these Cuban symbols serve to emphasize the economic aspects of the stratification; within vertically composed societies they may serve to foment interracial or intercultural solidarity, and thus foster feelings of national solidarity, within certain economic strata and their intelligentsia. The Cuban symbols may further stimulate national—or nationalistic—feelings of identity, insofar as the nation as a whole may be represented as the victim of foreign economic and political exploitation. In this light it becomes understandable that the majority of Puerto Rican independence movements and parties have adopted the Cuban symbols. This must not lead to the conclusion that elsewhere in the hemisphere nationalism is always accompanied by radical political or economic goals. Politically more conservative sectors certainly do not lack national fervor, which often expresses itself especially in the wish to preserve the traditional socio-cultural patrimony.

If we assume that some correlation exists between national identity, on the one hand, and the satisfactory functioning for a prolonged period of time of one national symbolism (as far as its relevance for

---

11. "There is no rejection of European culture in Afro-Cuban art, nor a search for anything specifically African, but rather a search for that which is Cuban through the (Cuban) Negro" Buero (1966:186).

interracial or intercultural relations is concerned) on the other, it seems that the Afro-Latin countries show a greater stability in the symbolic expression of their avowed national unity than the others. This would mean that in the Afro-Latin countries the subjective acceptance by the socio-racial strata of what are presented as "common" symbols is less critically scrutinized, less subject to doubts expressed along racial or cultural lines. It means, in short, that national identity in those countries is stronger. Even if one wants to interpret this phenomenon in terms of "brainwashing" or "oppression," and to view it as a lag in the process of becoming conscious of the black population groups in Afro-Latin America, one is still obliged to look for factors which can explain the continuity and effectivity of this cultural domination and inculcation in that part of the hemisphere.

Let us, at this point, recapitulate and round off some of the foregoing observations.

1. Political independence does not necessarily lead to the inclusion of the subordinated racial group in the national symbolism.

2. Inclusion of the subordinated racial group in the national symbolic pantheon is not necessarily the consequence of, or concomitant with, a radical improvement of this group's position in the national power structure. The symbolic inclusion may, as in Mexico and Haiti, respond to a change in the identity awareness of an upper stratum, culturally and economically removed from the subordinated group, yet linked with it through a socio-racial continuum. This latter link makes it precisely possible for the upper stratum to demand (or at least to accept) a *replacement* of European by indigenous symbols, without having to suffer from irreparable alienation as a consequence. (Where, as recently in Haiti, such a symbolic inclusion or even substitution is followed by harsh efforts to change the traditional socio-racial structure accordingly, the resistance of the upper strata is, of course, predictable.)

3. Where there is *no* socio-racial continuum, the substitution of the traditional symbolism by one representative of the lower racial segment leads to psychological exclusion of the creole-white (quasi-) endogamous population group, which lacks the subjective potential for identification with the new symbols. Where, as in most of the British, French, and Dutch areas, the overwhelming majority consists of blacks, such a substitution is nevertheless understandable. If, in some of these countries, and as a compromise, flags and mottoes now symbolize the racial diversity, it is really the racial or cultural *discontinuity* which is being symbolized, but it is being done in a fashion

(equally large circles, equally wide stripes) suggesting the *equivalence* of the segments. Such a symbolism, then, is not a reflection of real power or of numerical relations in the horizontally layered societies, but creates the fiction of a vertically segmented society, where all segments are equally powerful.

In the United States, where numerical proportions preclude a substitution of the traditional national symbolism by one representative of the subordinated segment, such a divided pantheon of symbols would seem to be the only viable answer to the current wishes of the black group. Such a symbolism would, with its suggestion of segmentation along vertical lines, be representative of a division in racial groups as unequal but equivalent parts, which is advocated—short of secession—by black militant movements. The United States is, indeed, the only one of all societies under discussion where—as a result of its peculiar numerical proportions—black militants try to change the society from horizontal to vertical segmentation[12] and where this change, short of exclusion, can be considered as a *final* goal.

4. The foregoing two points seem to warrant the conclusion that, in the horizontally layered American societies, the absence of a socioracial continuum[13] is a greater obstacle than is a pronounced cultural diversity, for the acceptance of any national symbolism, except of the "vertically divided" type.

5. Where, as in Afro-Latin America, there exists both a remarkable cultural continuity and a socio-racial continuity between the strata, there are absent per definition the objective and subjective conditions for clear-cut categorization and loyalty along racial or cultural lines.

In such a situation the question is not whether the Negro loses some of his militancy, as Talcott Parsons seems to suggest, but rather whether he, *qua "Negro,"* needs such militancy at all. Parsons's line of

12. Possibly accompanied by claims on certain political, economic and cultural autonomy.

13. Deutsch (1966:27) observes that "Most serious writers have agreed that nationality . . . has little if anything to do with race," which is of course correct in the sense that the formation of a national identity is not the privilege of the members of any "race." But one only needs to read in his book the index references to "intermarriage" to conclude that also Deutsch considers intermarriage between "distinctive units" within a national territory an important factor in the growth of national identity. Where in multiracial societies one or more "racial" groups abstain from intermarriage, the negative effect of such a socio-racial discontinuity on the "wide complementarity of social communication" which according to Deutsch (97) is characteristic of "membership in a people" can hardly be denied.

thought is ethnocentric, based as it is on the North American socio-racial structure.

While there is no need to dispute the objective fact of serious discrimination against the darkest strata in virtually all Afro-Latin countries, it makes subjectively a great difference whether the black stratum feels itself literally *related* to the higher strata or not. In the whole Latin area it is true what García-Zamor (1970:246) says about Brazil: "it is often quite difficult to distinguish between a Negro and a mulatto, or between a mulatto and a white, solely on the basis of physical characteristics," which is to say that there are many gradations between the main socio-racial categories (and *not*, as some believe, that an unequivocally negroid person will for social purposes be considered unequivocally white, as soon as he has fulfilled certain socio-economic prerequisites).

This must be taken into account by any North American who reads that "less than 2 percent of all civil servants [in Brazil] are Negroes,"[14] for *Negroes* means here those whose somatic traits make it impossible to consider them as part of even the darkest strata of the mulatto group. It is clear that, if one were to use the North American definition of *Negro* in Brazil, the number of Negroes in professional organizations and governmental bureaucracies would be rather higher.

One may further, like García-Zamor, be of the opinion that the Brazilian national ideology favoring racial miscegenation—which can also be found elsewhere in Afro-Latin America—with its emphasis on the "whitening" of the darkest part of the population "is in itself a manifestation of [the whites'] latent or camouflaged prejudice against the *prêto* [black] race" (García-Zamor 1970:248), but here again the danger of an interpretation from a U.S. point of view is great.

The essential point is that there *does* exist an inclusionist ideology of interracial mixing, and that it *can* exist because there is indeed a socio-racial continuum (the question whether demographic proportions really warrant the genetic feasibility of "whitening" the *whole* population, is not relevant for the ideology and its social function). That in such an ideology emphasis is placed on the "whitening" or "bleaching" of the darkest part of the population is virtually unavoidable in a multiracial society, where a racist ingredient in the mechanism of social selection (based on the dominance of the white

14. García-Zamor (1970:242-254, 251). Of course, also the different degree of economic development in both countries makes it difficult to compare the racial ratios in their respective bureaucracies.

somatic norm image) operates as it were by definition; under such circumstances the emphasis on "whitening" is functional for *all* groups involved. At the same time, who will want to deny that the operation of such a racist principle in *all* multiracial societies constitutes a source of social injustice and serious frustrations? It is for that reason that elsewhere (Hoetink, 1967:148 ff.) I have paid attention to the pathology of such societies.

But it is also clear that where the frequency of *connubium* between (often contiguous, yet different) socio-racial categories justifies the acceptance by all groups of an ideology of ultimate racial amalgamation, the vision of the future can be inclusion-directed for the darker strata, even if their *actual* self-perception is being influenced negatively by what are, ideologically speaking, still-functioning racist principles of selection. Under those circumstances, efforts, often under external inspiration, toward greater *exclusivity* (blacks versus whites), have fewer chances of success in the Afro-Latin countries than in the societies where a socio-racial discontinuity tends to foster an exclusion-oriented vision of the darker strata.

Thinking once again of Parsons's idea that "the" problem of racial relations is closer to "its" solution in the United States than in Brazil (or Cuba, or the Dominican Republic), we may now conclude that in reality there are here two very distinct problems, which tend toward two very distinct solutions. In the first case (to name but a few of the salient differences), we deal with a discontinuous structure in which *parts* of both racial groups aspire to inclusion of the black population on the basis of an ideology of social equality, which ideology is constantly being undermined by social reality, while in the other case we deal with a society having a socio-racial continuum, in which ultimate amalgamation is being put forward as a national ideology, which ideology finds some justification in social reality.

In the Afro-Latin ideology the inclusion of the darkest-skinned strata does not lead to exclusion of the whites, but rather to a change in both—admittedly most in the Negro—and their absorption in a new "race."

Earlier we saw how, in the Latin countries, dark heroes were incorporated in the national symbolic pantheon, or how they strengthened national awareness via national-religious symbolism. Such incorporation, we found, intensified awareness of national identity amongst the lower strata, though it is also possible to believe that such incorporation was made possible and admissible because of an already existing consensus or ideology, which was rooted in the continuity of the socio-racial structure. This consensus and this continuity, in turn, were favorably influenced by the rapid social mobility available to lower segments which accompanied political-military revolutions in many countries in the nineteenth century.

Other factors can similarly be seen as both cause and effect of both socio-racial continuity and national awareness. The remarkable cultural continuity—in religion and language, for example—in the Afro-Latin countries, was certainly facilitated by the channels of communication produced by the socio-racial continuum, while, reversely, these channels were widened and deepened by a common religion and language.[15] Such communication further both facilitated and was enhanced by certain patterns of interaction, which lend themselves well for "vertical" contacts and which therefore survived easily their transplantation from the South European or Mediterranean culture area: I think of patron-client relations, extended blood and ritual kinship patterns, of *personalismo* as a general cultural (and not exclusively political) phenomenon, and of patrimonialism as a cultural-psychological phenomenon.[16]

Nearly all of these patterns have to do with individual relationships between social unequals, with personal solidarities based on honor and loyalty, and with complementary and reciprocal relationships, which because of their personal-emotional charge give to communication an urgent—some would say oppressive—character, which communication has its structural parallel on the religious level in the relations between believer and personal, regional, or national patron saint.

The functionality of these vertical patterns of interaction in horizontally layered multiracial societies, such as the Afro-Latin ones, is so great, and their mutual interlocking is so stable, that it would be premature to dismiss their presence as the survival of an earlier socioeconomic stage, as some would like to. While some of these patterns also operate in the non-Hispanic areas, the impact of the *total* cluster can only be found in Latin America. Its culturally homogenizing effect seems clear.

It is interesting to observe how, in the Spanish Caribbean socie-

15. Cf. Hoetink, *Slavery and Race Relations in the Western Hemisphere* (forthcoming), for other factors influencing the expansion of Catholicism as compared to Protestantism.

16. Cf. Hoetink (1971).

ties, where no Amerindians have lived for a very long time, a historical continuity with the aborigines is being postulated, which is completely absent elsewhere in the Caribbean. Coulthard (1968:34)
observes that three of the best "indianista" novels were written "in
countries where Indians had long ceased to exist, Santo Domingo and
Uruguay." In Santo Domingo, at the end of the former century, an
outstanding political leader claimed that certain climatological laws
are changing the mulattoes' appearance into that of Indians (Hoetink,
1970:117-118). Today's children are often named after Indian *ca-
ciques*. The point here is not that this emphasis on the exotic Indian
may serve as an escape from the complexities of present-day socio-
racial relations, but rather that such a search for historical continuity,
for roots—however fictive—in one's own country, is hardly present
outside the Spanish Caribbean.

The greater pride of the former Spanish countries in their *colonial*
past may be seen as indicative of a greater measure of inclusivity, of
collective acceptability, which characterized the Spanish period in
retrospect and which contributed to the present sense of national
identity, as compared to the non-Iberian areas—with the possible exception of the French—where the metropolitan country is much less
perceived as a center of inclusive cultural expansion but at best as a
faraway political arbiter and commercial senior partner.

Sidney W. Mintz is also of the opinion that the Spanish Caribbean countries (including non-independent Puerto Rico) have "a
more defined national identity" than the non-Hispanic. In this context he speaks (Mintz, 1967:151, 152) of an already fixed "assimilation model" which made it possible for a country like Cuba sufficiently to absorb over 100,000 Chinese and massive importations of
African slaves in the last century, and a quarter of a million Jamaicans and Haitians early in the present century, and yet to be able "to
maintain its ideological identity as a nation," while the same cannot
be said of the non-Hispanic Caribbean areas, where large-scale immigration recently took place.

Mintz suggests as an important explanatory factor the "early
emergence of a stable creole culture" in the Spanish areas, so that important sectors of the population early considered themselves Cuban,
Puerto Rican, or Dominican, as opposed to Spanish or metropolitan.
This early cultural creolisation was, in Mintz's opinion, partly determined by "the very uneven development of the plantation system in
the Hispanic Caribbean, the early growth of peasant or yeoman sectors, and the attenuated influence of the metropolis in the rural areas

during the seventeenth and eighteenth centuries." He further pays attention to the development of different socio-racial structures by observing that the Spanish areas were those "in which genetic intermixture proceeded most rapidly and in which the rise of intermediate groups of freemen was rapid and continuous," while such groups "achieved statuses much closer to those of the planter groups than to those of the slaves."[17] Presenting what he cautiously calls a "caricature of historical reality," Mintz suggests (1967:147) that because in the Spanish areas "the masters came to stay, legitimized their unions with women of inferior status, and recognized their *own* alienation from the European past, creole culture in the most genuine, innovative sense could really begin to take shape."

In a recent important essay, Mintz (1970) has presented some of these thoughts again, be it in somewhat amended form. In his new article he states that Spanish administrative control over its colonies "was more rigid than that of the French and English" and that it is precisely this greater rigidity which may have contributed to a fuller growth of "creole identity" of the white settlers.

Further in this essay (1970:14) Mintz mentions once again the factors which he holds responsible for the development of a stronger "creole identity" in the Spanish Caribbean: "the types of local economic development; the presence . . . of colonial institutions within which all colonists could participate; the relative proportions of different social groupings, particularly of slaves and freemen; the distinctions of privilege established by the metropolis to separate 'creoles' from 'homelanders'; and the sexual and mating codes and practices in each colony."

In order to evaluate Mintz's stimulating and important suggestions, the hypothetical character of which he is careful to stress, it is necessary to observe that, in his use of the concept of "creole culture," two different phenomena have to be distinguished: (a) the development of a cultural-social identity of the *white settlers* vis-à-vis the metropolitan country and its direct representatives; and (b) the growth of a cultural-national identity, affecting *all* population groups. Though it is obvious that (a) may foster (b), there is no causal link between the two.

It is probable that in non-Hispanic societies where the absentee-

17. Mintz (1967:148). Although in the quoted text Mintz refers to Saint Domingue, it is clear from the context that he considers it valid for the Spanish Caribbean, too.

ism of the plantation owners for long periods led to frequent muta-
tions among the white group, which consisted largely of men
temporarily detached in the country, a strong sense of white creole
identity could not easily be formed. But there were non-Hispanic
colonies where, over long periods of time, a greater stability existed
among the white groups. There is no doubt that the white population
of Curaçao, for example, was subjected to both Latin and African cultural influences, which resulted in its "creolisation" (Hoetink, 1966:
137 ff.). Of course, this objective cultural adaptation has to be distinguished from the subjective awareness thereof: while vis-à-vis the
rest of Curaçao society and the neighboring countries, the Curaçao
whites invoked their Dutch cultural role, they came to recognize their
cultural "creole-identity" in their contacts with metropolitans; the
latter, in turn, reported vividly on these cultural "deviations."

The creation of such a creole cultural variant within the dominant
segment is conditioned by the degree of permanency of the white settlers, be they public servants, plantation owners, or yeomen; *qua*
cultural content, the creole deviation is determined by the culture of
the other population groups, by the contacts with the surrounding
cultures, and by the peculiar social structure of the colony, which demands cultural innovations; *qua* vigor and affirmative force, such a
creole variant will be influenced by the distinctions of privilege between creoles and homelanders, as Mintz suggests.

The question whether a strong *all-inclusive* awareness of cultural
identity came into being depended in part on channels of communication such as that constituted by the Catholic church in the Spanish
and French areas and within which indeed all colonists could participate, which was not the case with metropolitan religion in the Protes-
tant areas.

How great an obstacle a discontinuous socio-racial structure
could be for the development of a national identity out of a creole-
white separate identity vis-à-vis the mother country is made clear by
Gordon Lewis, (1968:168, 132), who suggests that one of the earliest
indications of a Jamaican "struggle toward nationhood" can be found
in "the efforts of the Jamaican settler-historians of the eighteenth
century, particularly Long and Edwards, to give a coherent creole
philosophical foundation to the struggle of the colonists against the
absentee metropolitan power"; but Lewis notes that this movement
"gradually [became] eroded as its wider and deeper growth within Jamaican soil was frustrated by the white distrust of the 'persons of colour' and by the joint insensate distrust that both white and colored

had for the black majority." "Similarly," he goes on to say, "the local-
ist loyalism of the great colored population of the later period was an
expression, likewise limited, of the continuing struggle against the social supremacy of the whites after their legal supremacy had been
broken." For Barbados, Lewis notes a parallel development: already
around the middle of the seventeenth century the local settlers were
characterized by a "separate and equal Barbadian identity" which
found its expression in political actions against the metropolitan power,
and which showed "how early in the colonization process a Creole society had been formed which, while not yet culturally homogeneous,
was already oriented in terms of separate colonial life." "But," Lewis
goes on, "with the development of a slave majority that theory of an
English community . . . degenerated, inevitably, into a defense of the
classes against the masses."

This latter observation brings us to the effects of the relative proportions of slaves, freemen, and whites on the development of national identity. No one would want to deny such effects, but they are
not easy to evaluate. If it could be established, that, as Mintz states,
"generally speaking, the Hispano-Caribbean colonies were never dominated demographically by inhabitants of African origin" (1970), then
even some causal relationship might be inferred. But several data
would be at variance with such a conclusion. Cuba in the years 1817,
1827, and 1841 had a majority of Negroes (as distinguished from coloreds) over whites.[18] And, more important, because it affected the
initial phases of culture contact, Santo Domingo had already in 1560
some 20,000 Negroes, 13,000 mestizos and mulattoes, and only 5,000
whites; around 1545, according to Benzoni, "the Negroes had multi-
plied in such a manner . . . that many Spaniards . . . did not doubt that
within a few years this island would become the property of the Negroes" (Cabral, 1967:80-82). This seems to indicate that a relatively
high degree of cultural homogenization in the Hispano-Caribbean societies could be achieved under sometimes adverse numerical conditions.

Finally, while I completely agree with Mintz that the development of an inclusive creole culture must be considered an important,
maybe even indispensable, condition for the creation of a strong sense
of national identity, I doubt whether a creole culture is a *sufficient*
condition for the fixation of an "assimilation model" such as he—
rightly, I think—postulates for the Hispanic Caribbean. The Deep

18. Cf. Pérez Cabral (1967:101) and the literature cited there.

South, characterized by a remarkable *cultural* homogeneity, did not produce a *social* assimilation model, comparable to the Hispano-Caribbean.

Yet it is indeed *social* assimilation which, in last instance, leads to sentiments of common descent and destiny, to an awareness of internal social cohesion, and to the subjective acceptance of the commonalty of collective experiences. It is also *social* assimilation which, once a population has achieved a certain degree of objective cultural homogeneity, helps to elevate this to a level of subjective solidarity, indispensable for a strong awareness of national identity.

If one wants to investigate the conditions which promoted social amalgamation in the Hispano-Caribbean multiracial societies, one has to start with the fact that very early in the history of all these societies, with a rhythm determined by economic and demographic conditions, a socio-racial continuum was being formed, while in the non-Hispanic Caribbean societies—no matter what their economic, demographic, and cultural differences were and are—the white creole group consistently has tried to abstain from such a national amalgamation.

REFERENCES

Barrett, Leonard E.
    1969   The Rastafarians: A Study in Messianic cultism in Jamaica. Rio
           Piedras: Institute of Caribbean Studies.
Bell, Wendell, and Ivar Oxaal.
    1964   Decisions of Nationhood: Political and Social Development in the
           British Caribbean. Denver: University of Denver.
Berghe, Pierre van den.
    1967   Race and Racism: A Comparative Perspective. New York: Wiley.
Buero, Salvador.
    1966   "Africa en América." Casa de las Américas 36/37:186.
Césaire, Aimé.
    1947   Cahier d'un Retour au Pays Natal. Paris: Présence Africaine.
           (First published 1939.)
    1955   "Discours sur le Colonialisme." Paris: Présence Africaine.
Coulthard, G. R.
    1968   "Parallelisms and Divergencies between 'Négritude' and 'In-
           digenismo'." Caribbean Studies 8, No. 1:31-57.

Deutsch, Karl W.
  1966   Nationalism and Social Communication. Second edition. Cambridge, Mass.: The M.I.T. Press.
Drimmer, Melvin, editor.
  1967   Black History: A Reappraisal. New York: Doubleday.
Fanon, Frantz.
  1953   Peau Noire, Masques Blancs. Paris: Editions du Seuil.
  1961   Les Damnés de la Terre. Paris: Maspéro.
Firmin, Anténor.
  1885   De l'Egalité des Race Humaines. Paris: F. Pichon.
Gamio, Manuel
  1916   Forjando Patria (pro nacionalismo). México: Porrua hermanos.
García-Zamor, Jean Claude.
  1970   "Social Mobility of Negroes in Brazil." Journal of Inter-American Studies and World Affairs XII, 1 (April): 242-254.
Hoetink, Harmannus.
  1966   Het Patroon van de oude Curacaose Samenleving. Aruba-Tiel: De Wit.
  1967   The Two Variants in Caribbean Race Relations. London: Oxford University Press.
  1970   "The Dominican Republic in the Nineteenth Century: Some Notes on Stratification, Immigration and Race." In Race and Class in Latin America, edited by Magnus Morner. New York: Columbia University Press.
  1971   El Pueblo Dominicano, 1850-1900: Apuntes para su Historia Sociologica. Santiago de los Caballeros: Universidad Católica Madre y Maestra.
  Forthcoming   Slavery and Race Relations in the Western Hemisphere. New York: Harper & Row.
Lewis, Gordon.
  1968   The Growth of the Modern West Indies. London: McGibbon and Kee.
Lewis, Sybil, and Thomas G. Mathews, editors.
  1967   Caribbean Integration: Papers on Social, Political and Economic Integration. Río Piedras: Institute of Caribbean Studies, University of Puerto Rico.
Leyburn, James G.
  1941   The Haitian People. Revised edition, 1966. New Haven: Yale University Press.
Lowenthal, David.
  1968   Race and Color in the West Indies. In Color and Race, edited by John Hope Franklin. Boston: Houghton Mifflin.
Maingot, Anthony P.
  1969   "From Ethnocentric to National History Writing in the Plural Society." Caribbean Studies 9, No. 3 (October):67-86.

Mintz, Sidney W.

1967 "Caribbean Nationhood in Anthropological Perspective." In Caribbean Integration; Papers on Social, Political and Economic Integration," pp. 141-155. Edited by Sybil Lewis and Thomas G. Mathews. Río Piedras: University of Puerto Rico.

1970 "Foreword." In Afro-American Anthropology: Contemporary Perspectives, edited by N. Whitten and J. Szwed. New York: Free Press.

1971 "Comments on the Socio-Historical Background to Pidginization and Creolization." In Pidginization and Creolization of Languages, Proceedings of a Conference held at the University of the West Indies, edited by D. Hymes. London and New York: Cambridge University Press.

Parsons, Talcott.

1968 "The Problem of Polarization on the Axis of Color." In Color and Race, edited by John Hope Franklin. Boston: Houghton Mifflin.

Pérez Cabral, Pedro Andres.

1967 La Comunidad Mulata; El Caso Socio-Politico de la República Dominicana Caracas: Grafica Americana.

Pool, Jonathan.

1970 "National Development and Language Diversity." Sociologische Gids 17, No. 2:86-102.

Price, Hannibal.

1900 De la Rehabilitation de la Race Noire, par la République d'Haiti. Port-au-Prince: J. Verrollot.

Price-Mars, Jean.

1928 Ainsi Parla l'Oncle. Reprint edition, 1954. New York: Parapsychology Foundation, Inc.

The Limitations of the "Segmented" Model in Explaining Race Relations in the Caribbean

MY REACTIONS to Dr. Hoetink's paper will be restricted to its ideological basis; to the utility or usefulness of a model for explaining social relations; to the value of the segmented model in reference to the Caribbean Society in general and its utility to the understanding of race relations and national identity.

Let me preface my comments about the presentation by pointing out the analogy between the events of tonight and a political process among the Zulu of South Africa. Those unfamiliar with the anthropological discourse will soon notice that all western social science partakes in the same body of concepts and is dominated by identical ideology.

Max Gluckman (1963:114) discussed, in one of his publications, two cases of what he calls "ritual of rebellion, an instituted protest demanded by sacred tradition which is seemingly against the established order, yet which aim is to bless that order to achieve prosperity."

He reported that, in Zululand, there existed a practice according to which women, who generally occupy an inferior position, are given a dominant role over men during the "first fruits ceremonies." He also argued that preceding the "first fruits ceremonies," the king of the Zulu participated in a ceremony during which the conflicts and contradictions of the society are given full expression. These ritualistic conflicts are interpreted by Gluckman (1963:110-115) as reinforcing mechanisms for the status quo.

This reference to the Zulu situation will help us in at least two ways: The events of tonight place Dr. Hoetink in a situation analogous to the rituals of rebellions described by Gluckman. In 1962, Professor Hoetink introduced me to the analysis of what is referred to as "segmented" and "plural" societies. In the rituals of tonight, Professor Hoetink is at a disadvantage. I was given the opportunity to read his paper in order to prepare my comments. He unfortunately will have to improvise in defending his position. I venture to guess that the organizers of the symposium hope that the "institutionalization of conflicts" we witness today will provide strength to the academic systems.

These comments lead me to the second reason for citing Gluckman: there are close theoretical and ideological similarities between the views expressed by Professor Hoetink and that of Gluckman. Five years ago, in my first systematic attempt to apply the concept of segmented society to my country, Haiti, I very early realized that this concept as reflected in the model had no explanatory power, it was antichange or reactionary. It looked at the social situation only from the point of view of the dominant group and therefore could make no prediction about structural change.

The Segmented Model Within the Modern Sociological Trend

Modern social science has recently moved toward including conflict among its concern. Lewis Coser (1964:31) has best summarized the dominant theoretical and ideological interpretation in the following statement: "No group can be entirely harmonious, for it would then be devoid of structure and process. Groups require disharmony as well as harmony, disassociation as well as association, and conflicts within them are by no means altogether disruptive factors."

Let's compare this statement with what Gluckman (1963:126, 17-18) says: "This acting of conflicts achieves a blessing, social unity." He goes on to say,

One has to think of civil wars as occuring constantly in the polity and involving contenders in a fight to seize the kingship rather than in a struggle for independence from it. . . . I knew too much of African history to believe that this was the only process at work, and that no sections will ever break out of the polity. But the process of civil war to maintain the kingship as a central process in the political system, might be present even where the king or chief has substantial secular power.

In this paper the nature of race relations, the strength or weakness of national identity, are analyzed within the framework of a model of "segmented society." From Dr. Hoetink's presentation, the segmented societies made up of different, and sometimes antagonistic social or racial groups, exist in a state of equilibrium—maybe unstable —which is maintained by the power of the dominant group (see Hoetink, 1967:Pt. II, Chap. II). He then proceeds to describe the complexities of this equilibrium and the conditions for its preservation. The establishment of harmony thus depends not in a remodeling of the society but rather in the presence or establishment of a "socio-racial continuum" which will foster harmony and strong national identity.

In the Caribbean, Professor Hoetink tries to give legitimacy to the segmented model developed by Boeke for the Dutch Colonies of the Far East. For the Dutch, pluralism and segmentation were the key analytical concepts for understanding of the colonial situation. In the Caribbean, M. G. Smith and Professor Hoetink respectively have risen as the main proponents of "pluralism and segmentation," while trying to make these models fit the Caribbean reality of today. M. G. Smith (1965) distinguished between social and cultural pluralism. Professor Hoetink (1967:Pt. II, Chap. II), on the other hand, borrowed from Frank Tannenbaum the concepts of Iberian and Anglo-Saxon variants and incorporated them into the segmented models.

Under Dr. Hoetink's pen (1967), the segmented society in its moment of origin consists of "at least two groups of people of different races and cultures, each having its own internal institutions and social structures." The Caribbean in this model consists of two polar types: the vertically and horizontally segmented societies, the differences between the two being the extent to which there exist a socio-racial continuum expressed in the vertical allocation of resources among the races and in the presence of a strong national identity to foster national solidarity.

To put it in a trite manner, by changing the racial ideology, you get rid of the social conflicts. It is not, therefore, surprising that some members of the U.S. Congress complained about the fact that the Black Panther party has decided to drop "racism" as its main concern to concentrate in the fight against imperialism.

To what extent does the segmented model reflect the social structure of Caribbean societies?

Social scientists have argued about the racial categories in Latin America in comparison with those of the United States. On the one hand, Herring, Gillin, Beate Saltz, and others, lumping phenotype with genotype, claim that there exist no racial but social prejudices in Latin America. On the other hand, Marvin Harris, Eduardo Seda Bonilla, and others have rightly argued that race prejudice is a type of social prejudice and therefore should be seen within the general class structure of the society. Eduardo Seda Bonilla presented a convincing case for his island, Puerto Rico. Professor Hoetink would like us to believe that the horizontally segmented society—that is, a society in which the socio-economic classes closely follow the race lines—exists in the Caribbean. This view is nothing but an illusion of the idealized categories used by Dr. Hoetink. Without explicitly stating it, the author accepts James Leyburn's characterization of Haiti's social structure in terms of a "caste" system. To convince Dr. Hoetink, one needs only to refer him to the saying that "a poor mulatto is a black; a wealthy black is a mulatto." Barbados is the only society which would most approximate the horizontally segmented society. Even in this case, Dr. Sutton (1969) and I (1970), in two different publications, have shown that the folk concept referred to as a "bracket system" provides a better understanding of the nature of the Barbados society.

The social structure of the Caribbean societies is rather characteristic of a period in which the traditional scale of values based on ethnic differentiation is being questioned. It would be more appropriate to conceive of these societies in the way Elliott Skinner (1960:905) has described Guyana, as "a society in flux with traditional group lines giving way at several points. The groups involved are not only trying to gain as much as they can from the economic system, but one is trying to monopolize those traits in Western culture that make for high status, while the other, through the process of acculturation, is trying to acquire them." The resistance to change is still very great because, in the postindependence period, these countries still remain under the control of the imperialistic powers. The group which in the past most approximated the imperialists, phenotypically and ideologically, is most likely to retain its dominant position, thus reinforcing cultural and ethnic differences. In the situation of highly mobile individuals from the less privileged groups, they "are even forced to adopt or maintain sentiments, and loyalties and identities in keeping with their new interest. In many instances, these interests unite them with individuals of many of the groups in the society, but invariably this conflicts with their group values" (Skinner, 1960:906).

Present-day Caribbean social structure reflects the neocolonial character of the relations between the social classes within these countries, and those with the industrialized societies. New activities are being initiated which require a disruption of the traditional system of allocation of wealth, and which demand a greater degree of vertical mobility for those who lacked it in the past. However, this new trend still favors those groups which, in the traditional system, most identify with the interests of these foreign powers. These are the groups which determine the nature and strength of national identity.

Segmentation and National Identity. Elaborating upon Tannenbaum's dichotomy, Dr. Hoetink sought out the relationship between socio-racial structure and national identity. He thus concluded that national identity tended to be stronger where there existed a fluidity of racial and cultural categories. This, according to Dr. Hoetink, was reflected in the national symbols, whose function was to reinforce national cohesiveness. Wherever there was a socio-racial continuum, the national symbols tended to represent all racial or cultural segments. To prove his arguments, Dr. Hoetink chose to discourse at length on the situation of Haiti. Dr. Hoetink got a good start by attributing the *mouvement indigeniste* to the well-to-do local middle class. But his emphasis on the ideology of racial identity prevented him from carrying the argument to its logical conclusions. A few examples will help to illustrate.

Referring to Haiti, the *négritude* or *mouvement indigeniste* was initiated by the black segment of the Haitian bourgeoisie in association with a few mulattoes. Dr. Price Mars, the main ideologue of the movement, asked the mulatto bourgeoisie to look back toward Africa for cultural and national revitalization. It is also necessary to emphasize that the support received by the *mouvement indigeniste* can in part be explained by the crisis situation of the moment. The behavior of American military occupation forces has destroyed any dream of the mulatto bourgeoisie of being considered equal to the white man. More important is the fact that the movement initially was strictly cultural in nature. Those who identified with the black masses politically moved to create the socialist party. When, about twenty-five years later, Duvalier attempted to enlist the disparate members of the movement into a political party, he could rely only on a small group of black intellectuals to formulate a common ideology which would facilitate their incorporation into the local bourgeoisie. This national identity Dr. Hoetink saw being reflected in the indigenist movement is nothing but the view of those from above.

With the exception of Dessalines, all the heroes included in the national pantheon have had a conciliatory attitude toward the Western European, this at the expense of the black masses. In many instances, Dessalines has been depicted as a "black savage" by the mulatto elite. Until recently, the black masses have had nothing to do with the formulations of a national identity. Let us look at another country.

Brazil is well known for its complex racial categories. Nevertheless, in the forties it experienced a black nationalist movement which has torn asunder the myth of a racially harmonious Brazil. Several writers on Brazil, such as Da Costa Pinto (1952) and Harris (1964) have shown that, in spite of the upper-class claim to racial democracy, the economy, the high positions in businesses, government, and diplomacy are in the hands of the brancos.

In the case of Brazil, as well as in the situation of the independent British Caribbean, the national ideology has always been formulated by the local upper white and/or brown-skin class in collusion with the colonial powers. One has to agree with Dr. Hoetink when he states that "cultural aspects are generally somewhat more heavily emphasized by those whose socio-economic position is relatively secure and who as a group are not bound to expect considerable advantage of radical economic and therefore racial changes." On the one hand, however, one need not look for the presence or absence of a socio-racial continuum to understand why the movements led by Duvalier in Haiti or the many government-supported Black Power movements from the Caribbean, the activities of LeRoi Jones in the United States, etc., emphasize a new cultural tribalism, and why, on the other hand, Abeng in Jamaica, the PPM of Barbados, the PPP of Guyana, the People Forum of Grenada, the Black Panther party in the United States, address themselves to the socio-economic situations of the whole area and that of the Third World. Difference in socio-racial structure is seen as secondary by the latter groups. The PPM in Barbados (1967), clearly expressed this view: "The PPM considers the Caribbean to stretch from Havana to Cayenne and to include all territories in the area that have suffered from colonies and plantation experience. We do not regard other Caribbean citizens as foreigners."

In the presentation, Dr. Hoetink has shown more of a mastering of a certain category of Caribbean literature than first-hand familiarity with the area. He has concentrated in those publications and arguments which tended to support the elitist point of view. Even the work of a "respectable writer" like Jayawardena on the East Indians of Guyana is ignored because the empirical facts tend to give more weight to a class then to a race-based interpretation.

In the concept of segmented society is a built-in bias toward the dominant group and/or colonial power. Neither the coercive power of the government in the plural society, nor the control of the dominant group, in the segmented one, is questioned. We are placed before a dilemma or a *fait accompli*. To repeat Schattschneider (1960), "the flaw in the pluralist heaven is that the heavenly chorus sings with a strong upper-class accent."

The nature of race relations and national identity must also be seen within the context of relations between the nation-states of the Caribbean and the empirical powers.

Race or ethnic relations in the New World have been marked since the intrusion of the Spaniards by a state of conflict which manifests the antagonisms inherent to the social structure. One can hardly mention a general theory which purports to explain the nature of and make predictions about race relations.[1] Thus, the Watts or the Harlem rebellions can only be explained in *a posteriori* terms. Ironically enough, it is those individuals who predicted the 1970 rebellion in Trinidad whom Dr. Hoetink accuses of making use in their analysis of "universalistic" categories.

Social scientists are now ready to explain these uprisings by referring to governmental inefficiency or other commonplace arguments. We must now ask: How is the relationship between the Caribbean and the imperial powers seen in the presentation?

In the last twenty years, anthropologists have recognized the necessity to incorporate in their analyses the outside influences affecting the societies under study. Marshall Sahlins's (1961:321-345) reanalysis of the Nuer materials is an eloquent case. With regard to the Caribbean, Robert Manners (1965:183), has argued that, "It is clear for the Caribbean at least, that a body of land entirely surrounded by water is no longer an island. . . . to study these islands, on their parts as if they were independent of outside influence and pressure, would be naive in the extreme." Professor Hoetink prefers to limit his analysis to the geographical limits of each society. While acknowledging the usefulness and academic legitimacy of the more encompassing approaches, he feels nevertheless ill at ease in their company, his objection being that these approaches, which are universalistic in na-

---

1. Professor Wallerstein, in this volume, must be commended for having demonstrated the usefulness of the concept of race in explaining group relations in Africa. His conception of race as a "status group" is methodologically a step toward a general understanding of race relations.

ture, can accommodate a variety of disparate societies. It is unfortunate that Professor Hoetink chooses to minimize the theoretical importance of the structural similarities between Haiti, Indonesia, and Ghana. Such reluctance may be interpreted as the expression of deep ideological division in the social sciences manifested in terms of "objectivity versus engagement." The paper is less convincing because of the author's unwillingness to delve into the influence of outside or foreign interests in the affairs of the Caribbean. Referring to Curaçao, Professor Hoetink said:

One may observe the fact that some of the complaints of the twentieth-century Curaçaoans against the policies of the Royal Dutch Shell or against the social behavior of its personnel curiously resemble the complaints of their eighteenth-century predecessors against the West Indian Company and its servants. In both cases, these criticisms result from the supremacy of a powerful economic organization, more backed than checked by the metropolitan power, in a small society whose own resources are too few to provide an adequate response.

Does this mean that to avoid a new uprising in the Dutch West Indies the Royal government of the Netherlands needs to keep close watch on the Royal Dutch Shell?

The principal shortcomings of modern social science are the neglect of general theory and the increasing reliance on abstract model. Western social scientists often forget that models are analogies and cannot explain social realities. David Kaplan (1968:244) has recently expressed the importance and limitations of a model in the following manner: "Though they (models) may constitute an important and perhaps even indispensable aid in arriving at explanation, they do not explain anything. A model can have explanatory power only if the various axioms or postulates of the model are assured a specific empirical content."

In this respect, it is advisable to mention Claude Levi-Strauss's (1963) useful distinction between conscious and unconscious models. Conscious models reflect the people's perception of their social structures. Unconscious models are the social scientist's comment about the society under study. The popularity of model building results from Robert Merton's (1968) attack on "Grand Theory" and his proposal that sociologists devote their attention to what he calls "middle-range theory."

In middle-range theory, individual social phenomena assume a life of their own and lend themselves easily to independent studies. Specific aspects of society can be isolated to be studied. In this context, race relations can become an independent subject of analysis outside the general characters of social relations in the society. Following Merton, the theoretical atmosphere was conveniently set for Dr. Hoetink to introduce his own brand of segmented society in the analysis of race relations.

Conclusions. Very recently Professor James Blaut (1970:65) bluntly stated: "All of Western science and historiography is so closely interwoven with western imperialism that the former can only describe and justify the latter, not predict it or explain it or control it . . . not even when human survival is at stake, as may now be the case."

Other social scientists such as Kathleen Gough Aberle (1968), Gunder Frank (1970), and David Horowitz (1970:1-10), to name only a few, share the same idea about the close dependence between western science (especially social sciences) and western imperialism. In this context, the segmented model originally devised as a means of analyzing the colonial situation at a given moment in time, has lost its significance for explaining race relations in the modern West Indies.

This presentation raises other more basic issues, but for lack of time we have limited ourselves to comments on the usefulness and ideological bias of the model. By refining the concept of segmented society, Professor Hoetink has given a great many of us from the Caribbean the opportunity to raise some fundamental questions. As Dr. Bryce Laporte, (1970) a former student of Dr. Hoetink, says: "For whom does pluralism work?"

To answer this question, many of us from the Caribbean stand with the suffering masses. It is more than obvious that in such circumstances, Dr. Hoetink's view will become obsolete, but not forgotten. We are certain he will make his the following thought, "for those who pay their obeisance in a true scientific spirit, the fact that science evolves beyond the points they have themselves attained is not to be interpreted as a betrayal of them. It is the fulfillment of their highest hopes" (Parsons, 1968:41). By taking the concept of segmented society to a high level of intellectual sophistication, Dr. Hoetink has provided us from the Caribbean with an opportunity to sharpen our intellect. This we will use for the benefit of the suffering masses of the Caribbean.

REFERENCES

Aberle, Kathleen Gough.
    1968 "New Proposals for Anthropologists." Current Anthropology 9, No. 5 (December).
Blaut, James.
    1970 Geographic Model of Imperialism. Antipode I (August).
Coser, Lewis.
    1964 The Functions of Social Conflict. New York: Free Press.
Costa Pinto, L. A.
    1952 O Negro no Rio de Janeiro. São Paulo: Companhía Editôra Nacional, Brasiliana, 276.
Frank, Gunder.
    1970 "On Dalton's Theoretical Issues in Economic Anthropology." Current Anthropology II, No. 1 (February).
Gluckman, Max.
    1963 Order and Rebellion in Tribal Africa. New York: Free Press.
Harris, Marvin.
    1964 Patterns of Race in the Americas. New York: Walker and Company.
Hoetink, Harmannus.
    1967 The Two Variants of Race Relations in the Caribbean. London: Oxford University Press.
Horowitz, David.
    1970 "Social Science of Ideology." Berkeley Journal of Sociology XV: 1-10.
Kaplan, David.
    1968 "The Formal-Substantive Controversy in Economic Anthropology: Reflections on its Wider Implications." Southwestern Journal of Anthropology 24:244.
Laporte, Simon Bryce.
    1970 "M. G. Smith's Version of Pluralism: The Questions It Raises." Comparative Studies in Society and History X, No. 1 (October).
Levi-Strauss, Claude.
    1963 Structural Anthropology. New York: Basic Books.
Manners, Robert A.
    1965 "Remittances and the Unit of Analysis in Anthropological Research." Southwestern Journal of Anthropology 21, No. 3:183.
Merton, Robert K.
    1949 Social Theory and Social Structure. Revised edition, 1968. New York: Free Press.
P.P.M.
    1967 Election pamphlet.

Parsons, Talcott.
    1968   The Structure of Social Action. New York: Free Press.
Remy, Anselme.
    1970   "Men's Clique in a Barbados Community." Mimeographed.
Sahlins, Marshall D.
    1961   "The Segmentary Lineage: An Organization of Predatory Ex-
            pansion." American Anthropologist 63:321-345.
Schattschneider, E. E.
    1960   The Semi-Sovereign People. New York: Holt, Rinehart and
            Winston.
Skinner, Elliott P.
    1960   "Group Dynamics and Social Stratification in British Guiana."
            In Social and Cultural Pluralism in the Caribbean, Annals, New
            York Academy of Sciences, v. 83, art. 5, edited by V. Rubin and
            others, pp. 904-912. New York: New York Academy of Sciences.
Smith, M. G.
    1965   "Social and Cultural Pluralism." In The Plural Society in the
            British West Indies. Berkeley: University of California Press.
Sutton, Constance.
    1969   "The Scene of the Action: A Wildcat Strike in Barbados." Ph.D.
            dissertation. New York: Columbia University.

Comment GERRY E. HENDERSHOT

Ethnic Stratification

EARLY IN his paper, Professor Hoetink notes that many popular approaches to the analysis of intranational conflict between racial and cultural groups are at a "high level of abstraction." So abstract are these approaches, in fact, that they tend to obscure important variations among nations, and lead—in the extreme—to the conviction that "when you have seen one 'Third World' country, you have seen all of them."

American sociologists have, perhaps because of their typically limited exposure to cultures other than their own, been more guilty than others of such overgeneralization—and I include myself in that indictment. Professor Hoetink has, therefore, done us a service by demonstrating that even within his area of specialization—the nations of the Caribbean and those which border it—there are significant differences in the interrelationships of national identity, culture, and race. I expect that the papers we will hear and discuss later in this conference will further emphasize the diversity of those relationships and the difficulty of developing general explanations.

Despite the difficulty, however, we will—and I believe we should —continue the search for explanations with cross-national applicability. As Professor Hoetink himself notes, such explanations "respond to the sociologist's avid need for wide generalization." For that reason my remarks will focus on those aspects of the paper which seem to me to hold the promise of a general explanation of the relationships between race and national identity. In doing so, I will be working from my own understanding of Professor Hoetink's ideas, an understanding which may be imperfect.

To begin, the object of analysis—the thing which is under investigation—is the ethnic stratification system of a nation. It consists of two or more hierarchically arranged categories of people who have, or at least believe they have, distinctive ancestries. More specifically, interest centers on those ethnic stratification systems in which recognizable somatic differences are of primary importance in the social definition of ethnic categories. Excluded are those stratification systems in which ethnicity is not important, and—with less rigor—those ethnic stratification systems in which somatic differences are not important.

Along what important dimensions do ethnic stratification systems vary? Although Professor Hoetink mentions many dimensions, the frequency of their use suggests three which are most important to his thought: the "angle" of the social barrier separating groups, whether horizontal or vertical; the "continuity" of social distinctions made among groups; and the "continuity" of cultural distinctions among groups.

With regard to the angle of barriers between groups, in some stratification systems membership in a particular group places individuals above some groups and below others—the barriers divide the society in *horizontal* layers; in other stratification systems, however, membership in a particular group, while clearly distinguishing the individual from other groups, does not place him above or below them; the barriers divide the society in *vertical* segments.

The angle of intergroup barriers may have important consequences for national solidarity. Professor Hoetink notes, for instance, that the prominent examples of viable heterogenous societies have *vertical* boundaries between groups. He suggests that in vertically segmented societies, individuals of different ethnic groups are more likely to make common cause with one another because of a similarity in socio-economic interests. In horizontally layered societies, where the ethnic and economic interests of each group tend to coincide, a commonality of interest is less likely to develop.

If vertical barriers are more conducive to intergroup solidarity, however, one wonders about recent developments in the United States. There, presumably, the barrier between whites and blacks has been shifting from horizontal to vertical, although the process is far from complete and its continuation is in doubt; yet black-white solidarity has not increased significantly, and it may have decreased. Perhaps the movement toward solidarity is not even in all stages of the transition; or perhaps the minimum of intergroup penetration and communication across vertical barriers—which Professor Hoetink believes necessary for solidarity—is not achieved in the U.S.

The second important dimension of ethnic stratification systems is social (or socio-racial) continuity. In some systems, notably the United States, the social definitions of ethnic categories are clear-cut and nearly immutable for the individual; one is black or white from birth and there are no significant intermediate categories. In other systems, however, such as that of Brazil, there are no clear distinctions between dominant and minority groups; rather there is a continuous gradation of somatically and socially defined ethnic types.

There are also variations in the continuity of cultural differences among ethnic groups, the third important dimension. In some societies the cultures of ethnic groups—their beliefs, values, and norms —differ significantly; in other societies, such differences may be almost entirely absent. The mulattoes and black masses of Haiti illustrate cultural discontinuity, and whites and blacks in the U.S. illustrate—according to Professor Hoetink—cultural continuity.

I think that these latter two dimensions—social and cultural continuity—can be usefully combined to create a typology of ethnic stratification systems. In fact, Professor Hoetink does so, at least implicitly. I would like to make that typology more explicit and formal.

National ethnic stratification systems can be categorized, at least in theory, as socially continuous or socially discontinuous; also, they can be categorized as culturally continuous or culturally discontinuous. Combining the two dimensions, there are four logically possible types. At one extreme are those systems which are socially and culturally continuous: there is a finely graded set of socio-racial categories with indistinct boundaries, and there are few significant differences in the values and norms of people in different categories; Brazil exemplifies such a system. At the other extreme are those systems which are discontinuous both culturally and socially: clear and firm boundaries separate the groups socially, and their values and norms are significantly different; if I am not mistaken, Professor Hoetink does not deal with this type at all. Do systems of this type exist? If so, how do they differ from the other types?

Between the two extremes are the mixed types: those, such as Haiti, which are socially continuous, but contain culturally different groups; and those, such as the United States, which are socially discontinuous, but are homogenous with respect to culture.

Professor Hoetink's data suggest that there may be systematic differences among the four types of society. For instance, in societies which are both socially and culturally continuous (for example, Brazil), there is a low probability of the formation of solidary and militant minority group movements; members of the lower strata, although seeing themselves as "different," and possibly suffering from that perception, also see themselves as socially "related" to higher strata; and they share the same beliefs, values, and norms. They do (or can) identify with the nation rather than with their minority group.

In the mixed types—those which have social or cultural continuity, but not both—solidary and militant ethnic movements have a higher probability of occurrence. Whether the discontinuity is social or cultural, minority group members see themselves as different and *un*related to other groups; their identity is, therefore, more likely to be with their ethnic group rather than with the nation, which must include members of other groups.

Whether the discontinuity is social or cultural also makes a difference: where there is cultural discontinuity, but social continuity, the goals of a minority movement tend to involve the dignity of the race, because the leaders of the movement, usually drawn from the higher levels of the lower strata, already enjoy considerable economic and political advantage. But where there is social discontinuity, but cultural continuity, the leaders of the movement are politically and economically disadvantaged, and their goal is the redress of those grievances rather than cultural dignity.

Finally, in the societies whose stratifications systems are both socially and culturally *dis*continuous—a type not discussed by Professor Hoetink—my hunch is that solidary and militant minority group movements have a low probability of occurrence. I have no evidence in mind to support that assertion, and perhaps it derives solely from a desire to maintain the symmetry of the typology.

If my remarks have any significance at all, it lies in their indication of ways in which Professor Hoetink's ideas might be formalized and generalized. Formalization and generalization inevitably lead to some loss of precision; on the other hand, they seem to me to be necessary if we are to move toward measurement and quantitative analysis of these important processes. And movement in that direction is necessary as a supplement to—*not* a substitute for—the provocative insights provided by the historical-cultural method of study employed by Professor Hoetink.

2 IRA KATZNELSON

The Politics of Racial Buffering in England, 1948-1968: Colonial Relationships in The Mother Country

IN "A Societal Theory of Race and Ethnic Relations," Stanley Lieberson (1961:902-910) distinguishes between two fundamental, contrasting types of racial and ethnic contacts: migrant superordination (the pure colonial case), where a minority migrant population imposes its will on an indigenous majority; and indigenous superordination (the voluntary migrant case), where a minority inmigrates to a situation where it is subordinate, if only temporarily. Lieberson argues that each of these contact situations produces a dynamic of its own. Colonial contact situations typically lead to a numerical decline of the indigenous population, new political boundaries, middleman minorities, and, ultimately, nationalist revolt. The immigrant case, on the other hand, is marked by the increasing assimilation of the voluntary immigrants into the ongoing social and political order and by striking cultural assimilation as well.

This typology ignores a third case, of which the British racial situation is a striking example: the case of voluntary migration that is at least partly a product of the colonial contact situation.[1] On the face of it, the movement of colored Commonwealth migrants to Britain since 1948 is an instance of the voluntary migrant case. Indeed, much

This paper develops out of a larger study comparing the political responses to black migration to the North in the United States, 1900-1930, and to the United Kingdom, 1948-1968. This study, *Black Men, White Cities*, by Ira Katznelson, will be published in 1972 for the Institute of Race Relations, London, by Oxford University Press. Copyright 1972 by the Institute of Race Relations.

1. For a discussion of American race relations in these terms, see Blauner (1969: 398-408).

race relations scholarship in Britain has adopted this orientation, focusing on acculturation and gradual assimilation. Sheila Patterson (1963:8-9), for one, has argued that "the new West Indian migrants to Britain are, in fact, passing through the same kinds of dynamic process in their relationships with the local population as do all other working-class economic migrants." Not only does this perspective ignore a considerable amount of empirical evidence on racial discrimination in England and the obvious point that, in contrast to white immigrants, the immigrants of color will be permanently visible (and in this sense, if in no other, will be a permanent minority), but it also ignores the colonial context of the movement to the Mother Country.

The movement of large numbers of colored colonized and formerly colonized migrants to the United Kingdom after the Second World War coincided with the liquidation of the British Empire, and, consequently, with a fundamental redefinition of British political relationships with Third World (non-European, non-Western, non-white) peoples. In 1948, there were few Third World people in Britain. In the same year, the Empire's citizenship provisions were redefined and codified by the passage of the British Nationality Act which divided British citizens into two classes: citizens of independent Commonwealth countries, and the remainder, lumped together under the rubric "citizen of the United Kingdom and Colonies." Two decades later, in 1968, the total colored population in England and Wales was estimated at 1,113,000, or roughly two percent of the total population, and the citizenship arrangements of 1948 were commonly acknowledged to have lost even their symbolic content.[2] The migration of Third World Commonwealth people to the Mother Country was thus linked in both time and space to Britain's colonial and postcolonial arrangements.

British race relations, therefore, can only be understood as an amalgam of Lieberson's two types. The immigrants have not arrived from anywhere; they have come from the British Commonwealth. And they have not moved to any urbanized, industrial locale, but to Britain. In Jerome Hartenfel's (1967:16) novel of West Indian immigration, the protagonist, a prospective migrant in his teens, muses:

I wanted to get out of the dirt, the noise, and the everlasting oppression of

2. The population estimate appears in Rose and Associates (1969:100); for a discussion of the citizenship issue, see Donald Rothschild, "Politics of Commonwealth Immigration: The Kenya Asian Crisis," unpublished paper.

hundreds of human beings crowded too closely upon me and upon each other; and I wanted to get out of being a black boy, out of that black skin that, as I saw it, made such conditions an unbreakable rule of nature and life. The first problem I hoped to solve by going to England; about the second I was less clear, but it seemed sufficiently interconnected with the first for me to hope my eventual journey to England might solve that, too.

As in any voluntary migration, the migrants were self-selected. In a real sense, the "children" of Empire were coming home. "Again and again," John Rex and Robert Moore (1967:156, 100) observe in their study of race relations in Sparkbrook, "as we read our research notes we find our West Indian respondents protesting they are not different from anyone else . . . West Indians come to England as to their mother country."

The Third World immigrants are not, of course, a homogeneous group; they are West Indians, Pakistanis, Indians, African Blacks, and African Asians whose social, cultural, and religious differences from each other are often greater than the intrinsic differences that distinguish them from white Englishmen. Nevertheless, they should be considered analytically as a single group because, as a collectivity, they form a meaningful stratification unit whose members share objective interests, similar vantage points, and a shared consciousness, actual or potential.[3] Most concretely, the immigrants share the dual bond of a colonial past and a skin color darker than white, as well as similar occupational and residential positions in England where they have acted as a replacement population in declining urban cores of industrial regions unable to attract a sufficient number of workers (Peach, 1968:82). Moreover, most British politicians, in their rhetoric, legislation, and deeds, have dealt with the country's Third World population as a single group.

Despite the intimate connection between the migration and the colonial experience, to date, even race relations scholars who reject the pure immigrant model have failed to deal with the British situation as a complex amalgam of the immigrant and colonial cases. Thus, for example, the most comprehensive study of British race relations yet published, which rightly stresses the interaction of the racial majority and minority, downgrades the significance of the colonial factor and, as a result, fails to analyze incisively the fabricated linkages of the immigrants and the polity (Rose and Associates, 1969). The study deals

3. For a discussion, see Etzioni (1968:98, 439).

at length with the origins, passage, and effects of immigration control
legislation and antidiscrimination legislation; but it has little to say
about the network of national and local institutions established to
manage the politics of race, which, I will argue below, give domestic
expression to classic colonial arrangements of political control.

Other research tries to transcend the immigrant and colonial dimensions by focusing on prejudice and discrimination.[4] The focus
on prejudice, as Schermerhorn (1970:6) notes, "has a subtle tendency
to psychologize group relations by seeing them as personality processes writ large." Consequently, it begs the questions: what are the
social, economic, and political origins of relationships of racial inequality, and what social, economic, and political factors sustain such
relationships? Thus those who focus on prejudice ignore the situations that produce and sustain prejudicial perceptions and attitudes,
and often engage in fruitless polemical argument about the number
and intensity of prejudiced Englishmen (Rose, 1969; Richmond,
1966), debate which usually has more to do with methodology than
objective reality. A focus on discrimination is also limited, and misleading, to the extent that it diverts attention away from concrete
structures, institutions, and relationships. Like prejudice, discriminatory acts have no meaning apart from concrete contexts.

Structure, then (which "may be defined as the relationships in a
social situation which limit the choice process to a particular range of
alternatives"), not behavior ("defined as the selection process in
choice, i.e., deciding between alternatives"[Apter, 1963b:732]) is the
logical starting point of analysis; to begin with behavior, stressing
perceptions, socialization, discriminatory acts, voting patterns, protest activity, and the like would assume a knowledge of structure and
the boundaries of choice possibilities. Without an analysis of structural relationships, an analysis of choice behavior can have little
meaning.

Many aspects of British race relations deserve, and to some extent have received, extended treatment (Sivanandan, 1967). Demographic, religious, educational, economic, family, and associational
issues, policies, and practices provide potentially fascinating areas of
inquiry. Based on a concern with the neglected colonial-immigrant
amalgam and with a first-order concern for structure, this essay ad-
dresses itself to a narrow, but vital range of questions: it explores British political responses to Third World immigration during the early,

4. For a summary, see Richmond (1966:181-209).

and relatively fluid, period of interracial contact; and examines the emergence, nature, and possible consequences of racial-political institutional relationships that link the immigrants to the polity through national and local buffering institutions in a manner strikingly different from the way in which white Englishmen are linked to the polity, thus producing a politics of race that contrasts sharply with the country's institutionalized politics of class and replicates aspects of the classic colonial pattern of indirect rule.

This paper begins with an examination of the Labour Government's White Paper of August 1965, which gave political expression to the immigrant-colonial amalgam. I will argue that the White Paper represented an effort to depoliticize race by dealing with both aspects of the British racial situation. A key feature of the White Paper was the establishment of national and local institutions to deal with the politics of race by mediating between the Third World immigrants and the polity. These structures are then examined with particular reference to their implications for immigrant leadership, participation, and decision-making capabilities. The paper concludes with an analysis of the colonial features of these linkages, their consequences for racial justice, and the directions they point to for future research.

On 2 August 1965, the Labour Government published a White Paper which set out "the Government's future policy on immigration to Britain from other parts of the Commonwealth and on the problems which it has given rise" (Government White Paper, 1965:2). This policy had

two aspects: one relating to control on the entry of immigrants so that it does not outrun Britain's capacity to absorb them; the other relating to positive measures designed to secure for the immigrants and their children their rightful place in our society and to assist local authorities and other bodies in areas of high immigration (Government White Paper, 1965:2).

The White Paper spoke of "the need to control the entry of immigrants to our small overcrowded country," in announcing that the annual rate of issue of labor vouchers would be cut drastically to 8,500 a year, of which 1,000 would be allocated to Malta. Category C vouchers, for those who did not have a specific job to come to and/or lacked special qualifications or skills, would be permanently discontinued (Kaufman, 1965).

The limitations on voluntary immigration were linked in the White Paper to the establishment of new institutional mechanisms, officially sponsored yet largely voluntary, to link the immigrants and the local and national political systems. The document announced a new National Committee for Commonwealth Immigrants which would "co-ordinate on a national basis efforts directed towards the integration of Commonwealth immigrants into the community." In particular, the Committee would be required to:

(a) Promote and co-ordinate the activities of voluntary liason committees and advise them on their work;
(b) Where necessary, assist in the recruitment and training of suitable men and women to serve these committees as full-time officials;
(c) Provide a central information service;
(d) Organize conferences, arrange training courses and stimulate research;
(e) Advise on those questions which are referred to them by Government or which they consider should be brought to the attention of Government (Government White Paper, 1965:16-17).

The National Committee's personnel was to consist of a chairman, deputy chairman, and eighteen other members, all voluntary, part-time, and unpaid. The Government's unsuccessful attempt to persuade Lord Butler (the Conservative Home Secretary who introduced controls on Commonwealth immigration in 1962) to accept the chairmanship of the National Committee (NCCI), and the subsequent appointment of the Archbishop of Canterbury to the post, graphically symbolized the Government's hope to depoliticize race.

British politics, Samuel Beer asserts (1965:69-102, 319-390), have entered the collectivist age, but, one is tempted to add, the liberal collectivist age. The political model which saw the rational, independent individual as the source of action has been replaced by a politics of rational independent groups. The liberal assumptions of rationalism, independence, and tolerance have carried over into the group politics of the mid-twentieth century. Thus the "rational" conflicts of class can be managed and institutionalized. Indeed, the increasing institutionalization and coherence of the politics of class is the most salient feature of twentieth-century British political history.

From the turn of the century to the First World War, as the country faced substantial labor unrest, the Labour party resembled a pressure group, and the trade union movement grew rapidly, class conflicts appeared to threaten the transformation of the polity itself. These fears, or hopes, were not borne out. To paraphrase George Woodcock, the Labour movement moved out of Trafalgar Square into the committee rooms. The Parliamentary Labour party was absorbed into the political system as it assimilated traditional political attitudes and broadened its class base. The unions developed into a "rational" interest to be tolerated, consulted, and conciliated. Though fundamental relations of property and power were not altered, the development of a stable, coherent, manageable politics of class defused class conflicts (Foot, 1968:277; Hall et al., 1967).

However managed and defused, class is still at the core of the British political dialogue. As a result, for the mid-twentieth-century British politician, class issues present few unknowns. In discussing issues of class, he knows, broadly, what is expected of him; his rhetoric and behavior conform on the whole to relatively clear-cut norms. For the typical politician, on the other hand, domestic racial issues, when first raised, were worrying, confusing, incoherent, anomic. Consequently, most British politicians have been anxious to depoliticize race, to make the politics of race coherent by creating policies and institutions *outside* of the usual political arenas that are capable of eliminating race once and for all as a public political issue, thus permitting them to deal with the more congenial, well-defined issues of class. The White Paper of August 1965 can only be understood in these terms.

The attempt to develop a coherent politics (or nonpolitics) of race has passed through three distinct, yet chronologically overlapping, stages: prepolitical consensus (1948-1961), fundamental debate (1958-1965), and political consensus (1963-present).

I. Pre-Political Consensus

In the early and middle 1950s, race, in Deakin's phrase, "only touched the periphery of political debate" (1968:26). Both the labour and Conservative parties were in substantial agreement, if not on what to do, at least on what not to do: either for purposes of immigration control or domestic politics, race would not be treated as a relevant political category. That there were any problems of discrimination, prejudice, integration, and social deficiencies was implicitly denied.

In this period, the issues of race were raised only sporadically in the House of Commons, and never by the Conservative Government or Labour Opposition front benches. On 5 December 1958, in a revealing debate, David Renton, Joint Under-Secretary at the Home

Office, rose to reject a private member's motion proposed by Cyril Osborne, a Conservative MP who led a small but vocal backbench lobby in favor of limitations on Commonwealth immigration, which urged "Her Majesty's government to take immediate steps to restrict the immigration of all persons, irrespective of race, color, or creed who are unfit, idle, or criminal; and to repatriate all immigrants who are found guilty of a serious criminal offense in the United Kingdom." Despite the disclaimer, there was little doubt that Osborne had Third World immigrants in mind. Just a month earlier, he had stated that "it is about time someone spoke out for the white man in this country, and I propose to do so," and had called for the control of immigration, "particularly of coloured immigrants" (Great Britain, 1958:596, col. 1552); Foot, 1965:129).

Renton, speaking for the Government, deplored any step which would breach "the principle of the open door upon which most of us agree," stating that "this country is proud to be the centre of an interracial Commonwealth . . . As a result of that, we have always allowed any of the people in what was the Empire and is now the Commonwealth to come to this country and to go from it as they please" (Great Britain, 1958:596, col. 1579-1580). And, he concluded, "both the Government and, I am glad to record, the Opposition front bench do not see the necessity for any general control of immigration."

This shared party position developed logically out of the essentially paternal view of the Empire and Commonwealth that was shared by those who differed over the future of Britain's colonial possessions (see Horowitz, 1970:169-185). Britain, both Labour and Conservative members argued, was the center of the Commonwealth; immigration from the Commonwealth must not, therefore, be restricted. As Henry Hopkinson, the Minister of State for Colonial Affairs had put it in 1954, "We still take pride in the fact that a man can say *civis britannicus sum* whatever his color may be, and we take pride in the fact that he wants and can come to the Mother Country" (Great Britain, 1954:532, col. 827). Much as Harold Macmillan justified decolonization in paternal terms (he spoke, in 1960, about "the development of nations in the world to which we already stand in the relationship of parents," and argued that decolonization was "the logical result—indeed the triumph—of Britain's imperial policies" [Horowitz, 1970:182]), his Government and the Labour party appealed to the Commonwealth ideal to resist the politicization of race and preserve the prepolitical consensus.

II. Fundamental Debate

Largely as a result of the violent racial clashes that erupted in London and Nottingham in the summer of 1958,[5] this ennobling ethos of paternalism failed to prevent the movement of the politics of race from the periphery to the center of political debate. A Labour MP noted astutely in the Osborne private member's motion debate of December 1958, "I feel this debate originates out of what happened at Notting Hill Gate and Nottingham, and try as we will we cannot divorce ourselves from these events, for I am certain if those incidents had not occurred we would not have a debate on this issue" (Great Britain, 1958:596, col. 1564). Before the summer of 1958, Ray Gosling (1962:9) has observed, "the country was in a state of racial innocence: its experience with people of black, brown, or yellow skin was colonial, tolerant, often smug. Now all that was changed. Notting Hill and Nottingham have become loaded words." The nonpolitical consensus that had kept race out of politics was upset. Color was now revelant politically, and, respectable or no, it would be dealt with politically.

The search for a coherent politics of race between the summer of 1958 and 1962 was primarily a search for coherence *within* each party. Though the ideological differences dividing the parties had narrowed in the 1950s, their hierarchies of interests and social priorities, as well as their membership's social characteristics, remained distinct (Beer, 1965). As a result of these differences, as well as the differences in perspective between governing and opposition, the reactions of the Conservative and Labour parties to the politicization of race differed strikingly. Thus when the Government announced in the Queen's Speech of October 1961 that it intended to introduce legislation to control immigration from the Commonwealth, the Labour party demurred and vigorously resisted the bill.

In making policy, the Conservative Government had to take into account the views not only of the parliamentary party, but also those of the party's constituents, public opinion as a whole, and the Civil Service. Within the parliamentary party, the Osborne group of backbenchers lobbied for control. Paul Foot's (1965) competent survey of race and immigration in British politics attributes the passage of the Commonwealth Immigrants Act largely to the activities of these MPs. Not surprisingly, members of the control lobby also opt for this interpretation. Harold Gurden, for example, who represents

---

5. For an account of the violence, see Wickenden (1958:23-35).

the Birmingham constituency of Selly Oak, is convinced that his lobbying efforts were instrumental in convincing Butler to favor controls; "I let him know we meant business, and raised the issue at a meeting of the 1922 committee where I found more party support than opposition. We had sunk our teeth in the issue and would not let go. Butler knew we meant business. I think that is why he came around."[6]

This interpretation is only partially accurate. Butler has forcefully denied that pressure from the control lobby convinced either him or the Cabinet to bring in legislation. "I was used to pressure from this group in the party. I took their views for granted."[7] But the activities of the parliamentary control advocates were indirectly significant in convincing the Government to curb immigration in two respects. Ironically, their activities had the effect of increasing substantially the numbers of immigrants, many of whom came to beat the mooted ban. Until 1960, the rate of immigration into the United Kingdom varied directly with the state of the British economy; in 1960, 1961, and the first six months of 1962, there was a major break with the trend. Though the British economy was depressed, immigration rates reached a record rate. The rush to come reflected the migrants' uncertainty about the future (Peach, 1968:46-47).

The control lobby was also influential indirectly in that their efforts helped shape local party and general public opinion. "The lobbyists arguing for control," writes Deakin (1968:45), "became siren voices offering a solution where the Government could only proclaim with diminishing conviction the indivisibility of British citizenship." In both 1958 and 1961, Conservative conferences passed resolutions opposed by the Government calling for immigration controls. By 1961, every major survey on the subject revealed a large majority in favor of restrictions on Third World migration.[8] And, too, available evidence indicates that a significant number of civil servants coun-

6. Interview with Harold Gurden, MP, at the House of Commons, 6 March 1969.

7. Interview with Lord Butler, Trinity College, Cambridge, 2 March 1968.

8. A survey conducted in 1960, based on a quota-type sample of 604 manual workers or their dependents in six large urban English constituencies, found that "83 percent . . . favored government action to restrict colored immigration; Labour and Conservative voters supported this view with almost exactly the same frequency." In May 1961, the Gallup poll found that only 21 percent of the British public favored free entry, 67 percent advocated restrictions, 6 percent wanted blacks completely excluded, and 6 percent were undecided (McKenzie and Silver, 1968:152; Supplement to the Institute of Race Relations, 1961:1.)

seled the Government to bring in immigration legislation (The Economist, 1958:189, p. 767; Butler interview, 1968). Thus constituency and public opinion, backbench pressures, Whitehall advice, and of most immediate importance, the sharply rising immigration figures convinced the Government to abandon its support of unrestricted Commonwealth entry.

The reaction of the Labour party to the politicization of race took place in the context of internecine party quarrels between rival leadership groups, each with substantial constituency support. Before the General Election of 1959, the party had managed to paper over its ideological cracks to fight the election apparently united. But with the party's crushing defeat (the Labour party polled almost 1,750,000 fewer votes than it had in 1951, and 200,000 less than in 1955), its synthetic unity was shattered. A partisan observer (Miliband, 1964: 344) noted that

the battles which broke out in the Labour party after the General Election of 1959 were not only about nationalization or nuclear strategy. They were the specific expressions of a more basic question, namely whether the Labour party is to be concerned with attempts at a more efficient and more humane administration of capitalist society; or whether it is to adapt itself to the task of creating a socialist order.

Hugh Gaitskell, the leader of the Labour party, who supported the first option and who attributed the party's defeat to its lack of appeal to marginal middle-class voters who were repelled by the ideological baggage of nationalization and unilateralism, urged the party at the postelection November 1959 Conference to abandon Clause Four, the socialist core of its 1918 constitution.[9] Largely because of trade union opposition, Gaitskell did not get his way and was compelled to accept a compromise draft of principles which were appended to Clause Four.

When the Government introduced the Commonwealth Immigrants Bill in late October 1961, the Blackpool Party Conference had just voted to reverse the party's 1960 decision taken at Scarborough in opposition to the leadership to support the unilateral renunciation of nuclear weapons. The Clause Four and nuclear weapons disputes left deep wounds which had to be healed if the party were to regain popular esteem. The party needed an issue on which it could unite

9. The conference was held 18-19 November 1959.

enthusiastically on principle. Immigration control was such an issue.

Though a small number of Labour MPs were dissatisfied with Gaitskell's uncompromising opposition to control legislation, the vast majority of the party was finally united behind its leader. In particuular, Gaitskell's adversaries on the left were jubilant. In an article which summarized their view, Michael Foot (1961:5) wrote in the *Tribune:*

No praise is too high for the manner in which it was done. Hugh Gaitskell in particular debated with a devastating passion which spread terror and shame along the Government benches . . . The spectacle of the Labour party asserting its principles in the face of what is supposed to be the popular need of the moment and resolving to withstand all the pressures of expediency is something fresh and exciting . . . The Party is united, and not merely united but exhilarated.

The search for coherent racial policies within the parties had destroyed the prepolitical consensus and had produced, for the first and last time within Parliament, a debate which found the parties divided fundamentally on the issues of race.

III. Political Consensus

To borrow a metaphor from Robert Paul Wolff (1965:45ff.), the territory of liberal group politics is like a plateau that drops sharply on all sides to a deep valley below. Legitimate, "rational" interests, ideas, and groups are placed on the plateau itself, and are tolerated and conciliated. But those ideas, interests, and groups in the valley are outside of the political process of discourse, compromise, and accommodation. In the 1950s, by bipartisan consent, the unformulated, incoherent politics of race were kept in the valley. But as a result of the factors discussed above, the Conservative party placed immigration controls on the political plateau; by virtue of this new position, the advocates of controls now had to be bargained with and conciliated. They were included in the broad embrace of liberal tolerance.

The prepolitical consensus, paradoxically, had managed to devise the politics of race by the agreement to leave them unformulated. With the Commonwealth Immigrants Act, however, the politics of race, by being partially modeled, became incoherent. Not surprisingly, therefore, the parties moved between 1962 and 1965, haphazardly, obliquely, but unmistakably, toward a new consensus, politically arrived at, which, it was hoped, would be capable of relegating race

from the political plateau to the valley below. The definition of this
political consensus, expressed in the White Paper of 1965, was made
without Third World immigrant participation or access to positions of
political control. There were in this period (and to date) no colored
MPs, and, with the exception of the Campaign Against Racial Discrimination (CARD) which was founded in December 1964, whose principal concern was antidiscrimination legislation, and whose interracial,
intellectual, middle-class membership was hardly representative of the
immigrant community, there were no organized groups with access to
national decision-makers who could articulate and transmit the views
and demands of the Third World immigrants. Thus the powerless immigrants were the objects, not the subject-participants, of the political
consensus.

At the Second Reading debate on the Commonwealth Immigrants
Act in November 1961, the Labour party had elevated the principle
of the open door to the level of ideological commitment. But by the
Third Reading in February, Labour had subtly, but significantly,
shifted its ground. Speaking for his Front Bench, Denis Healy (Great
Britain, 1962:654, col. 1271) discussed what Labour's attitude toward
the Bill would be when it next won power:

If the information collected by a serious survey of the whole problem revealed
that immigration control was necessary, we should regard it as essential
to consult other Commonwealth Governments to see how this could
be achieved with minimum damage to their interests and to their confidence
in our loyalty and good will.

The parties no longer divided over the *principle* of controls, but over
consultations and timing.

In complementary fashion to the changes in Labour's rationale,
the Government had modified the bill at the committee stage: it would
expire in eighteen months instead of five years; it recognized common-
law marriages and illegitimate children for the purpose of defining
wives and dependents; it now made explicit provisions for Commonwealth students and set up a system of entry certificates; and, perhaps most important, the Home Secretary announced that he would
appoint a Commonwealth Immigrants Advisory Council to advise
him and to co-ordinate governmental race policies. Thus by the message of the Commonwealth Immigrants Act, immigration controls
(following Wolff's metaphor) were firmly entrenched on the political
plateau, while the idea of special institutional mechanisms to deal with

the domestic politics of race were ascending the steep cliffs. The outlines of the political consensus later expressed in the White Paper
could dimly, but surely, be perceived.

By March 1965—after Hugh Gaitskell's death, Harold Wilson's
assumption of the Labour leadership, the 1964 General Election shock
of Smethwick (where an explicitly racist campaign produced a Conservative victory in a safe Labour seat) that embarrassed the Conservatives and jolted the Labour party, but before the expected 1966
General Election—the development of the bipartisan consensus was
acknowledged. On 23 March, Peter Thorneycroft, the Conservative
Shadow Cabinet spokesman on race and immigration, initiated a
Commons debate to propose "a drastic reduction in the inflow of
male immigrants . . . through the granting or not granting of vouchers; and, of course, also in tightening up provisions against evasion."
On the positive side, he advocated devoting "our utmost energy to
promoting the absorption of these communities within the fabric of
the civilisation of which we in these islands are so proud." Controls
and integration measures, he stated, are "two sides of the same
medal." He concluded by commending the work of local voluntary
liaison committees (discussed below) and the original National Committee for Commonwealth Immigrants which had been set up in April
1964 (Great Britain, 1965:709, cols. 334-345).

Speaking for the Labour Government, Herbert Bowden noted
that the "voucher problem" and evasions were under review and
would be dealt with, and reminded the House that the Government
had announced that it would "see what measures might be adopted
. . . to regulate the flow of immigrants to the United Kingdom, including the need to prevent evasion of control" (Great Britain, 1965:709,
cols. 352-353). The days of fundamental debate were over. "On both
sides of the House," a Conservative MP noted, "we are coming together on perhaps two aspects . . . to have a balanced policy towards
immigration and immigrant communities in our midst—control and
adjustment" (Great Britain, 1965:709, col. 434). A Labour Member
endorsed the view that we must try "to take a bipartisan approach"
and search "to see how far we can speak as a House of Commons
rather than as parties" (Great Britain, 1965:709, col. 391). All the
speakers' remarks could have come from either side of the House.
This remarkable accord was codified and given systemic expression in
the White Paper published just fourteen weeks later.

The structural-behavioral distinction discussed earlier provides
the basis for distinguishing critical from routine periods and decisions.

Thus critical decisions are structural decisions that not only limit but shape the direction of choice; critical periods are the historical periods when critical structural decisions are made. In the period of migration of Third World people to Britain, the most critical structural decision made was the establishment of national and local institutions to deal with the issues of race.

British politics in the liberal collectivist age are above all the politics of institutionalized class conflict. The structural arrangements announced by the political consensus White Paper did not integrate the immigrants into the class-based framework, but rather set up alternative political structures to deflect the politics of race from Westminster to the National Committee for Commonwealth Immigrants, and from local political arenas to voluntary liaison committees.

As a result, the Third World population has been linked to the polity indirectly through buffer institutions. This mediating, buffering role[10] has been acknowledged explicitly by NCCI. "The National Committee and the voluntary liaison committees," NCCI's 1967 report (1968) asserts, "have to steer the most difficult course of all. The concept 'liaison' indicates the tightrope on which they must walk . . . Success depends on retaining the confidence of the authorities in order that one's views will be heeded when it comes to policy-making. No less important is the confidence of the immigrants." The national and local committees were not meant to be spokesmen for the newcomers or organized pressure groups. Rather their orientation was consensual; NCCI's 1967 guidelines (1967) on the formation of local committees stressed that "it should be emphasized at every stage that this is *not a committee to serve the interests of one section of the community but a committee to promote racial harmony. It is therefore beneficial to all.*" Local representation, the guidelines urged, should include party representation, service organizations and clubs (Rotary, Chamber of Commerce, Working Men's Clubs, etc.), voluntary and statutory service organizations (Council of Social Service, Family Welfare Association, Probation Office, the Police, the Welfare Officer, etc.), and visible immigrant leadership: "There may already be immigrant associations in the area which can be approached for representation, but

10.   Buffering has been defined by Manfred Halpern as being that form of organized encounter between individuals or groups where "the tension that accompanies changes in the balance of costs and benefits in encounters between self and other is managed by intermediaries. Such a position may be occupied by a mediator, arbitrator, broker, or by a concept . . . Buffering allows for change by permitting indirect and limited forms of conflict and collaboration" (Halpern, 1969:63).

if not, the officers of appropriate High Commissions may be able to supply some names, as also may the National Committee for Commonwealth Immigrants" (1967).

The nature and impact of these buffering institutions can be best examined by looking at a concrete case, Nottingham, an East Midland City with a population of 320,000, including 15,000 predominantly West Indian Third World immigrants whose economic and demographic characteristics are typical of areas of immigrant settlement. I have selected this city because the institutions developed there became the model for the White Paper network of organizations, and because in Nottingham buffering institutional arrangements are most developed. Not surprisingly, the National Committee for Commonwealth Immigrants (1968) has singled out its Nottingham liaison committee for special praise:

The Nottingham Citizens Consultative Committee, one of the oldest in the country, continues to be among the leading groups. Because of its early start it was able to anticipate and minimize many of the difficulties such as housing shortage, discrimination in employment, problems of immigrant relations, and youth problems. After so many years of solid work and pioneering activity, the Nottingham committee may well set an example in this field from which many of the newer committees will benefit.

By discussing the institutionally structured politics of race in Nottingham—the limiting case—it is possible to illuminate indirectly the politics of race in other British cities.

Like their national counterparts, before 1958 Nottingham's political community dealt with the issues of race by denying them political recognition. Yet the prepolitical period of race relations in Nottingham is of considerable interest. During the middle 1950s, quasi-political mechanisms were established which, after the violence of 1958, provided the city's political community with the means to institutionalize the new politics of race with a minimum of disruption and change.[11]

In May 1954, when the city's predominantly Jamaican colored population numbered between 700 and 1000, the Council of Social Services and the Council of Churches decided to found the Notting-

---

11. The term *political community* is used to describe the city's politicians because the cozy atmosphere of Nottingham's council politics makes reference to party divisions often misleading and irrelevant. Close bipartisan consultation, a club for former Lords Mayor and, above all, the policy of allocating a high proportion of council committee chairmanships to the minority party, dampen issue partisanship.

ham Consultative Committee for the Welfare of Colored People "to help the local colored community to settle down as happily and as easily as possible."[12] No colored immigrants were present at the founding meeting. A second planning meeting was called for September to "hear from the colonial peoples themselves what they felt they needed." Accordingly, three members of the nonpolitical Colonial Social and Cricket Club, including its Secretary Eric Irons, were invited to represent the city's West Indians. Of the twenty-nine individuals who attended the first official meeting of the committee, only six were West Indian and all were members of the Colonial Club. The other participants were delegates appointed by the city's leading voluntary organizations, including the Rotary Club, the YMCA, the Trades Council, and the Salvation Army. The formal political community was not invited to participate.

The new committee was meant to link West Indian and local community leaders, but the attempt suffered from serious shortcomings. With the exception of a hard core of interested whites, the voluntary agency representatives contributed little. More significant from the perspective of the Third World population was the dual nonrepresentative nature of the committee. Not only were there few West Indian members, but they were hardly representative of their community. Most of the Colonial Club's approximately twenty-five members were "old settlers" who had served with the RAF during the Second World War, married white wives, and had middle-class occupations. They were on the whole uninterested in politics.

If, with John Rex and Robert Moore (1967:13), "we understand urban society as a structure of interaction and conflict," and if we view competition for the allocation of scarce resources as a political process involving political decisions, then it is clear that the immigrants, who comprised an identifiable group competing for homes and jobs, needed access to positions of political control. Yet the most obvious access point, the Consultative Committee, was overtly nonpolitical.[13]

In fact, however, the committee's official nonpolitical position had political ramifications, for it helped to isolate the political community from potential immigrant political demands. Thus the council could avoid taking the political risks of a program designed to assure a fair allocation of resources to the newcomers. Immigrants who

12. Interview with Miss D. M. Wood, Founding Secretary of the committee, 24 April 1968.

13. For a more detailed discussion, see Katznelson (1970:431-446).

sought the assistance of their councillors and who complained of discrimination were often directed to the politically impotent Consultative Committee.[14]

After the violence of the summer of 1958, the parties responded to the politicization of race by acting in concert to resolve their common problem by attempting to formulate race relations and domesticate racial conflicts. In February 1960, the Council appointed Eric Irons, the leader of the Colonial Club West Indians on the liaison committee, to the specially created post of Organiser for Educational Work Amongst the Colored Communities. His appointment was complemented by official recognition of the Consultative Committee as a quasi-political institution, and the award of an annual grant of £500.

Thus within a year of the disturbances, the political community had established officially sanctioned access points, both within and outside the local authority, for the immigrant population. Neither access point provided for direct access to the political community; each acted, instead, under the conceptual heading of liaison, as political buffers. Immigrant needs and demands were filtered through them: Iron's office dealt with individuals, the Consultative Committee with immigrant groups.

The buffering race relations structures have occupied an anomalous, powerless position. Created and supported by the local authority, their political independence is compromised. The committee was meant to link immigrant organizations and the political community; but, in terms of power, this liaison function was a one-way process, for the committee's functions, powers, and legitimacy were defined from above, while the predominantly nonpolitical immigrant groups who served on the committee were essentially powerless.

Furthermore, by providing access to the immigrants' conspicuous, moderate, largely middle-class *élite*, the committee has not only been unrepresentative, but it has also muffled immigrant protest and divided the Third World Population. The politicization of the black community is not only not encouraged, but has been actively discouraged; stability and harmony are stressed at the expense of political organization. Irons's 1965 report to the council is instructive in this regard. After the publication of the Labour White Paper in August, many of Nottingham's immigrants felt betrayed, and there were fears that dependents might be excluded. As a result, a number of politically oriented immigrant organizations, principally the Indian Workers As-

14. Wood interview.

sociation and the Afro-Asian West Indian Union, met an unusually
favorable response from their normally politically quiescent communities. Much like the effect Enoch Powell's speeches were to have
three years later, the insecurity caused by the White Paper promoted
immigrant political consciousness (See Heilpern and Hiro, 1968:11).
It was in this context that Irons (1965:1) reported in November:

The past year has been a difficult one for the immigrant communities
. . . They have been under considerable social pressures, *particularly from
within their respective racial groups.* These pressures have tended to
undermine the confidence of the immigrants and have been therefore a real
test of the effectiveness of the work that has been carried out in the City over
the years.
    The difficulties were surmounted largely because of the intelligent and
reasonable manner in which the majority of the colored community reacted
to the situation . . . and the splendid liaison work and very flexible policies
adopted by Local Authority departments and other statutory bodies . . .
    Nevertheless, the strain experienced has underlined the *need for a
much stronger stabilizing influence amongst the immigrants* [italics added].

There is striking agreement among the committee's supporters
and detractors that, above all, the existence of the committee has in-
sulated the political community from pressures for change in the racial status quo. "We have succeeded," a white founding member
boasted, "and this is our most important achievement, in acting as a
safety valve . . . We prevent trouble."[15] One of the Committee's
most vocal West Indian critics noted too that "there is no doubt the
committee is deliberately used as a political safety valve. Whites are
involved directly in politics; blacks are expected to be involved indirectly."[16]
    The existence of the buffer institutions has benefited a small
group of predominantly middle-class colored "leaders" who have been
granted not direct access to positions of political control, but a measure of paternal patronage in the form of seats on the committee, contacts with local political and voluntary elites, the appointment of two
black magistrates, in addition to Irons's post at the Education Office.
But most of all, the city's buffering institutional structure has benefited
the city's politicians, for it has permitted them to manage the politics

    15. Interview with A. F. Laird, founding Chairman of the committee, 14 April
1968.
    16. Interview with O. G. Powe, Secretary of the Afro-Asian West Indian Union, 9
November 1968.

of race with a minimum of dissension while simultaneously being able to assert that Nottingham has coped well with the immigration, citing Irons's office and the Consultative Committee as evidence. Thus, for example, the leader of the council's Conservative majority stated, "I am proud of our bipartisan approach to these matters . . . I am sure we have no immediate problems in this area. We are very pleased with the committee and with Mr. Irons's welfare work."[17]

While Nottingham's Third World population was expected to act as if color were irrelevant, the political community viewed them as a group apart. Immigrant participation, established through the Consultative Committee and Irons's office, precluded direct access through the parties to the competition for positions of political power and control. Immigrant patronage, in this situation, is meagre, doled out to a token, unrepresentative group of powerless leaders. Despite Nottingham's rather elaborate structure of buffering racial mechanisms, at the end of 1968 there were no black councillors, no black members of school management boards, no black policemen, no blacks employed by the Housing Department. On the assumption that a system's output is in part a reflection of the process and structure of the system itself, Nottingham's buffering mechanisms, which have been emulated on a national basis, must be found wanting.

A key feature of the classic colonial situation, indirect rule through a broker, native leadership, has been replicated in the Mother Country (see Crowder, 1970:26-36; Apter, 1963a:119-158). "In one sense," Eric Irons (1962:2) wrote in his 1961-1962 report to the Nottingham Council, "the organizer looks upon his functions as being that of an 'interpreter' between the new and established communities, in that he is in direct, personal contact with the colored communities and his advice and help are often sought by statutory and voluntary bodies in their approach to these sections of the population." The operative phrase, nationally and locally, has been "for immigrants." The process of making decisions and creating institutions "for immigrants" has made participation by the Third World population not only difficult, but also, from their perspective, often meaningless and absurd.

In their attempt to depoliticize race, British politicians had to deal with the immigrant-colonial amalgam. Immigration from the Commonwealth has been severely curtailed, and quasi-colonial institutional structures have been established to deal with the issues of race. As a result, the Third World population has been institutionally

17. Interview with Alderman Derbyshire, 19 March 1968.

separated from the society-wide, largely class-based network of political institutions and associations, and it has been unable to compete
effectively for the scarce resource of political power.

The 1965 political consensus has taken race out of politics, then,
in two respects. Immigrants' felt needs and demands are dealt with by
quasi-political bodies like NCCI (now the Community Relations Commission) and the Race Relations Board, which administers the country's
antidiscrimination legislation, rather than by Parliament and the Government directly. In neither institution are Third World representatives selected by the immigrant communities themselves. Secondly,
since 1965, the front benches of both parties have accepted the dual
framework of very strict immigration controls coupled with antidiscrimination legislation and quasi-political buffering institutions.
These institutions (there are now 78 local committees) have pursued
an elite, consensual strategy, leaving the mass of Third World immigrants politically unanchored.[18]

Britain's Third World population could have been linked to the
polity either by a legitimately color-blind policy that would have permitted them to divide, like other Englishmen, as individuals based on
class rankings (individual integration) or by a recognition that color is
an independent political category, thus encouraging the immigrant
population to organize as a group to join the political process as partic-
ipant-equals (pluralist integration).[19] The first alternative clearly
would have been preferred by a majority of the West Indian immigrants who were moving away from a color-ascriptive society; they
wanted and expected to be accepted as Englishmen. The politicization
of race after 1958 and the systemic expression of the folk prejudices
of British society in immigration control legislation, however, made
individual integration for most impossible. The second possibility,
that of pluralist integration, has been achieved only in the inadequate
form of buffering.

In conclusion, I have argued that British race relations can only

18. In preparing his forthcoming Ph.D. thesis, Daniel Lawrence found in a random
sample of 122 male colored immigrants drawn from Nottingham's Central Parliamentary
constituency that 75 percent had not heard of the Consultative Committee; 19 percent
claimed to have knowledge of the organization, but in fact knew almost nothing about
it; of the 6 percent who knew something of the committee, two individuals were members of immigrant organizations that had served on the committee. I am indebted to Mr.
Lawrence for this information.

19. Here I am referring to structural, not cultural integration.

be understood as an amalgam of the colonial and voluntary migrant cases. The Labour Government's White Paper of August 1965, "Immigration from the Commonwealth," gave political expression to the immigrant colonial amalgam in an effort to take race out of politics. A significant feature of the politics of race in Britain has been its nonintegration into an institutionalized class-conflict framework. For British politicians, the issues of race were incoherent and anomic; accordingly, they have sought to take race out of politics. This central feature of domestic racial politics produced a political consensus that strictly controlled Third World immigration, and that—in the key structural decision of the period—linked the immigrants to the polity indirectly through quasi-colonial buffer institutions. These arrangements made meaningful immigrant political participation difficult, produced a group of broker leaders, formalized the institutional separation of the colored population, and made it unlikely that the Third World immigrants would secure an equitable share of the scarce resource of political power.

This discussion is a corrective to the dominant research foci in the literature on immigrant assimilation, prejudice and discrimination, and points the way to neglected research concerns. As such, it represents the beginning, not the conclusion, of analysis. In part, then, this essay should be read as an implicit research agenda. Much needed are studies of the buffering institutions and their consequences for social and economic mobility, immigrant participation rates, perceived satisfaction or deprivation, patterns of conflict and accommodation; in short, research on the ways in which the political consensus buffering institutions define the limits of choice and racial justice.

REFERENCES

Apter, David.
    1963a   Ghana in Transition. New York: Atheneum.
    1963b   "Comparative Politics and Political Thought: Past Influences and
            Future Development." In Comparative Politics, edited by Harry

Eckstein and David Apter. New York: The Free Press.

Beer, Samuel.
  1965   Modern British Politics. London: Faber.
Blauner, Robert.
  1969   "Internal Colonialism and Ghetto Revolt." Social Problems 16
          (Spring): 393-408.
Crowder, Michael.
  1970   "Indirect Rule—French and British Style." In African Politics and
          Society, I. L. Markovitz. New York: The Free Press.
Deakin, Nicholas.
  1968   "The Politics of the Commonwealth Immigrants Bill." The Politi-
          cal Quarterly (January-March): 26.
The Economist.
  1958   189 (29 November):767.
Etzioni, Amitai
  1968   The Active Society. New York: The Free Press.
Foot, Michael.
  1961   "The Way to Beat the Tories." Tribune, 24 November.
Foot, Paul.
  1965   Immigration and Race in British Politics. London: Penquin Books.
  1968   The Politics of Harold Wilson. London: Penguin Books.
Gosling, Ray.
  1962   "Twistings in that Poor White Boy." New Society (29 November).
Government White Paper.
  1965   "Immigration from the Commonwealth." 2 August.
Great Britain. Parliament.
  1954   Hansard's Parliamentary Debates (House of Commons) 532 (5
          November).
  1958   Hansard's Parliamentary Debates (House of Commons) 596 (5
          December).
  1962   Hansard's Parliamentary Debates (House of Commons) 654 (27
          February).
  1965   Hansard's Parliamentary Debates (House of Commons) 709 (23
          March).
Hall, Stuart, et al.
  1967   New Left May Day Manifesto, 1967. London: (Pamphlet).
Halpern, Manfred.
  1969   "A Redefinition of the Revolutionary Situation." Journal of In-
          ternational Affairs XXIII (Winter): 63.
Hartenfels, Jerome.
  1967   Lazarus. London: SCM Press.
Heilpern, John, and Dilip Hiro.
  1968   "The Town We Were Told Was Tolerant." The Observer, 1
          December.

Horowitz, Dan.
  1970   "The British Conservatives and the Racial Issue in the Debate on
          Decolonization." Race XII (October).
Institute of Race Relations.
  1961   Supplement to the Institute of Race Relations Newsletter. (August.)
Irons, Eric.
  1961-1962   "Report of the Organiser for Work Amongst the Coloured
          Communities." City of Nottingham Education Committee. Feb-
          ruary 1961-March 1962.
  1965   "Report of the Organiser for Work Amongst the Coloured Com-
          munities." November.
Katznelson, Ira.
  1970   "The Politics of Racial Buffering in Nottingham, 1954-1968."
          Race XI (April).
Kaufman, Gerald.
  1965   "Dutch Auction on Immigrants." New Statesman, 9 July.
Lieberson, Stanley.
  1961   "A Societal Theory of Race and Ethnic Relations." American
          Sociological Review 26 (December):902-910.
McKenzie, Robert, and Allan Silver.
  1968   Angels in Marble. Chicago: University of Chicago Press.
Miliband, Ralph.
  1964   Parliamentary Socialism. London: Merlin Press.
National Committee for Commonwealth Immigrants.
  1967   "Notes for Guidance on the Formation of a Voluntary Liaison
          Committee." Unpublished.
  1968   Report for 1967. London: H.M.S.O.
Patterson, Sheila.
  1963   Dark Strangers. London: Tavistock Publications.
Peach, Ceri.
  1968   West Indian Migration to Britain. London: Oxford University
          Press.
Rex, John, and Robert Moore.
  1967   Race, Community, and Conflict. London: Oxford University
          Press.
Richmond, Anthony.
  1966   "Britain." Research on Racial Relations, UNESCO. Amsterdam:
          UNESCO.
Rose, E. J. B., and Associates.
  1969   Colour and Citizenship. London: Oxford University Press.
Schermerhorn, R. A.
  1970   Comparative Ethnic Relations. New York: Random House.
Sivanandan, A., Editor.
  1967   Coloured Immigrants in Britain, a Select Bibliography. London:
          The Institute of Race Relations.

Wickenden, James.
    1958   Colour in Britain. London: Oxford University Press.
Wolff, Robert Paul.
    1968   "Beyond Tolerance." In A Critique of Pure Tolerance, by Robert
            Paul Wolff, Barrington Moore Jr., and Herbert Marcuse. Boston:
            Beacon Press.

Race and Color:
Overriding Issues of
the Twentieth Century

AN ATTEMPT will herein be made to evaluate the analytical and developmental efforts to deal with the subject of "The Politics of Racial Buffering in England, 1948-1968: Colonial Relationships in the Mother Country."

In doing this, the relationship and its appropriateness to the over-all theme of "Racial Tensions and National Identity" will be examined. This will be done through an application of some of the factors and principles conducive to the phenomenon of racial tension. The specific situation in England will then be examined in relationship to these factors and principles. Finally, the relevance of the principal paper in coming to grips with and enhancing understanding of these phenomena will be taken into consideration.

Behavioral scientists in the United States have been somewhat preoccupied with the issue of adjustment. They have been fixated on factors conducive to the realization of peace, harmony, equilibrium, balance, etc. They have, as a consequence, generally avoided the study of phenomena which relate to conflict. This kind of avoidance of what may be considered substantive and crucial issues of Western civilization and the American society have minimized the possibility of meaningful contributions in this area. Serious and concerted efforts to come to grips with the basic understanding of wars, riots, intergroup and interracial conflicts have not been made in a scholarly way. This is particularly true in the areas of interracial, interethnic and intercultural conflicts.

It is of interest that scholars in a highly aggressive, competitive, and achieving society have studiously avoided the objective analysis of the phenomena of conflict and violence which have formed such integral parts of the culture of Western civilization and which have been regarded in the United States society as "American as apple pie."

In view of the existence of situations and circumstances leading to conflict, it becomes legitimate to make a systematic attempt to look at how and where people meet and to examine closely and objectively resultants and concomitants of this kind of meeting.

It is important at this juncture to develop some principles for explaining what the expected outcomes are when persons who are defined or who define themselves as racially and/or culturally different come in contact with each other in certain racial and/or cultural "frontiers"—where people meet (see Frazier, 1957).

Of primary importance in this assessment is the place of the meeting. It is of significance that the meeting takes place in England, and not in the West Indies; in Brazil, and not in South Africa; in the northern part of the United States, and not in the southern part.

The ethos, the ideological stance, and the values of the social structure are important. The nature of the economy is also important: is it agricultural or industrial? Is it an expanding economy, affording employment opportunities to those coming in, or is it closed, with no room for expansion and with a high unemployment rate even for the indigenous people? These are indeed crucial questions.

What are the values or the ideological stances of the people in that social structure with respect to strangers or newcomers? Do they believe, as is the case in Brazil, that all persons and human groups must be assimilated? Do they have highly developed beliefs in ethnocentrism leading to the maintenance and perpetuation of in-groups and out-groups? If the existence of these groups is recognized, then to what extent are they regarded as antagonistic, co-operative, or pluralistic? To what extent are these newcomers regarded as transient or temporary, and to what extent, irrespective of length of residence, is the meeting place regarded as "home"?

The fact that Europeans did not regard the West Indies and West Africa as settlement areas is important in evaluating the nature of intergroup relations in these areas. These were plantation colonies located in geographical areas where climatic conditions were not conducive to European settlement. Europeans remained in these areas for a short period of time as colonial officials or as plantation managers. They referred to and thought of England as "home."

The situation was quite different in Kenya, which was considered suitable for European settlement. As a consequence, Europeans occupied the "white" highlands and relegated the indigenous people to the inhospitable areas of the hinterland.

This phenomenon partially accounts for the fact that when these plantation-economy colonies no longer proved profitable, they were given their political independence with relative ease, as compared to the nature of the struggle epitomized in the Mau Mau rebellion in Kenya and the intransigence of the European power elite in Rhodesia and in South Africa in giving any semblance of democratic and equalitarian treatment to the indigenous people of these areas.

Within this context, one can more readily understand the nature of white-black relations in the United States, the treatment of the Australian aborigines, and the virtual extermination of the indigenous population of Tasmania.

The intensity of the conflict will understandably increase if the physical characteristics of the "out" or "stranger" group make the members highly visible and therefore easily identifiable.

The nature of the contact is also of importance. If these newcomers come in as individuals over a fairly long period of time, the nature of the contact will be different in outcome and consequences than when they come in large numbers over a short period of time. The latter phenomenon is more likely to intensify the conflicts.

The situation in England can now be analyzed to see the relevance of this theoretical system.

The critical issue related to the racial situation is the sudden influx of a significant number of non whites—known in England as "colored" people. This happened in the mid 1950s and early 1960s. As recently as 1950, there were in England no more than 100,000 "colored" persons with origins in Africa, the Caribbean, and Asia. Most of these people lived in such selected areas as Cardiff, London, and the major ports of the northeast coast.

Today, there are approximately one million nonwhites in Britain. This constitutes two percent of the total population of Britain. This was brought about primarily by an increase in the rate of immigration of Pakistanis, Indians, and West Indians. The West Indians number about a half million, with approximately the same number coming from a combination of Indians and Pakistanis. There are only about 50,000 Africans, most of whom are from West Africa. Jamaicans constitute the majority of the West Indians.

In less than twenty years, therefore, Britain experienced an increase in its nonwhite population to the tune of almost one million people. Most of these individuals were highly visible in physical characteristics and pigmentation. Their visibility became more obvious throughout Britain because they were no longer concentrated in a few seaport cities but, on the contrary, were found in the large industrialized and urbanized areas. England's racial and ethnic problem was no longer localized, but now had a national thrust.

These new immigrants, somewhat different from the old ones, came not as individuals but in family groups, indicating quite clearly their intentions of remaining in the country. There was, then, obvious competition with whites, particularly those located at the lower socioeconomic strata, for jobs, for housing and for other indices of status and survival.

Even at a time when England was experiencing an expanding economy and jobs were relatively plentiful and easily available, nonwhites —particularly West Indians—were experiencing discrimination in varying degrees of intensity.

This was particularly frustrating to these nonwhite immigrants because discriminatory practices were quite contrary to their expectations about their treatment in England. They had believed in the fairness and the honesty of Englishmen and therefore strongly expected to be given equality of opportunity. The realization that Britain was a country where nonwhites were treated with hostility and where those in power and positions of influence discriminated against them was indeed traumatic and disillusioning. This was the feeling which was very prevalent among West Indians where the majority found life below their expectations (Daniel, 1968:32). The two prime discriminatory areas were housing and employment. There was at this time a shortage of housing in England. Here the color gradient was a factor in that the darker West Indian was discriminated against to a greater degree of intensity than Pakistanis, Indians or Cypriots. It is interesting to note that Cypriots, Hungarians, and others who came from the Middle East were most likely to be discriminated against over the telephone.

As could be expected, there were adequate rationalizations for these discriminatory practices. They were couched within the framework of broad generalizations and stereotypes. This bears out the significance of the in-group/out-group, they-we concepts strongly supported by feelings of ethnocentrism and the proneness to deny acceptance and to refer to these nonwhites as aliens, foreigners, outsiders.

According to Bell, "Colored people were seen as an alien group, as outsiders. Preference should be given to 'our own people'" (Daniel, 1968:96). Therefore, it is quite apparent that although members of the out-group were exposed to prejudice and discrimination in some form, it was found to increase in intensity as the group became darker.

It is so easy to account for the origins of prejudice only in terms of the sudden influx of nonwhites in the late 1950s and the early 1960s. This is, of course, an oversimplification. Prejudice against dark peoples was institutionalized at the covert level and seemingly occupies an important part of the psyche of the English people. The concern about color, particularly blackness, is deeply entrenched in Western civilization, particularly in Britain, and it is vividly caught in the literary expressions of England, particularly in Elizabethan literature. This is important particularly when one recognizes the cultural proneness of Englishmen *not* to express their real feelings openly. The meanings are latent rather than manifest, covert rather than overt. They are prone to circumlocution and understatements.

The British government has played a minor and relatively ineffective role in influencing the tone and direction of race relations in Britain. There have been no indications of strong affirmative action on the part of the government. When some action has been forthcoming, it has tended to articulate the prejudicial feelings and beliefs, the fears and insecurities of the British populace. A primary example of this has been the recent passage of legislation to restrict immigration of nonwhites into Britain. This has been followed by the frequent racist remarks made by elected officials, such as Enoch Powell. The absence of strong indications of condemnation on the part of the leaders of both political parties bears fitting testimony to this position.

The political stance which the British government took toward the Rhodesian situation *vis-à-vis* the situation in Guyana is further supportive. On the one hand, as in the case of Rhodesia, the government was reluctant to impose rigid sanctions and was adamantly opposed to any show of force to persuade the power elite in Rhodesia to involve the blacks of that country in the operations of the government. When, however, conditions in Guyana were not favorable to the British government, it did not hesitate to dispatch warships to these shores.

All indications are that hostility will increase in the future. As the rate of expansion of the economy decreases and the competition for jobs and housing increases concomitantly with a greater concentration of blacks sustained by a higher birth rate, the latent prejudices of whites will be manifested in overt forms of discrimination and conflict.

One of the basic and significant characteristics of the nonwhite immigrant population of Britain is its youthfulness. Most of the children of these households were born in Britain. The younger generation of blacks will become more impatient and, as a consequence, will become more militant, with possibilities of violence and further conflict. There are stirrings of the Black Power movement in England. The movement will continue to grow, strengthened by the activities of the movement in the United States and in the Caribbean.

The Black Power movement in the Caribbean is of particular significance here. This movement reached a peak in Trinidad and Tobago when an attempt was made to overthrow the government accompanied by an army mutiny and civilian rioting on April 21, 1970. Blacks in Trinidad and Tobago and in Britain feel very close to the Black Power movement in the United States: although he is an American citizen, Stokely Carmichael, who gave leadership to the movement in the United States, was born in Trinidad.

The influence of the Third World ideology must not be ignored. These different "out-groups" in England are becoming more and more cognizant of the need for and importance of forming coalitions as a means of increasing their effectiveness as a socio-political force. The trend is toward a viable *rapprochement*.

How relevant are the above points to the specific contents of the paper to be discussed?

An interpretation of the relationship between the nonwhite immigrants and the indigenous people within the framework of the immigrant-colonial dimension fails to contribute markedly to any further clarification and understanding of the phenomenon.

Race and color became significant precisely as a result of the expansion of Europe and the subsequent colonization of these areas. The justification for this kind of exploitation revolved around the concept of superior-inferior races. These immigrants into England, quite contrary to other kinds, represent this traditionally oppressed and exploited group.

References are therefore made to immigrants who are defined as racially different. These immigrants come additionally from colonial situations which have strong racial connotations and denotations.

It is conceivable that the variables of class and race are interrelated. It is quite clear, however, in terms of actual behavior, that race consistently takes precedence over class in most social situations.

What therefore becomes sociologically meaningful and significant is *not* what persons verbalize about race, but the things which they take for granted and which explicitly and implicitly affect the decision-making process.

This explains the apparent consensus on the part of the two major political parties in Britain on issues relevant to that of race.

Nonwhite politicians are virtually nonexistent in Britain. The small percentage of nonwhites in Britain is by no means the important explanatory factor for this phenomenon. The over-all climate in Britain is not conducive to nonwhite political activity. There is no strong sense of political belonging. Political buffer groups have therefore been set up, appointed and superimposed to give some semblance of representation and involvement. This is a device commonly resorted to in biracial societies. This has been a successful technique to maintain and perpetuate the superordinate position of the dominant group. They are not effective representatives of the groups they are supposed to represent because these groups were not chosen by them. The stance has been paternalistic. Decisions are made without the advice and consent of the affected persons.

It is of significance that West Indians hold more positions of political leadership in the United States and particularly in the state of New York than they do in Britain. They appear to be more numerous and prominent in the areas of law, medicine, government and politics than their proportion in the total black population would warrant.

Four of the six elected office holders in the Bedford-Stuyvesant district in Brooklyn, including Shirley Chisholm, the first black female in the U.S. House of Representatives, are West Indians. Hulan Jack, the first black borough president, and Basil Patterson, state senator and the unsuccessful running mate of Arthur Goldberg for lieutenant governor of New York, are West Indians.

A comprehensive comparative socio-political analysis of these two "frontiers" would certainly give additional insights into the nature of race relations.

The ineffectiveness of buffer groups in the United States has led to other dimensional manifestations of the political process to affect the nature, direction, and intensity of social change. The results have been increased militancy in protests, mass demonstrations, etc. As a consequence, one envisions further such political expressions emanating from nonwhites in England.

Race and color have indeed become the overriding issues of the twentieth century. Britain has played a role in exacerbating the impact of these issues; wittingly or unwittingly, she has not contributed to defusing these issues, but on the contrary, by her lack of positive, moral leadership, has fostered and increased their importance. The impact of her failures on young blacks in Britain may very well be cathartic and Fanonian.

The increasing militancy of the young nonwhite generation intensified with the related stances of Black Power and Third World ideologies may conceivably provide the kind of political leverage which is "liberating" and will tend to eliminate the socio-political invisibility of nonwhites in Britain.

REFERENCES

Daniel, W. W.
    1968   Racial Discrimination in England. London: Penguin Books.
Frazier, E. Franklin.
    1957   Race and Culture Contacts in the Modern World. New York: Alfred A. Knopf.

3 MARTIN KILSON

Dynamics of Nationalism and Political Militancy Among Negro Americans

AS A form of political behavior, nationalism is usually viewed as an outgrowth of a need for identity on the part of groups or individuals who, because of power differentials between such groups and a dominant strata, have been denied the right of what may be called identity fulfillment (cf., e.g., Essien-Udom, 1963). The utility of this conception of nationalistic political thrusts or movements is that it facilitates analysis of outward manifestations of such political tendencies, their paraphernalia, their conspicuous symbolism and ideological articulation, all of which distinguish nationalist politics as much more visible than other types of political behavior. Yet there is a serious limitation to this conception of nationalistic political tendencies: it emphasizes the form rather than the content. When it is viewed from the vantage point of the content of a nationalistic political tendency, one is interested less in the outward manifestations—usually centered upon ethnic, religious, caste, and other subcultural features of a group —than in the question of politics as power—the question, that is, of who gets what, how, why.[1]

Thus Lenin's quip that if you scratch a nationalist, underneath will appear an incipient bourgeois, offers a power-oriented perspective on the nature of nationalist tendencies. The same is true of an obser-

1. For an example of this approach to nationalism, cf. Carr et al. (1939).

vation by Karl Marx (n.d.: 180) in the mid-nineteenth century on the nature of the term *national wealth:*

The term *national wealth* has only arisen as a result of the liberal economists' passion for generalization. As long as private property exists, this term has no meaning. The *national wealth* of the English is very great and yet they are the poorest people under the sun. One either dismisses this term completely, or one accepts such premises as give it meaning.

And in attempting to give a power-focus to an analysis of African nationalist development in Sierra Leone, I remarked in 1966 (1966:90) that "stripped to its essentials, the anticolonial nationalism that emerged after World War I was merely the ideological projection of the expanding appetite of middle-class Africans for new jobs and related perquisites which only the government could provide."

Viewed, then, from this vantage point, one is likely to obtain a more politically valid comprehension of nationalist (and militant) political tendencies among black Americans. Like other nationalist tendencies elsewhere in the world, those among Negroes have displayed outward manifestations such as the assertion of a black ethnicity over and against the dominant white ethnic or cultural patterns. Although this feature of modern nationalist tendencies is often seen in terms of what I call identity fulfillment, it is better to think of the conspicuous or outward manifestations of nationalism in instrumental terms. Nationalist paraphernalia, then, are nothing more than one of the means by which the leadership endeavor to regulate or control their followers, the masses.

It remains, however, to determine why a given leadership adopts a nationalist political style, by which I mean the intense manipulation of ethnicity and ethnic experience for political (or political-economic) ends. Things being equal, it is likely that an emergent leadership which is deficient in the usual political resources (e.g., money, prestige, influence, organization) is more inclined to rely upon the nationalist style than leadership well-endowed in these resources. This proposition applies to most nationalist leaders among American Negroes since World War I; they have been men of lower-middle-class and marginal middle-class background, and occasionally of skilled working-class origin. Yet another set of circumstances under which a nationalist style will be adopted involves the rapid sharpening of the perception of relative deprivation by an established elite or leadership. This situation characterizes the growth of a nationalist and militant political style among some middle- and upper middle-class Negroes since the early 1960s, and this latter situation has become even more intensified in the past several years in consequence of the relatively rapid growth of the black middle classes, while the relative gap between the elite rewards available to the black as against the white middle classes remains large.

The masses or popular strata, on the other hand, interact with nationalist tendencies from a unique set of circumstances. For one thing, the popular strata, unlike the leadership, depend upon nationalism for the primary definition of political interest. Throughout the modern era, both within the West and outside it, the popular strata have relied upon nationalism especially in order to give political coherence to their frustrations and grievances. This situation has characterized the growth of greater political articulation among the black American masses as it has among other masses elsewhere in the world. Indeed, in the past decade the growth of greater political articulation through nationalism among the black American masses has outstripped the growth of nationalist political articulation among the black middle classes. As a pattern of modern nationalist development, this situation is unique, and one important consequence of it has been a major decline in the legitimacy of the established black leadership groups, and particularly in the style of leadership heretofore associated with these groups.

The Historical Pattern

There were two important nationalist tendencies among American Negroes before World War II. One, the so-called New Negro movement, was a race-conscious literary and artistic tendency, made up largely of the intellectual elements within the black leadership group (see Bone, 1958). By drawing upon the folkways of blacks, the New Negro movement, also called the Harlem Renaissance movement, endeavored to redefine the meaning of Negro life in ways free of white American influences. The intellectual roots of the New Negro movement owed much to Paul Lawrence Dunbar, a rather bourgeois gentleman, whose novels and poetry drew heavily upon Negro folk materials —speech, lore, humor, wit, etc. (cf. Dunbar, 1930).

Politically, the New Negro movement was inarticulate: it was largely a cultural nationalist assertion of the needs of a special segment of blacks rather than a political assertion. A few writers and artists in the movement did, however, acquire political ties during the late stages of the movement in the 1930s, but these ties were with white radical groups, mainly socialists and communists. It is indeed a striking feature of the New Negro movement that, though it coexisted in time with a politically oriented populist nationalist movement of blacks— namely, the Garvey movement—the members of the New Negro movement remained for the most part separate from it.

There are several reasons for this: for one thing, the Garvey movement, officially called the Universal Negro Improvement Association, depended heavily upon charismatic leadership, which was not predisposed to permit intellectuals an independent or critical relationship to the movement. Moreover, the leader, Marcus Garvey, who designated himself provisional president of Africa, possessed a strong ego and nursed intellectual ambitions of his own. Though he had little formal education and thus is more properly described as a "para-intellectual" rather than a full-fledged one,[2] Garvey wrote numerous pamphlets and was fond of appearing in academic garb at public rallies (see Cronon, 1955). To the leaders of the New Negro movement, however, Garvey was something of an upstart who chanced upon an important issue. Alain Locke (1925:15), the finest theoretical thinker in the New Negro movement, remarked in 1925 that "Garveyism may be a transient, if spectacular, phenomenon, but the possible role of the American Negro in the future development of Africa is one of the most constructive and universally helpful missions that any modern people can lay claim to."

Matters of social class and style also contributed to the failure of the Garvey movement and the New Negro movement to join forces. The Garvey movement, led by small businessmen (largely West Indians) was a petty bourgeois affair: it was less interested in the intellectual aspects of black nationalism than in translating black awareness into material benefits—especially economic benefits. Indeed, the leadership of the Garvey movement was virtually obsessed with manipulating black nationalism for economic goals of the bourgeois type; the use of nationalism for political goals of long-run benefit to the typical Negro (e.g., gaining greater access to city machines, strengthening and disciplining the urban Negro vote, etc.) was an uncommon feature of the Garvey movement, and this was precisely because of the leadership's equation of nationalism with bourgeois economic activity.[3] On the other hand, the intellectuals in the New Negro movement,

2. I develop this concept (1969a) of para-intellectual in terms of a special strata of nationalist or militant Negro leadership.

3. Garvey's concern with economic activity is covered in Cronon (1955). In Kilson (1971), I deal with the small political role of the Garvey movement.

though from bourgeois families, were antibourgeois in outlook. They sympathized with the anticapitalist views then current among many American intellectuals and in general saw economic matters as humdrum. They also had little taste for the popular, though politically superficial, appeal of the Garvey movement which stirred thousands of working-class and lower-middle-class urban Negroes with ideas of blackness. "We've got to teach the American Negro blackness," declared Garvey in 1924. "Give them black ideals, black industry, black United States of Africa and black religion."[4] The particular style of acculturation to intellectual life and pursuits that characterized most intellectuals in the New Negro movement inhibited them from embracing the populist, opportunistic, facile, and raucous style of the Garvey movement.

Thus by the end of World War II the first two major nationalist (and militant) tendencies among black Americans in this century possessed no effective links between them. Today, however, this situation is quite different: many Negro intellectuals participate in or are sympathetic to a popular-based nationalist militancy which is often xenophobic toward white society and rejects the established intellectual style. What postwar changes brought this situation about?

Context of Black Militancy

For nearly two decades after World War II the Civil Rights movement was the major political articulator of Negro interests. But the composition and structure of the Civil Rights movement seriously restricted both the range of interests it articulated and the style in which it did so. The Negro lower class and working class (and even the lower-middle class) had little influence in the organizations that constituted the Civil Rights movement (e.g., NAACP, Urban League, SCLC, CORE, and Negro professional associations). This movement was, then, a rather oligarchical affair: the black bourgeoisie defined the goals, tactics, and methods of the Civil Rights movement: the working-class and lower-class blacks were mainly acted upon by the movement.[5] Furthermore, like most oligarchies, the leadership of the

4. Quoted in Opportunity: Journal of Negro Life (September 1924): 284.
5. Incidentally, in the years between the two world wars, had the white-controlled city political machines outside the South discarded their racist ways and included the black working and lower class in their political process, thereby lending political efficacy to the Negro popular strata, it is unlikely that the middle-class blacks and the Civil Rights movement would have virtually monopolized the political articulation of Negro interests after World War II. (See Kilson, 1971.)

Civil Rights movement was self-perpetuating: the Negro popular strata, in whose name the movement's leaders spoke, had no direct say in the selection of leadership.

The composition of the Civil Rights movement had another feature which is crucial to understanding the movement's transformation in the 1960s—namely, alliance with the liberal segments of the white intelligentsia. This alliance provided the Civil Rights movement numerous benefits: money, professional skills, legislative alliances (federal and state), access to strategic institutional roles, etc. But it also had certain drawbacks: it fostered a rather uncreative relationship of dependence between the established Negro leadership and white liberals. This, in turn, caused the established Negro leadership in the 1950s to neglect a most pressing requirement of their organization's survival —namely, the expansion of these organizations among the Negro popular strata. With the exception of the rise of the Montgomery Improvement Association (and later the SCLC) led by Martin Luther King, which emerged in response to the special needs of Negro popular strata in Montgomery, Alabama, the established Negro leadership did not cultivate the Civil Rights movement in this regard in the 1950s. As a result, a political vacuum occurred in the Negro community, especially outside the South, in the urban ghetto, but also within the South.

The Negro popular strata, especially in the urban areas outside the South, experienced important socio-economic gains in the 1950s, including a growth in social expectations. But these gains were associated in the Negro popular mind less with a sense of satisfaction than with a sharpening perception of the relative socio-economic gap separating blacks from whites. Thus by the late 1950s the popular strata in the Negro ghetto were ripe for mobilization into a more developed and assertive political force than they had ever constituted heretofore. But the established Negro leadership in the Civil Rights movement failed to undertake this mobilization. The relationship of dependence which characterized this leadership's alliance with white liberals had dulled its perception of the unique political needs of the Negro popular strata and also induced a certain lack of nerve among the Negro civil rights leaders. In the end, a political vacuum emerged in the urban ghetto outside the South (and even in the South) and a new type of leadership and style called black militancy arose to fill the vacuum.

Sociology and Style of Black Militancy

Unlike leaders of the Civil Rights movement, leaders of the black militant groups who have given articulation to the political needs of the Negro popular strata since the 1960s are largely of lower-class, working-class, and lower middle-class backgrounds. One set of these leaders appeared initially outside the South and functioned within a religious black militant format—namely, the leaders of the Nation of Islam, the Black Muslim movement, the prominent figure among whom was Malcolm X.[6] Another set of these leaders appeared initially within the South, functioning within the Civil Rights movement and through secular political channels, but seeking to redefine the Civil Rights movement. The Student Nonviolent Coordinating Committee (SNCC) was the agency of this set of black militant leaders in the early 1960's, and these leaders—especially Stokely Carmichael, James Forman, and Rap Brown, all from working-class and lower middle-class backgrounds and the first in their families to attend college—brilliantly utilized the SNCC to launch a new perspective toward Negro protest.

In the years 1964-1966, the SNCC, now seeking beachheads in cities outside the South, began to differentiate itself from the established Negro leadership in the Civil Rights movement through the agency of a new ideology. Low in usual political resources, ideology was the only important political weapon available to the leaders of the SNCC. The doctrine of "Black Power," basically a militant and more political variant of the Garvey movement's form of nationalism, was their major ideological formulation, which was first enunciated in mid-1966. Within the South the SNCC had only limited success in using Black Power to acquire a sizable political following separate from the established groups in the Civil Rights movement. Outside the South, however, in the black urban ghetto, the doctrine of Black Power received much more attention from the Negro popular strata. More than in the South the Negro popular strata outside had experienced enough social-economic change in the 1950s to have acquired a sharpened sense of relative deprivation and thus a need for political articu-

6. Malcolm X's background might be described as upper working-class or perhaps lower middle-class, insofar as his father was what Negroes call a "jack-leg" minister (that is, not formally trained for clergy). But Malcolm X's life style as a boy and young man was very much lower-class. (See Malcolm X, 1966.)

lation (leadership) on a scale unprecedented.[7] The riots, which commenced in 1963 and had become a political force by 1966, graphically underscored this popular need for leadership, and the SNCC leaders, shrewdly manipulating the doctrine of Black Power, made the first bid to fill this vacuum.

But, interestingly enough, the militant leaders of SNCC did not succeed in filling the political vacuum which the riots of the 1960s drew attention to. Instead they were replaced by another set of nationalistic militants (exemplified by leaders of the Black Panther party) who for the most part are of marginal (unskilled) working-class and lower-class backgrounds rather than from the upward-aspiring solid (skilled) working class and the lower middle class, which was the case for most SNCC leaders who had also attended college, usually the first of their families to do so. The difference in family background not only meant that the militant leaders who superseded the SNCC in the urban ghettos from the mid-1960s onward seldom entered college, but, more important, that they had experienced the variety of pathological and antisocial tendencies that pervade the life of the Negro lower class and the marginal working class.[8]

Thus the leaders of black militant groups like the Black Panther party, organized in some 30 cities; the West Side Organization, based in Chicago; and the New England Grass Roots Organization (NEGRO), based in Boston, are largely school dropouts who have held a variety of "hustling roles" within the ghetto—such as pimp, numbers writer, narcotics pusher, small-holdup man, etc.[9] These hustling roles lent the leaders of these militant groups a special legitimacy—a value the militant leaders of SNCC, of skilled working-class and lower middle-class origin, did not claim—for segments of the Negro lower

7. On the socio-economic gains of Negro popular strata in 1950s, see U.S. Bureau of Labor Statistics (1967). Marx first articulated the concept of relative deprivation in his pamphlet "Wage Labor and Capital" (1849:87):

> A noticeable increase in wages presupposes a rapid growth of wealth, luxury, social wants, social enjoyments. Thus, although the enjoyments of the worker have risen, the social satisfaction that they give has fallen in comparison with the increased enjoyments of the capitalist, which are inaccessible to the worker, in comparison with the state of development of society in general. Our desires and pleasures spring from society; we measure them, therefore, by society and not by the objects which serve for their satisfaction. Because they are of a relative nature.

8. On pathologies of the black ghetto, see Clark (1965).

9. On background of these particular militant leaders, see, e.g., Cleaver (1968); Steel (1969:19); Ellis (1969).

classes celebrate hustling roles, according their occupiers a certain folk status as "culture heroes" (see, e.g., Malcolm X, 1966; Keil, 1966; Liebow, 1967).

For the most part, however, the occupiers of hustling roles who have become nationalistic militants are usually individuals with high native talent and exhibit high need achievement. Apart from the opportunity to seize leadership roles provided by the riots of the mid-1960s, the fact that leaders of groups like the Black Panther party and the West Side Organization possess high native ability must have been determining. To some extent the measure of this native talent was the success of these leaders in using certain skills associated with leadership within the black lower classes—especially verbal skills and a variety of interpersonal skills concerned with the facile manipulation of others for a short-run benefit (cf. Kochman, 1969). These skills have been readily adapted to the new militant political roles now held by lower-class and working-class leaders, and a number of them have even turned to writing political pamphlets, books, articles, etc. They are, in short, what I have called "para-intellectuals," by which I mean self-made (or nonformally trained) intellectuals who are articulators of the interests and outlook of the Negro lower classes.

Thus the rise of the militant leaders who superseded the SNCC leaders in controlling the militant politics in the urban black ghetto in the 1960s represents a major change in the political relations of black and white America, particularly in the style of these relations. There is, for the first time, an ascendancy of lower-class criteria (that is, experiences and situations associated with lower-class Negroes) in the legitimation of Negro leadership, especially nationalist and militant leadership but also more established or usual Negro leadership.

This does not mean, of course, that the established leadership among blacks has been totally stripped of legitimacy, but that it can continue legitimacy only to the degree that it comes to terms with the new lower-class black forces which now have an independent form and structure within the politics of the Negro subsystem and thus also in the political relations of blacks and whites. Thus such tendencies among lower-class blacks as violence, vulgar language, and uncivil style are now not uncommon among established black leadership groups. It is also not uncommon among established black leadership, seeking to recover from the threat posed by the lower-class and working-class black militants, to find the outward manifestations of the new nationalistic militancy like the "Afro" hairstyle and what I call the language of blackness, usually militantly antiwhite expressions.

Of all the forces that contributed to this radical change in Negro leadership patterns, none is quite as significant as the riots that commenced in 1963-64. What the riots did was to politicize the heretofore relatively inactive popular strata. Participation by these strata in the riots was symptomatic of a leadership vacuum in the ghetto. The riots uncovered the prevalence of numerous aggrieved and politically inarticulate groups who were in search of leadership. These groups included school dropouts—who are legion in the black ghetto—welfare mothers—equally legion—unskilled workers in need of stable jobs, and skilled workers seeking redress from racist practices in trade unions, among other aggrieved groups. Thus in politicizing these groups—that is, in giving them a primary platform or arena for political definition —the riots clearly performed a major function.

Data on the participation of lower-class and marginal working-class Negroes in the riots of the 1960s may provide some measure of the class attributes of this politicizing function performed by riots. Surveys of rioters done for the Kerner Report (1968) show that in Detroit, in the 1967 riot, 38.6 percent of a random sample of 44 arrested rioters fell in the lower income range of less than $2,000 to $5,000, and 13 percent of this sample fell into the marginal working-class to skilled working-class income range of $5,000 to $7,500. A similar survey in Newark found 60.6 percent of the rioters falling within these two income ranges.

The occupational position of the rioters in Detroit and Newark was comparable to their income category: 50 percent of 125 arrested rioters surveyed in Newark in the 1967 riot were unskilled (remainder were semi-skilled) and 61 percent of a sample of 104 rioters in Newark were unemployed for a month or more in the year prior to the riot, and at the time of the riot unemployment gripped 29.7 percent of a sample of 84 rioters. Similarly, when measured for educational attainment, the majority of the rioters surveyed in Detroit and Newark in 1967 also ranked low: 60.5 percent of a random sample of 43 rioters in Detroit had education ranging from less than sixth grade to some high school; and 65.1 percent of a random sample of 106 rioters in Newark fell into this same educational category.

Perhaps the most striking feature of the data on the majority position of lower-class and marginal working-class Negroes in the riots of the 1960s is that this majority of rioters were from the better-off, not the poorer sections of the Negro popular or lower strata. Thus only 13.6 percent of a random sample of 44 rioters in Detroit had less than $2,000 income, and 4.7 percent of a random sample of 104 rioters in

Newark in 1967 fell into this income category. An analytically important conclusion emerges from these data: political (nationalist) militancy is a function not merely of a depressed or oppressive status but
more significantly of a changing status and of expectations of further
change consequent upon the use of militancy.

This proposition is supported by another set of data on the 1960s
riots, namely, data concerning middle-class participation in the riots.
Some 16.2 percent of a sample of 43 rioters in Detroit in 1967 had college education, as did 5.7 percent of a sample of 106 rioters in Newark;
and 18.2 percent of a sample of 44 rioters in Detroit were in the
$7,500-to-$12,500 income category and 2.3 percent had upper middle-
class income of $15,000, while in Newark 15.4 percent of a random
sample of 104 rioters were in the $7,500-to-$12,000 income bracket
and 1 percent in the $10,000-to-$12,500 category.

The crucial feature of middle-class participation in the riots of the
1960s is that there was any participation at all. Things being equal,
rioting is not a political behavior expected of the middle classes. But
then, things are clearly not equal in regard to the black middle classes;
they displayed in the early 1960s at least as sharp a sense of relative
deprivation as lower-class and working-class Negroes. Moreover, giv-
en their greater political experience and their need to maintain a leadership position in the Negro community, the black bourgeoisie could
not let nationalistic militancy become a monopoly of lower-class and
working-class militant leaders. Thus, in part, the black bourgeoisie has
adopted a variant of nationalistic militancy, including some riot participation, in order to guarantee its political status. Furthermore, a sizable number of middle-class Negroes now derive a profound catharsis
and therapeutic gain from adopting a political style in black-white interactions which was heretofore verboten.[10]

Political Structure of Black Militancy

Like many modern nationalist tendencies, current nationalistic
militancy among Negroes is high in ability to articulate demands for
black self-determination in political matters but low in actual capacity

---

10. On verboten features of traditional black-white political interactions, and particularly on the passive leadership style of middle-class blacks, see Myrdal (1954:709-
780). On the catharsis Negroes experience from aggressive or militant behavior toward
whites, see, e.g., Wright (1940). See also LeRoi Jones's two plays, "Dutchman" (1964)
and "The Slave" (1964).

to realize this. This has in turn produced a variety of curious relationships between the dominant white society and militant black nationalism. For example, among nationalist-minded Negro students in white colleges a fixation on black consciousness and identity has produced a movement for so-called black studies.[11] Like other aspects of black nationalist militancy, the black studies movement is caught in a contradiction: it is seemingly motivated by an intense sense of alienation from white culture and institutions but, alas, chooses white colleges and universities as its main arena of action.

This apparent contradiction in the black studies movement has not escaped criticism from certain of its supporters. One critic, Professor Vincent Harding of Spelman College, a Negro institution, has called for a lessening of activity in behalf of black studies on white campuses in order to allow more effective growth of black studies in Negro colleges (see Harding, 1969). This criticism has a point, but not a very sharp one: it amounts to little more than rearguard action. Most Negroes attending college are now on white campuses (perhaps 65 percent) and this trend will increase in the future. Furthermore, the brightest Negro students are attracted increasingly to white campuses, both within and outside the South; and despite severe alienation and the absence of a set standard toward white institutions, these students possess enough common sense to recognize that a superior education is a more likely possibility at Wayne State University or at Duke University than at Grambling College. Thus the contradiction reflected in Negro students' choice of white campuses as the arena of action for black studies is merely another facet of the longstanding ambivalence underlying black-white interactions in American society; many blacks genuinely dislike or hate whites, and vice versa, yet simultaneously recognize that they need whites—and vice versa. There is simply no significant conception, existentially speaking, of being a black or white American which excludes this sort of ambivalence.[12]

There is, in fact, no major black nationalist political group that exists in any significant sense free of white ties and support. The federal government, dominated by whites, is the source of funds—the patron, as it were—for hundreds of small black militant community organizations that emerged following the riots of 1964 and 1965. These black militant organizations obtain federal aid through the Economic Opportunity Act of 1964 and could not exist long without federal aid

11. For analysis of black studies movement, see Kilson (1969b).
12. I am influenced in this viewpoint by Ellison (1964).

(see Levitan, 1969). The West Side Organization, a militant group, is a case in point: formed in 1964 by lower-class and working-class para-intellectuals, the West Side Organization, initially funded by white charity funds, performed a small range of social services for the Chicago ghetto poor. But under stimulus of the 1966 riots in Chicago, the OEO requested the West Side Organization to submit proposals for community development, emphasizing employment services. The OEO funded this operation at nearly $100,000 and these funds in turn enabled the West Side Organization to become a viable concern (see Ellis, 1969:7ff., 107ff.).

Outside the federal government, white radicals, and, to a lesser extent, white liberals, have been a major source of funds, skills, and equipment for black militant organizations. The most prominent of these organizations, the Black Panther party, derives nearly all its finances from white radicals. In this way, the Panthers finance a weekly newspaper, the *Black Panther*; they are virtually the only black militant organization with such an organ, and their national prominence is a function of this organ. White funds also aid the Panthers' effort to supply social services in the cities where they are organized (nearly 30 such cities, more than any other black militant group). But the Panthers' propaganda to the contrary, none of these services is particularly extensive (e.g., the much-trumpeted breakfast program for ghetto children reaches no more than 20,000 [*Black Panther*, 1969]), though even these are more than other black militant groups can claim and would be unthinkable without the support the Panthers gain from white allies.

Indeed, it is a unique feature of the Black Panther party that, of all black militant organizations, it was the first to renounce racial xenophobia toward whites as such, common to most black nationalistic groups, and to forge alliances with whites, albeit radical ones. This is a mark of political realism, and though the Panther party can hardly become a popular force among whites as long as it persists in a fixation on violent symbolism and restricts its allies to white radicals, the very fact of such allies remains a sign of realism on the part of the Panthers. Blacks clearly lack the resources for viable political self-determination and those nationalistic Negro groups who propagate self-determination indulge in sheer fantasy.

Conclusion: An Evaluative Note

Thus an analysis of the political structure of black militancy indicates few viable organizations that depend upon Negro resources. The black popular supporters of these organizations are, after all, weak in political resources. As a result, white charity groups, white radicals, and the federal government are the major sources of financial support of black militant organizations. Recently, some white charity bodies have drastically reduced their support of black militant groups—especially those groups who seek, as it were, to have their cake and eat it too, which is to say they persist in xeonphobic public stance toward whites, but take their funds. Also the Nixon administration in Washington has drastically reduced federal spending under OEO and Model Cities, causing a major loss of funds for black militant organizations.

Thus there are currently many signs of declining organizational viability for many black militant organizations (save the Black Panther party, whose white radical allies persist in large-scale support). This situation is not, however, all bad. Most of the hundreds of black militant organizations that formed since 1964 were precarious operations. Many were concerned more with seizing for their aspiring leaders a share of the spoils from white charities and the federal government than with the provision of leadership and services for the neglected constituencies in the Negro ghetto like semi-skilled workers, street gangs, school dropouts, welfare mothers, etc. The decline of this variety of black militant organization need hardly be mourned.

On the other hand, some of these organizations do provide, after a fashion, a modicum of political structure for the ghetto lower strata. They lend some assistance to the masses' political striving and some hope that in time better means will be forthcoming. The West Side Organization in Chicago falls into this category of militant organizations, and its demise due to a disinterested federal administration would be sad.

Perhaps the worst feature of the demise of black militant organization is that the large number of Negro youth in ghettos will be left without political direction. All black nationalistic tendencies lend some measure of political direction to ghetto youth, and it would seem very much in the interest of the wider integration of blacks into the American body politic that such direction continue to be available. This is borne out by data gathered in a Harris poll which asked Negroes the question, "Can blacks win rights without violence?" Some 31 percent of the sample felt that blacks could not progress politically without violence, while 58 percent felt that they could. More significantly, younger Negroes were more strongly in support of violence as a political instrument than were older blacks. Thus 65 percent of those 50 years of age and above favored the question, compared to 58 percent of those 22 to 29 years of age and 55 percent of those 14 to 21 years of age (Time, 6 April 1970).

It is, then, clear that federal resources are required in order to lend viability to those black militant organizations which provide ghetto services to the poor and lend political direction or coherence to Negro city youth. No doubt means more effective than black militant organizations must ultimately be fashioned for these tasks, but meanwhile black militant groups are available and should be utilized. If not, it is likely that the standardless features of black nationalist militancy, always close to the surface anyway, may gain greater currency, causing a major setback in the long-run political institutionalization of the Negro subsystem in American society.

Finally, it must be asked specifically what is the over-all impact of the new forms of black nationalistic militancy upon interactions between Negroes and whites.

At one level, it is unmistakably clear that black nationalistic militancy since the 1960s has polarized the perceptions of black-white interactions. For example, more than ever before there are individuals and groups among Negroes who articulate a view or description of the past and present status of blacks which differs fundamentally from views or descriptions articulated by whites. Similarly, more than ever before Negroes will express a desire to participate in all-black political and cultural activity, separate from associations with whites. Moreover, these expressions of all-black preferences are, of course, surrounded with a tremendous amount of black nationalist ideological activity and symbolic manifestations.

Indeed, at no other period since World War I can one find, as one can find today, extensive nationalistic ideological activity at every level of the Negro American social structure. Thus upper middle-class Negro students are as likely to be involved in some aspect of nationalistic ideological activity as working-class and lower-class Negro youth in the urban ghetto.

There is, then, evidence of greater polarization in black-white relationships, especially at the verbal, ideological, and symbolic levels. But, alas, things are never quite as they seem: for the most striking feature of the rise of a more pervasive black nationalistic militancy in the 1960s is that greater black-white polarization at the verbal and ideological levels is not perfectly continuous at the institutional level. *In other words, despite the sharp ideological polarization of Negroes and whites, there is more, not less, common participation by Negroes and whites in the same institutions.*

This paradox is most apparent, of course, in higher educational institutions. I have already noted the fascinating paradox of growing ideological articulation of nationalistic militancy among Negro college students, in the form of the black studies movement; yet this same articulation of something all-black over and against something white takes place on white college campuses, where Negro students are increasingly to be found and increasingly choose to go. In other words, this instance of a fierce assertion and articulation by black students of an ideological and cultural distinctiveness has not been continuous with a growing institutional distinctiveness or polarization in higher education. In fact, it has resulted in a heretofore unprecedented rate of increase of Negro students attending white colleges.

Even more striking illustration of the proposition that greater ideological and verbal polarization between blacks and whites has not been continuous with greater institutional polarization is the fact that all major new black militant organizations rely heavily upon white support, white finance, and other forms of white reinforcement. This is seen most prominently in the Black Panther party which, at one level, articulates a fierce form of black ideological militancy over-and-against whites; but at another level has the closest institutional ties with white progressives and white radicals that one can imagine. Indeed, the Black Panther party was the first prominent black militant group to admit openly, and I think correctly, *that the greater ideological polarization of blacks and whites should not result in greater institutional polarization or separatism.*

Instead, the leaders of the Black Panthers argue, like good Marxian dialecticians who understand the role of paradox in social change, that greater black-white ideological polarization should be an instrument of greater institutional identity or harmony between Negroes and whites. The Panthers have, of course, a special revolutionary view of how such institutional identity will ultimately evolve, though I do not think their view is correct. But I do think their general comprehension of the paradox of black militant ideological development in contemporary American society that I have delineated is correct, for there is a lot of evidence to support it. It is, indeed, a profound irony of American social and political change that the more use a given ethnic community makes of its ethnicity to redefine power differentials between itself and other groups, the more likely is the disappearance of ethnicity in the long run.

REFERENCES

The Black Panther.
>   1969   December 27.
Bone, Robert A.
>   1958   The Negro Novel in America. New Haven: Yale University Press.
Carr, E. M., et al.
>   1939   Nationalism. London: Oxford University Press.
Clark, Kenneth B.
>   1965   Dark Ghetto. New York: Harper & Row.
Cleaver, Eldridge.
>   1968   Soul on Ice. New York: Random House.
Cronon, Edmund.
>   1955   Black Moses. Madison: University of Wisconsin Press.
Dunbar, Paul L.
>   1930   Collected Poems. New York: Dodd, Mead and Company.
Ellis, William.
>   1969   White Ethics and Black Power: The Emergence of the West Side
>   Organization. Chicago: Aldine Press.
Essien-Udom, E.U.
>   1963   Black Nationalism—A Search for an Identity in America. Chicago:
>   University of Chicago Press.
Ellison, Ralph.
>   1964   Shadow and Act. New York: Random House.
Harding, Vincent.
>   1969   "New Creation or Familiar Death?" The Negro Digest (March).
Jones, LeRoi.
>   1964   Dutchman. New York: Apollo Editions.
>   1964   The Slave. New York: Apollo Editions.
Keil, Charles.
>   1966   Urban Blues. Chicago: University of Chicago Press.
Kilson, Martin.
>   1966   Political Change in a West African State. Cambridge: Har-
>   vard University Press.
>   1969a   "New Black Intellectuals." Dissent (July-August).
>   1969b   "Anatomy of the Black Studies Movement." The Massa-
>   chusetts Review (Autumn).
>   1971   "Political Change in the Negro Ghetto." In Key Issues in the Afro-
>   American Experience, edited by N. Huggins, M. Kilson, and D.
>   Fox. New York: Harcourt Brace Jovanovich.
Kochman, Thomas.
>   1969   "Rapping in the Black Ghetto." Trans-Action (February).

Levitan, Sar A.
   1969   "The Community Action Program: A Strategy to Fight Poverty."
          Annals. American Academy of Political and Social Science (Sep-
          tember).
Liebow, Elliot.
   1967   Tally's Corner. Chicago: University of Chicago Press.
Locke, Alain.
   1925   The New Negro. New York: A. and C. Boni.
Malcolm X.
   1966   Autobiography of Malcolm X. New York: Random House.
Marx, Karl.
   1849   "Wage Labor and Capital." In Selected Works, by Karl Marx and
          Frederick Engels, vol 1. Reprint edition, 1951. Moscow: Foreign
          Language Publisher.
   n.d.   Economic and Philosophic Manuscripts of 1844. Moscow: Foreign
          Language Publisher.
Myrdal, Gunnar.
   1954   An American Dilemma. New York: Harper and Brothers.
National Advisory Commission on Civil Disorders.
   1968   Report. (Kerner Report.) New York: Bantam Books.
Opportunity: Journal of Negro Life.
   1924   (September):284.
Steel, Ronald.
   1969   "The Panthers." The New York Review of Books. (September
          11):19.
Time Magazine.
   1970   95: (April 6).
U.S. Bureau of Labor Statistics.
   1967   Social and Economic Conditions of Negroes in the United States.
          Washington: U.S. Government Printing Office.
Wright, Richard.
   1940   Native Son. New York: Harper and Brothers.

The Dialectic
Inner-Dynamic

DR. KILSON'S paper calls for an analytical approach with some illumination of the typological guideposts and with some additional review pointers to do justice to the rich content of his presentation.

Dr. Kilson looks at the dynamics of nationalism and political militancy among Negro Americans as a dialectic process which in the long run will lead to the political institutionalization of the Negro subsystem in American society. This projective proposition sounds axiomatic. But there is good reason to assume that Dr. Kilson would be responsive to a challenge of the validity of this proposition. He could have introduced existential or even revolutionary propositions but refrained from doing so.

From his selected vantage point, Dr. Kilson develops a system of polar positions which in dialectical interaction may lead to a synthesis in terms of the proposition which he has advanced or may end in a failure to solve the black-white dilemma in American society. He considered such a failure as possible but not as probable.

There is a dialectic inner-dynamic in the black movement which parallels the dialectic dynamic of the black-white confrontation. When Dr. Kilson speaks broadly of dynamics he thinks, so it seems, of the black-white polar forces which dialectically interact by a sequence of changing casts in the drama but which, notwithstanding, are moving steadily toward the projective goal of the institutionalization of the

Negro subsystem in American society.

The first set of polar positions is the self-identity drive (nationalism): in Riesman's terms "an inner-directed drive" as opposed to the political power drive—in Riesman's terms "an other-directed drive," the synthesis being the gaining of political power for the black community through the medium of national self-assertion. The Garvey movement and the New Negro movement before the second World War operated in this framework without noticeable success other than politicizing the Negro masses.

The second polar position emerged two decades after the second World War. The Civil Rights movement (e.g., NAACP, Urban League, SCLC, CORE, and Negro professional associations) and the liberal white intelligentsia became the challengers of the white establishment.

Yet, the black polar position was not firmly established as long as the Civil Rights movement included liberal whites who provided partially strong leadership and deprived the upcoming Negro leadership of a clear sense of independent action and decision-making.

Therefore a third polar position came on the scene through the emergence of the Black Power ideology which helped to transfer the leadership of the black movement to a black intelligentsia from black middle class. The Student Nonviolent Co-ordinating Committee (SNCC) was born. The new leaders—especially Stokely Carmichael, James Forman, and Rap Brown, all from working-class and lower middle-class backgrounds and the first in their families to attend college—brilliantly utilized the SNCC to launch a new perspective toward Negro protest. It was a manifestation of black political self-assertion.

The fourth polar position soon followed suit when, in the process of dialectical polarization, the black masses rioted in frustration because they remained excluded from active participation. They called for leaders from the marginal working class and the lower class with whom they could identify. This change of leaders finalized the polarization by including the black masses actively in the black social movement. The Black Panthers symbolize this new black leadership as the last set of final polar positions.

Dr. Kilson considers the progressive emerging of polar positions as a process of politicization of the Negro masses with enough momentum to challenge successfully the white power structure.

The inner-dialectic of the black movement is finally solved by the common awareness of the deprivation under which all sectors of the black society suffer. Coalitions with white liberal and radical sectors of the white society are not ruled out, as Marx would consider such coalition workable and desirable in his theory of the class struggle. Dr. Kilson considers these coalitions as crucial for giving the black radical leader the resources to keep the ghetto masses politically organized, to motivate them to develop their community, and, above all, to become forceful and recognized conflict partners in the black-white confrontation. The proposition and typologies offered in Dr. Kilson's paper render themselves exceedingly well for developing further research designs in the area of his inquiry. Such inquiry could be extended to existential or revolutionary or even anarchical propositions which would lead to a different set of typologies and research designs.

4 STANLAKE SAMKANGE

A Historical Perspective of Racial Tensions and National Identity in Rhodesia

IT WAS Linnaeus who, while looking for a unit from which systems of classification could be built, made the species his unit and further grouped them to form the genus. According to Philip Mason (1970:11), "Below the species was a subdivision, sometimes described as a subspecies, less precisely, a race. This was applied to distinguish a population which had been isolated from the main body of the species long enough to develop some differences." According to Dr. N. A. Barnicot (Mason, 1970:11), "The members of a species share certain features, which are presumed to be inherited, which distinguish them clearly from other species, and interbreeding leading to the production of intermediate forms does not occur in nature." We thus have, in the species, as well as in the race, shared inherited features, a clear distinction from other species, and the fact that fertile interbreeding does not occur in nature. As Philip Mason (1970:11) points out, "Neither of these two latter points applies to local differentiations of the same species, which will interbreed when they meet, and which will then produce a variety of intermediate forms."

Mason (1970:12) continues, "The importance of this for man now becomes clear. Man is one species; he shares many inherited features with other men and every kind of man is much more like a man than he is like any other species; he breeds with all other kinds of men and produces offspring who are fertile. The races of man are local variations, the differences between them are considerable. . . . but they are not of such a nature as to provide absolutely sharp boundaries."

Therefore, while discussing the subject of race relations in Zimbabwe, known as Rhodesia today, or, indeed, anywhere else on the face of the earth, it is important to bear in mind the essential unity of men.

All men belong to one and the same species; racial differences are purely and simply local variations and manifestations of men's ability to adapt themselves to their cultural and physical environment.

In this paper, we shall endeavor to trace the attitude concerning race which various groups, now comprising the population of Rhodesia, manifested when they first came into contact with one another. We shall suggest why they held certain notions about people of a different racial group and why they adopted a certain attitude toward them. We shall try to see to what extent these group attitudes have been affected by actual contact with one another over a number of years.

Racial groups comprising the population of Rhodesia today are: Africans; people of European descent; people of mixed race known generally as Coloreds; and Asiatics, almost always called "Indians."

Africans

The Mashona

Africans, numbering over five million, are by far the largest single racial group in Rhodesia. They comprise the Shona-speaking tribes, also by far the largest group among Africans; as well, the Amandebele in the west and the Amatshangane in the east. The Mashona have a long and proud history. Archaeological evidence shows Rhodesia to have been part of an area occupied by Iron Age people who entered it in waves from A.D. 300 to the beginning of the second millennium. Among those immigrants were the ancestors of the Mashona, who, as pointed out in the writer's *African Saga: Introduction to African History* (1971), "dominated the area and became rulers of the land." They constructed several "dzimbabwe"—royal residences in stone—the largest and most famous of which is Great Zimbabwe, seventeen miles from Fort Victoria. Zimbabwe—big house of stone—is situated in a valley in which is a rocky hill. On this hill, with walls built into its granite rock, stands a citadel, access to which could only be gained through easily defensible approaches. In the valley is a great wall surrounding a huge conical tower and several buildings connected by a labyrinth of walled passages. The walls are thirty feet high and fifteen feet wide. They are evenly and neatly built of stone bricks, without mortar.

When Europeans first saw Great Zimbabwe in the nineteenth century, the ruins immediately became one of the wonders of the world. The question was, who built them? They were described as "a mystery," "a riddle," and "an enigma." Their construction was ascribed to Phoenicians, Egyptians, Cretans, Etruscans, Sabeans, Persians, Summerians, Dravidians—anyone except the Mashona. But, as Europeans developed some understanding of African history, they discovered what Africans had known all along: that the Zimbabwe were built by the Mashona. Europeans not only found that there were several other "dzimbabwe" built of stone in other parts of the country at Mapungubwe, Dhlo-Dhlo, Khami, Naletale, etc., but they also found that some of these places had been occupied comparatively recently. Clearly, the mystery, riddle, and enigma of the Zimbabwe had existed only in European minds, some of whose scholars, even today, still try to pretend that these "ma dzimbabwe" are not the work of Africans.

Perhaps the most remarkable aspect of Shona dominance over this area is that, as Edward Alpers (1967:5-6) points out: "There is no indication that they achieved this dominance by violent means. In fact the archaeological record suggests exactly the opposite, for . . . Shona culture coexisted with earlier cultures and never completely replaced them. Similarly, the key to Shona dominance would seem not to have been superior military power, although this may have been a contributory factor, but rather the possession of superior organizational skill." The intellectual capacity and organizational skill of the Mashona is shown, among other things, in powerful religious concepts connected with the worship of Mwari, the Supreme Divine Being, through ancestors and tribal spirits—"mhondoro"—expressing themselves through mediums called "svikiro." Since the power of Shona kings and chiefs was ultimately based on the influence and sanction of Mwari, the religious apparatus by means of which communication between Mwari and the people took place was a potent instrument in the integration of social, political, religious, and economic factors into the Mashona way of life.

Shona organizational skill also showed itself in economics. Shona states had a firm economic base founded on agriculture and trade with Arabs from the east coast of Africa. This trade, which dates from the time of the Empire of Zanj, in the second half of the first millennium, was primarily in the export of ivory, copper, and gold. Ivory in particular was greatly in demand for the making of bracelets and trinkets in India, since Indian elephant ivory was considered too hard and brittle. In exchange, the Mashona imported glass beads, cloth, porcelain, etc. This long-distance trade was organized on a large scale and was facilitated by the security of movement assured by Shona rule.

Early in the fifteenth century, there arose a dynasty among the Mashona, later identified as Va Rozwi, whose kings became known as Mambo and earned the praise-name Mwene Mutapa. When the Portuguese came, at the beginning of the sixteenth century, the Rozwi Empire of Zimbabwe had virtually divided into two empires. At this time, the dynasty of Changamire controlled the larger and more important portion and its influence and strength grew from day to day.

On the other hand, the Mwene Mutapa's empire and power were shrinking. Portuguese designs and circumstances were such as brought them into contact with the Mwene Mutapa portion of the Rozwi Empire. The Portuguese were, therefore, not especially conversant with the area ruled by Changamire; and the Mwene Mutapa, understandably, tried to use the Portuguese to retrieve lost ground. About 1692, Nyakambira challenged the authority of the Mwene Mutapa, who called on the Portuguese for assistance. Nyakambira solicited the support of Dombo, the reigning Changamire. Dombo's army marched to the Zambezi and forced the Portuguese to flee to Tete and Sena. After this, Dombo became the real heir to the Rozwi Empire, while the Mwene Mutapa, although not completely finished, was virtually a puppet of the Portuguese.

Rozwi Changamire rule was disrupted, eventually, by the Nguni warriors of Zwangendaba in 1830 and by the Amandebele under uMzilikazi, ten years later (Samkange, 1971).

Contrary to popular opinion among Europeans, the Mashona, threrefore, clearly, had a worthy way of life, a tradition, a civilization to preserve and protect when Europeans first came into contact with them. They did not in any way cringe to the Portuguese, the first white men with whom they came into contact. They more than held their own against them in diplomacy, as well as on the battlefield. Thus, when the invaders of the British South Africa Company, the so-called "Pioneer Column," entered Mashonaland in 1890—making that land, according to white historians, the only country in the world that was never invaded, only "pioneered"—the Mashona had a history of contact with white men.

Drawing from their past experience, the Mashona adopted a friendly attitude toward British South Africa Company invaders arriving at Harare (Salisbury) in September 1890. Their spirit mediums advised the Mashona not to be afraid of, or hostile to, the white men, since they were only traders, but to take them a black cow and offer it to the visitors as a greeting gift. This was done, and the chiefs received in return gifts of cloth and blankets. The Europeans then told the Mashona that they were looking for gold and asked for help in prospecting as well as peace to enable prospectors to carry on their work. Some of the Mashona acted as guides to gold-bearing areas; others volunteered labor in return for cloth; Chief Whata hoped to ally himself with this new power and sent his relatives to serve the whites and to be educated.

The Mashona attitude to white men, therefore, was one of friendliness to people whom they regarded as mere traders, or visitors and transients in their country. They offered to help, guide, and work for these white men they thought were their guests, and even tried not only to learn the visitors' ways, but also to involve them in their own domestic quarrels. This was all on a man-to-man basis, on the basis of racial equality. There was, at this time, no tension, no conflict, no friction.

The Amandebele and Amatshangane

Both the Amandebele and the Amatshangane, on the other hand, had a different attitude from that of the Mashona toward Europeans. Both groups had migrated from fear of the wrath of Shaka, the Zulu king; both had fled northwards into the present day Transvaal, where both had encountered Europeans and had been driven further north into present-day Rhodesia. Unlike the Mashona, therefore, the Amandebele and the Amatshangane were not disposed to be friendly to white men. They were hostile. This hostility resulted in Mzilikazi, first king of the Amandebele, closing his country to all but a few white traders and hunters: "I do not want to hear the cry of a white child," he said, "nor the bark of a white man's dog, nor the lowing of a white man's calf" (Preller, 1963:32).

Even though the Amandebele had been forced by the Boers to flee from the Northern Transvaal, most of their warriors considered themselves more than a match for the white men, and they were eager to wash their spears with the blood of Europeans. The Ndebele attitude toward white men in the 1890s was therefore unco-operative, arrogant, and hostile. This applies also to the Amatshangane. There was, therefore, tension between these groups, even before they came into contact in present-day Rhodesia.

Europeans

People of European descent entered Rhodesia from South Africa. They were Boers, i.e., Afrikaners and Englishmen resident in that country. Europeans in Rhodesia now number about 250,000. In 1652, Jan Van Riebeek proclaimed the first ordinance of white South Africa to the first settlers on board the ships *Dromedaris, Reiger,* and *Goede-hoop,* forbidding intercourse with and provocation or ill treatment of natives on any pretext, on pain of fifty lashes administered, right or wrong, in the presence of natives to prove to natives the friendly intentions of the authorities. Ever since that time, white men in South Africa have persistently clung to the notion that racial friction can be prevented by varying degrees of the separation of racial groups. Netherlanders and Hugenots, the core of the Boers, were Calvinists, accustomed in their theology to thinking in terms of the elect, pre-destined by divine grace for salvation and separation from the damned. As a result, when the Boers embarked on the Great Trek to the north in the 1830s, it was with the declared intention of main-taining in their new republics so-called just and proper relations be-tween master and servants. It was one of the first principles of these Boer Republics that there would be no equality between black and white in church or state. Thus, religion played an important part in forming the racial attitudes of white men who later went to Rhodesia.

Sex was also a factor. The existence of a large colored population in the Cape still bears testimony to the encounter of the first predomi-nantly male white settlers with Hottentot and slave women. Being Calvinists, whites reacted to these furtive, loveless, short, animal-like affairs with a strong sense of guilt and shame which drove them to shun their own offspring, whom they regarded as having been born damned.

There was another element in the attitudes of white men who went to Rhodesia: the influence of British officials, some missionaries, and British public opinion. Some British government officials were sus-ceptible to influence by missionaries sympathetic to black men. In the course of time, Boers cried out in the famous Piet Retief Manifesto: "We complain of the unjustified odium cast upon us by interested and dishonest persons under the cloak of religion whose testimony is believed in England to the exclusion of all evidence in our favor"

(Grahamstown *Journal*, February 2, 1837).

White men who went to Rhodesia were, thus, people who regarded black men as inferior or damned folk, condemned to be forever hewers of wood and drawers of water for Europeans. They knew, however, that voices of protest against their attitude toward and treatment of Africans would be heard in Britain. They braced themselves for such protests. In fact, it became part of the administrator's function to have a good explanation ready, as Dr. Jameson, Rhodes's right-hand man, shows when he wrote: "I am getting some knocks re. late treatment of the impertinent natives; but it was necessary, and expecting a snubbing from higher quarters, I took all necessary precautions to have a good explanation. Of course, Iverson (Loch), has to protect himself with the home people, so strictures don't bother me, and on the whole he has been very nice. Rhodes's return will keep all that kind of thing straight" (Samkange, 1969:242).

Because the Amandebele were known to be arrogant, unco-operative, hostile, and quite capable of putting 20,000 warriors against Europeans, the British South Africa Company's invading column bypassed and avoided Matebeleland when it invaded Mashonaland in 1890. Because Europeans who entered Mashonaland were imbued with ideas of superiority, regarding themselves as the elect of God and considering the Mashona as forever damned and condemned to bondage, they completely misunderstood and misinterpreted Mashona history, culture, and attitude toward them.

"Either owing to the intense stupidity of the Mashona or his knowing nothing," wrote the Native Commissioner, Salisbury (Ranger, 1967:2-3), in January 1896, "I have been able to discover very little of his origin or history. . . . Unlike the Zulus the Mashona have no folklore and are content to enjoy today and think nothing of yesterday or tomorrow either for that matter. . . . I do not think it is more than a hundred years since this country was first occupied or invaded by Mashonas."

Mashona chiefs were considered completely impotent. "There is no such a thing as a chief in my area. Those who are called chiefs have not the slightest authority; they are defied even in their own Kraals," wrote the Native Commissioner, Hartley (Ranger, 1967:3), in December 1895 from the village of Chief Mashayangobe. Mashayangobe later led the 1896-1897 resistance to white rule in Western Mashonaland.

"Among the Mashonas there are only very faint traces of religion," wrote the Jesuit missionary, Father Hartman (Ranger, 1967:3), in 1894. "They have hardly any idea of a supreme being. . . . The Mashona are united as a commonwealth by nothing except the unity of their language."

Europeans made such an inaccurate assessment of Shona history, culture, and character largely because of the preconceived ideas they held about black men, ideas derived from the white man's religious and social experiences at the Cape in South Africa. Race relations in Rhodesia were thus damaged beyond repair. Europeans were to pay dearly for this myopia, this self-deception.

In 1896 what is quite wrongly described by white historians as the "Matebele and Mashona Rebellion" broke out. The Mashona had not, up to this point, been subjects of the British government or the British South Africa Company. How could they revolt against a government whose subjects they were not? In this African resistance to white rule, brilliantly masterminded by Shona priests and chiefs, 10 percent of the European population of the day lost their lives; a percentage much higher than that of European victims of the Mau-Mau. Marshall Hole, the Resident Magistrate of Salisbury and settler historian complained that

this sudden departure on the part of the Mashona tribes has caused the
greatest surprise to those who from long residence in the country thought
they understood the character of these savages and to none more than
to the Native Commissioners themselves. . . . With true Kaffir deceit they
have beguiled us into the idea that they were content with our administration
of the country and wanted nothing more than to work for us and trade with
us and become civilized; but at a given signal they have cast aside all
pretence and simultaneously set in motion the whole of the machinery which
they have been preparing.[1]

After the storm had passed, the first native Commissioner of Mrewa in central Mashonaland confessed: "We had underrated the Mashona. We knew nothing of their past history, who they were or where they came from, and although many of the Native Commissioners had a working knowledge of their language, none of us really understood the people or could follow their line of thought. We were inclined to look down upon them as a downtrodden race who were grateful to the white man for protection" (Ranger, 1967:2). White men continued to look down upon the Mashona, and indeed upon all

---

1. Acting C.N.C. to Acting Administrator, 30 March, A 10/1/1-, reported by
Marshall Hole, 29 October 1896, A 1/12/36, as cited by Ranger (1967:1).

black people, as a downtrodden race who should be grateful to the white man for civilization. Now, not only the Amandebele and the Amatshangane, but also the Mashona, who hitherto had been friendly and co-operative with Europeans, were counted as hostile. Race relations worsened as Africans entered the twentieth century aggrieved, sullen, and resentful of the white man's attitude toward them, although they tried not to show it. Europeans on the other hand, entered the twentieth century mistrustful and fearful of the Africans, arrogant toward them, and having shed none of their ideas about the superiority of the white race.

In 1923, European settlers in Rhodesia acquired political power as British South African Company rule came to an end and a new era of "responsible government" began. Under the cloak of Rhodes's empty slogan of "equal rights for all civilized men north of the Limpopo," a constitution purporting to grant equal voting rights to all people, regardless of color, who satisfied certain qualifications, was given. The qualifiations, though simple, disenfranchised almost the whole African population. Saying this disenfranchisement was merely temporary and would last only until Africans were able to qualify and register for the vote in large numbers—a state of affairs the British government persuaded itself to believe would happen sooner or later—it retained an imperial veto on all legislation which exclusively affected Africans.

The value of the imperial veto in Southern Rhodesia has often been questioned. Its critics point to the fact that no British government ever exercised it. In its defense, it is stated that the very fact that the Rhodesian government was required to justify to the British government (and, indirectly, to the British public) proposed legislative measures, exclusively affecting Africans, inhibited the Rhodesian government from enacting extremely harsh legislation against Africans and thus contributed toward better race relations.

One of the results of the use of the imperial veto in Rhodesia, however, was that the legislators (who were all white until the 1923 Constitution was replaced by a new one in 1960) sometimes resorted to stratagems to avoid submitting to the British government proposed legislation exclusively affecting Africans. From assurances given in the lobbies, members understood that certain proposed legislation was, in fact, intended to apply exclusively to Africans even though it was not being tabled in the House as such. They shared the Rhodesian government's desire not to place the British government in such a position that it could, through the exercise of its veto, call for justification of the measures proposed and open the white Rhodesian government's motives and intentions to public scrutiny and criticism in Britain. A gentlemen's agreement to pass the legislation without debate or division was often made, and the legislation was put in the statute book. When times were bad and the going rough for the government, legislation intended to repress Africans only was used against Europeans. The Todd government deported a European trade unionist and the Whitehead government banned the Rhodesian Republican party, using legislation tailor-made—though not enacted exclusively—for Africans.

From 1923 to the advent of the Central African Federation in 1954, most Rhodesian legislation affecting Africans appeared, on the surface, to be nonracial. Africans could register as voters, for instance, or stand as members of Parliament. In fact, qualifications for the vote were raised every time they came within the Africans' grasp. As a result, no African ever stood for election for the South Rhodesia Parliament during this period. Most things, including entrances into public buildings such as post offices, were segregated. Africans were not even permitted to drink "European beer." It is one of the writer's doubtful claims to fame, or maybe notoriety, that the political chore of proposing, at the 1956 United Rhodesia party Congress in Gwelo, the resolution which brought about legislation permitting Africans to drink "European beer and light wines," was entrusted to him. Yet, the country enjoyed, during this time, an undeserved and unearned reputation as being better than South Africa.

In 1930, the Land Apportionment Act was enacted, giving the lion's share of the land to the few Europeans and depriving the majority of the population of the right to live and own land in most of the country. This law has been amended several times.

When the government found that the Land Apportionment Act had not apportioned sufficient land to Africans, they were settled on "European farms and estates." After their numbers had greatly increased and suitable land nearby was no longer available, Africans were told to leave the farms and estates.

This resulted in the endless, fruitless, countless litigation of the 1950s which was conducted mainly by Benjamin Burombo's Southern Rhodesia British African Voice Association. The bitterness these evictions and removals engendered and the hardships people suffered dramatized the problem of land hunger among Africans to such an extent that it became a fruitful rallying cry for recruiting new members into the first modern African mass movement—the "new" African National Congress which became such a thorn in the flesh of the government that it was banned in 1959 and a thousand of its leaders detained. The passing of the Land Apportionment Act made the mass evictions and removals inevitable (Samkange, 1968).

The damage caused to harmonious race relations in the country by the administration of this Act therefore cannot be exaggerated.

For purposes of the Land Apportionment Act, a native was defined as one who has the blood of the aborigines of Africa and lives in the manner thereof. This means that one could have the blood of the aborigines of Africa flowing in one's veins and not be a native so long as one did not live in the manner thereof—whatever that means. Under this definition, Coloreds—people of mixed blood—could be classed as not natives if they did not live according to the manner thereof. Coloreds often went to all sorts of trouble to secure this status, which meant receiving higher wages than those normally paid to "natives," exemption from carrying passes, occupation of better houses, etc., etc.

They were obliged to shun their African relatives, sometimes describing their own mothers as their "nannies" in accounting for the presence of "native women" in their homes. Coloreds, therefore, as a rule, did not identify themselves with Africans. It paid them not to associate with Africans. They preferred to be part of European society. This society, however, did not welcome nor accept them even though they were better treated than Africans.

Among themselves, Coloreds were further divided into Euro-Africans—those with white and black parents—and Cape Coloreds—descendents of whites, Malay slaves, and Hottentot women at the Cape. The latter considered themselves superior to the former because Cape Coloreds had no black parents. Some of the Euro-Africans objected to this name because *Euro-* was shorter than *African;* they preferred to be called Afro-Europeans.

Coloreds and Euro-Africans occupy the same residential areas as "Indians" and often discriminate against each other. Coloreds and Indians in Rhodesia number about ten thousand. Politically, they have always identified themselves with Europeans. Only in the 1960s, when Africans made a determined bid to seize political power and appeared to be succeeding, did some Coloreds and Indians identify themselves with Africans. Even today, Coloreds and Indians are languishing in restriction camps as members of the Zimbabwe African National Union and the Zimbabwe African Peoples' Union.

In 1948, The Native Urban Area Accommodation and Registration Act was passed, requiring a strict enforcement of pass laws in urban areas on the South African model. The philosophy underlying this law was imported from South Africa, as were its administrators, such as Mr. Ballenden, the Salisbury City Council's first Director of Native Administration under this Act. An African was required to have, on his person, at all times, on pain of immediate arrest and imprisonment, a Registration Certificate, a pass to seek work, a pass to reside in a stated urban area, a pass to walk through the city after dark, a pass to show that he had undergone medical examination and was free from disease, a pass to show that his hut tax had been paid, etc., etc. There were often such long queues of people waiting to get passes that it took days if not weeks of waiting, waiting, and waiting in a line to get one pass. White officials insisted on every African applicant's respectfully standing whenever the officials appeared on their frequent visits to the toilet nearby—treatment calculated to impress every black man with the superiority of the white race. It did much more: it created bitterness and resentment of white men which, one day, was bound to explode into the open.

When the Central African Federation was created in 1954, white politicians took pains to tell their supporters that, as far as Southern Rhodesia was concerned, they would continue to enjoy their privileged status politically, socially, and economically; that in fact, with the advent of Federation, they would enjoy their privileged status in Northern Rhodesia (Zambia) and Nyasaland (Malawi) as well and save these countries from Colonial and eventual black rule. Africans in Southern Rhodesia opposed Federation because they did not want other Africans in the north to be subjected to the "Native Policy" of Southern Rhodesia; for, although they themselves had nothing more to lose, since they had lost everything, they believed that their position was bound to be affected and their status improved by the existence in the north of other Africans in positions of power and authority.

When the Federation was imposed against the will of the majority of Africans in the three territories, Africans in Southern Rhodesia hoped that all the talk about partnership would change European attitudes toward them and usher in a new era of racial harmony and cooperation. They virtually disbanded their nationalist organizations and joined European-run political parties. This was the era of interracial associations and multiracial parties. They flourished. The Southern Rhodesia Labor party which, alone of the white political parties had heretofore accepted African members, now had difficulty keeping its African members from being lured to the ranks of its opponents.

Mr. Garfield Todd, a missionary, became Prime Minister. He knew many Africans personally and was known by many more. He continued to be friendly and approachable, and he did not lose the common touch, even though he was then walking with kings. For the first time in the history of Rhodesia, Africans referred to the government as "our government." It is correct to say that the climate for good race relations in Southern Rhodesia has never been better than it was at this period—soon after the beginning of the Federation.

Unfortunately, the experience of Africans with political parties dominated by Europeans soon made them realize that these parties could never serve the true interests of Africans. For instance, it was widely known that most Africans in Southern Rhodesia wished Mr. Joshua Nkomo, President of the African National Congress, and the writer, its Secretary General, to represent them in the Federal Parliament. The Federal party selected two "good boys" on the staff of a local newspaper and a predominantly white electorate confirmed their choice. The Federal party obviously knew what it was doing, for, on crucial issues such as the famous Yamba motion opposing discrimination in the post offices and an important constitutional amendment in which opposing votes would have deprived the government of a two-thirds majority, these "good boys" either abstained or voted with Europeans against the advice, wishes, and interests of their own people. Africans lost confidence in multiracial parties and organizations. Some began to say that, although Federation's motto was "Magni esse, me reamur"—May we deserve to be great—its motto really was: "With Partnership on our lips and Apartheid in our hearts, may we appear to be great."

A "new" African National Congress was formed in 1957 with Mr. Joshua Nkomo, President of the "old" one, as president. The writer was, at the time, studying in the United States. The African National Congress, as we have already pointed out, became such a thorn in the flesh of the government that it was banned, and more than a thousand of its leaders were imprisoned in 1959.

For a time, Mr. Garfield Todd, now no longer Prime Minister, became president of the Central Africa party in which the writer was vice-president. Although this party attracted large numbers of Africans, it unfortunately lacked European support to make it truly multiracial. Its African members eventually found their political home in the National Democratic party which had succeeded the banned African National Congress. Politics in Rhodesia had polarized according to race. The National Democratic party was banned and the Zimbabwe African People's Union was formed to succeed it. It split and some of its members formed the Zimbabwe African National Union. Both were banned in 1964, but they continue to operate from bases outside the country.

European political parties also experienced changes. The United Federal party, which replaced Garfield Todd as Prime Minister with Sir Edgar Whitehead and continued to welcome Africans into is ranks, was defeated by the Rhodesia Front led by Winston Field campaigning on the issue of community development—which is another way of spelling Apartheid. The Rhodesia Front victory made Rhodesia virtually a one white-party state. In less than a year, Winston Field was replaced by Ian Smith as Prime Minister. Ian Smith led Rhodesia into the Unilateral Declaration of Independence and isolation by the world community of nations except South Africa and Portugal. Today, Rhodesia is slowly but surely becoming the fifth province of South Africa. Not only its racial attitudes, but its economy also is being integrated into that of South Africa.

With African freedom fighters periodically crossing the Zambezi and engaging the country in guerilla warfare; with the Rhodesian army, air, and police forces on alert all the time; and with the country in a continuous state of emergency, tension between the races has never been greater nor race relations poorer. How and when all this will come to an end, no one can tell. What we can say with certainty, however, is that one day, an African government, a government of sons of the soil, by sons of the soil, for sons of the soil, shall preside over Zimbabwe. For the problem of eradicating pockets of white rule in Southern Africa is not the most formidable problem Africa has had to face. The problems of slavery, which lasted 500 years, and Colonialism, whose first phase is only beginning to come to a close now, appeared even more formidable in their time. Yet both came to an end. It took time to eradicate them; a long time, when viewed in terms of a man's life, but only a moment when regarded in the context of the history of a continent. It remains the writer's unshakable conviction that the sons and daughters of Zimbabwe shall overcome and shall, like their forefathers, rule in Zimbabwe.

Nationalism and National Identity

As regards nationalism and national identity, it will be seen that the country has never enjoyed a single nationalism nor have all its people been identified as a single unit. Race and racial privilege have facilitated the growth of two nationalisms in the country: African and European nationalisms.

Africans draw strength and unity from the past, from being discriminated against on grounds of color and from being oppressed as a group. They stand together as Africans and fervently sing the African National Anthem, "Ishe Komborera Africa" or "Nkosi Silela i Africa" which is sung in many tongues by other Africans from the Cape to Kenya. Authorities, fearful of it, have banned this anthem in the schools of Rhodesia.

Europeans stand together united by privilege. To maintain their privilege, they must remain a separate group into which no African can enter. There was a time, for instance, when an African could not belong to the police force—the British South African Police, as it was called. He could only be what was called a "black watcher"—"ma burakwaca," as they were known in Shona. Later, Africans were allowed to become members of the B.S.A.P., but it was specifically provided that every African, no matter how long he has served in the force, would be inferior to a European, even though the latter was a mere recruit. During the war, whites belonged to the "Royal Rhodesian Regiment," while Africans served in the "King's Africa Rifles." Even the Boy Scout movement was, once, for whites only, Africans being called "Path Finders." In sports, until fairly recently, only Europeans could, as in South Africa, represent Rhodesia. Consequently, Africans always supported and cheered the visiting team. This still happens in South Africa, today.

Under such circumstances, it was difficult to build a single nation embracing black and white races. Europeans tried to make loyalty to the Queen the one thing that bound both black and white together. This was unreal for most Africans. They could never sing "God Save the Queen" with the same fervor that they felt for the African National Anthem. Now, even the Europeans no longer want God to save the Queen, and the British flag no longer flies over Rhodesia. Rhodesia now has a new flag and a new anthem, both meaningless to most Africans.

There are thus, mainly, two races and two nationalisms, symbolized by Zimbabwe for Africans and Rhodesia for whites. Whites venerate Rhodes, while Africans see nothing to admire in him and think he was just a rogue.

Only once, during the prime ministership of Sir Edgar Whitehead, was a conscious and deliberate effort made to weld white and black into a single nation in Rhodesia. A "Build a Nation" campaign was organized. It appeared, however, to concentrate on Africans, rather than Europeans, and it was associated with a recruitment drive for Sir Edgar's party. It appeared, to most Africans, to be an attempt to divert them from seeking Uhuru. The "Build a Nation" campaign was a flop.

The country remains a land of two races, two names, two nation-alisms—one black, the other white, with no embracing national iden-tity and no sense of nationhood.

REFERENCES

Alpers, Edward.
    1967   "The Mutapa and Malawi Political Systems." In Aspects of Cen-tral African History, edited by T. O. Ranger. London: Heine-mann.
Cory, G. E.
    1910   The Rise of South Africa. London: Longmans, Green and Co.
Fouche, Leo.
    1936   "Foundations of the Cape Colony." In The Cambridge History of the British Empire, vol. VII. Cambridge: Cambridge University Press.
Frank, T. M.
    1960   Race and Nationalism: The Struggle for Power in Rhodesia-Ny-asaland. New York: Fordham University Press.
MacCrone, I. D.
    1937   Race Attitudes in South Africa: Historical Experimental and Psy-chological Studies. (Published on behalf of the University of the Witwatersrand.) London: Oxford University Press.
Mason, Philip.
    1954   An Essay on Racial Tension. London: Oxford University Press.
    1958   The Birth of a Dilemma. London: Oxford University Press.
    1970   Race Relations. London: Oxford University Press.
Preller, G. S.
    1963   Lobengula. Johannesburg: Afrikaanse Pers-Boekhandel.
Ranger, T. O.
    1967   Revolt in Southern Rhodesia 1896-7, A Study in African Resis-tance. London: Heinemann.
Rose, A. M.
    1951   The Roots of Prejudice. Paris: UNESCO.
Rose, Holland J., et al., editors.
    1936   The Cambridge History of the British Empire, vol. VIII. Cam-bridge: Cambridge University Press.
Samkange, Stanlake.
    1968   "The Establishment of African Reserve." Ph.D. dissertation, In-diana University.

1969   Origins of Rhodesia. New York: Praeger.
1971   African Saga: Introduction to African History. Nashville: Abing-
        don Press.
Theal, G. M.
1900   South Africa, The Cape Colony, Natal, Orange Free State, South
        African Republic, Rhodesia, and all other Territories south of the
        Zambezi. New York: G. P. Putnam's Sons.

The Uses of History

PROFESSOR SAMKANGE has studied the history of his country more thoroughly than any other man alive. He has also taken quite an active part in *making* the political history of Rhodesia over the past two decades. Thus, his comments may be appropriately viewed from either of the two perspectives which Dr. Samkange has taken: that of the scholar and that of the politician.

His paper reflects the high level of scholarship of Samkange's larger study, *The Origins of Rhodesia* (New York: Praeger, 1969), from which it is derived. Being brief, however, it can cover only selected aspects of the historical record. It is here, in the selection and interpretation of the historical data, that Samkange the politician becomes apparent. As I see it, the paper formulates the region's *past* in a way that is most congenial with *his* vision of its *future*. It is as this sort of effort that I would like to interpret the present paper.

Men of all nations, of course, have long made use of the past in legend, religion, and history to try to fix the future. Every aspiring nation, be it territorial, religious, or ethnic, builds an ethos of "manifest destiny." Dr. Samkange makes quite clear his view of the manifest destiny of the territory presently called Rhodesia. He says that though it may take many generations and no one can tell how it will come to pass, still, one day, "a government of sons of the soil, by sons of the soil, for sons of the soil, shall preside over Zimbabwe."

Who are included among Samkange's sons of the soil? The paper is devoted in large part to analysis of each distinct ethnic group now resident in Rhodesia. In each case, two questions are posed. First, how long has the group been in the territory? And second, what is its trustworthiness in dealing with other ethnic groups? Some groups are described in consistently positive and others in consistently negative terms. From this, it is apparent that the future is said to belong to the virtuous, long-resident groups.

Most clearly, whites are excluded from ruling the future Zimbabwe. They came late and repeatedly dealt deceitfully with all other groups. The fate of the Coloreds and Indians is not so clear, because, while they were late arrivals and historically identified with whites against Africans (all negative factors), Samkange notes that many have recently supported the African liberation movement (a positive factor).

A much more complex question of "manifest destiny" arises in relation to the several African tribes of present-day Rhodesia. While Samkange concludes his paper by pointing to an all-African community, this united community is welded together, as he recognizes, in large part by an opposition to colonialism. As the evidence of other new African nations sadly attests, African unity begins to evaporate the day that the colonial flag is finally pulled down. Thus, while the author concludes with a section appealing for pan-Africanism, he earlier makes a number of somewhat invidious comparisons between tribes which are now resident in the territory called Rhodesia. These comparisons have to do with length of residence and the relative virtues which are the factors we identified earlier as determining who will ultimately be included as "sons of the soil."

The first African group to be discussed are the Shona. Samkange has no doubts concerning their territorial claim, for their ancestors have lived in the area for one thousand years. They are always described in positive terms. They are said to have become rulers of the area through their intellectual capacity as expressed in superior political, economic, social, and religious organization rather than by military domination. Contacts with whites also show the Shona in a positive light. They dealt honorably with the Portuguese and English in their early contacts. That the Shona later involved Europeans in their internal struggles is interpreted positively as a sign of their "cleverness." Even their killing of ten percent of the European settlers in 1896 is described as "brilliantly master-minded by Shona priests and chiefs." Throughout the discussion the Shona are shown to have what Samkange calls "a worthy way of life."

The two other tribal groups in Rhodesia are described together. These are the Ndebele and the Shangan. They are described as proud, warlike people whom the early English pioneers feared and whose territory they thus avoided. Like the Shona, these groups are always referred to in terms which stress their positive virtues. But, are they sons of the soil? That depends on what length of residence is required. As Samkange notes, they entered Rhodesian territory in the eighteenth century fleeing from the Impis of the Zula king Shaka and the white settlers of the Transvaal. Thus, they are relative newcomers to the area. That Samkange intends them to be among the rightful heirs to the land is suggested by his laudatory descriptions of their activities and his avoiding detailed discussion of the historical record of their immigration into Rhodesia. Their entry was at least as filled with conflict as the later entry of Europeans, for they took much of the Shona's territory by force and enfeebled the Shona kingdoms.

In the discussion following the presentation of the paper, Dr. Samkange made it quite clear that he includes all black Africans in the definition of "sons of the soil." The facts of history are, however, continually open to interpretation. Each new historian can put them to his own uses. Thus, for example, the *same* criteria of "manifest destiny" that Samkange has used to show that all black Africans and only black Africans have rights in Zimbabwe could be used by a Shona historian to prove that the Shona and only the Shona are the rightful sons of the soil.

5
JOHN SAUNDERS

Class, Color, and Prejudice:
A Brazilian Counterpoint

UNTIL RECENTLY, the objective study of race relations in Brazil has been notably hampered by two pervading biases. The first of these, held by foreign, mostly American, scholars and observers of Brazilian society, stemmed from the model of Negro-white relations provided by the American South, whose major features are: racial castes maintained and enforced by the application of the descent rule which relegates all persons of known Negro ancestry, however remote, to the black caste; overt, legally sanctioned discrimination and public and private avoidance accompanied by systematically applied boundary maintenance mechanisms; and, finally, a high degree of homogeneity of racial attitudes and prejudices among the white population. Brazilian scholars, on the other hand, have experienced the effects of the Brazilian racial mystique which maintains that in Brazil there is equal opportunity for all to advance according to individual merit, that, therefore, skin color or other phenotypical features have no social meaning, that prejudice and discrimination are nonexistent, that there is, consequently, a complete racial democracy.

Each of these biases acted in its own way to blind the observer to social reality. The foreign scholar, encountering a situation of racial

I am grateful for critical comments by Werner Baer, Vanderbilt; Maxine Margolis, Florida; and J. F. B. Dasilva, Notre Dame.

contact and interpersonal relations very different from the southern model, found it difficult to perceive in the far more complex and more harmonious Brazilian situation manifestations of prejudice and discrimination which, furthermore, were generally denied by his informants. The Brazilian scholar influenced by the prevailing national racial ideology which points with pride to Brazilian superiority in this area of human relations, suffered from the same difficulty, particularly in dealing with historical materials. Both groups were, by and large, white, and therefore subject to a common communications barrier when discussing race with persons of color. These biases gave rise to two myths, that of the friendly master (slave-owner) and that of racial democracy in which manifestations of prejudice and discrimination were said to be due to the social class status of the person and not to his color.

The myth of the friendly master (see, for instance, Freyre, 1959: 114-120) and the happy slave living in symbiotic harmony has been certified, and the testimony of a long line of peripatetic Europeans who made trips to Brazil in colonial times and committed their observations to paper now need to be re-evaluated. Boxer (1963:101-121), Harris (1964a:65-78) and Nogueira (1955:443) document the inhumane treatment to which plantation slaves in Brazil, as everywhere, were subjected. The dissatisfaction of slaves with their lot is amply confirmed by the numerous *quilombos* or runaway slave colonies, by high suicide rates, the large number of runaways, and the short life expectancy of slaves.

In this paper, however, our interest is in the nature of contemporary race relations in Brazil and with stating some propositions that will aid in the understanding of this complex phenomenon. We shall rely especially on research undertaken since about 1950 which was given impetus by a grant from UNESCO.

The Descent Rule and Color Typing

Among the more important phenomena for understanding race in Brazil are color typing and the absence of a descent rule, which are interrelated. In Brazil, demographic, economic, and historical factors contributed to create a large population of persons of mixed racial ancestry. Portugal, having a population of one million or so at the time of the colonization of Brazil, was not anxious to send large contingents to the new world and, indeed, discouraged emigration (Harris, 1964a:82). Consequently, the large importation of African slaves soon converted that class of the population and its mixed blood off-spring into a decided majority. In 1819 the negroid population of Brazil outnumbered the white population by three to one (Harris, 1964a:121). The chronic labor shortage and the small number of Portuguese "compelled [them] to create an intermediate free group of half-castes to stand between them and the slaves because there were certain economic and military functions for which slave labor was useless, and for which no whites were available." (Harris, 1964a:86-87). These functions were related mainly to control of the plantation labor force through capturing runaway slaves and overseeing, but military duty was also an important role performed by the free half-caste population, as was labor performed in the raising of cattle, for cowboy slaves could not be trusted not to run away, given their unavoidable freedom of movement.

Thus, at the time of abolition there had been in existence for nearly two centuries a substantial population of mixed bloods and free blacks as well, which through extensive miscegenation and frequent recognition of kinship between persons of different color made it a practical impossibility to establish patterns of segregation and discrimination on the basis of two "social races" and the application of a rigid descent rule, the situation that eventually evolved with particular vehemence in the American South. The practical consequence of the absence of descent rule is that it is not possible, except when distinguishing between extremes, to make sharp distinctions between racial types.

In the absence of sharp culturally defined distinctions between racial categories, governed by a descent rule, race becomes a matter of individual perception and definition, which involves a loose consensus among a group with regard to color types and the particular individuals who fall within them. If persons are to be classed according to the visual perceptions of those doing the classifying, then in a racially heterogeneous population two categories are obviously inadequate. A minimum of three is required and the possibilities are virtually endless when, as is the case in Brazil, the three major racial stocks of the world are present in all kinds of mixtures. Thus, every study which has undertaken to examine racial typing in Brazil has turned up a multiplicity of terms corresponding to different combinations of white, black, and Indian, as well as terms for white and for black. Furthermore, this multiple racial typing is found from one end of the nation to the other. Wagley (1953:130) found five terms in an Amazonian community; Pierson (1951a:190-191) reports five terms in a

São Paulo community, and twenty in Bahia (1942:139-140); Hutchison, also referring to Bahia, notes twenty-one (1957:117-121).

It has been my experience that probably without exception at least five terms descriptive of racial type are in use in any Brazilian community. Harris and Kottak studied racial categories systematically in the fishing village of Arembepe not far from Salvador, Bahia. They report (Harris and Kottak, 1963; Harris, 1964b; Kottak, 1967) a highly complex racial nomenclature consisting of forty different terms based, as are racial typings elsewhere in Brazil, on a variety of phenotypical characteristics—skin color, hair color, hair texture, shape of nose, shape of lips, and others. Furthermore, Kottak (1967:44) reports agreement on the terms white (branco) and black (preto) but wide disagreement on the meaning of intermediate terms. Harris (1964b), points to ambiguity in defining terms indicative of mixed racial characteristics and ambiguity in classifying specific individuals as to racial type. Arembepe, admittedly, appears to be an atypical case with regard to the extraordinarily large number of racial terms used by its residents. It is also atypical of most Brazilian towns in that its economic mainstay is fishing, and because all of its population belongs to the national lower class. Yet, Nogueira (1955:551), studying a community in Southern Brazil, reached essentially the same conclusions.

These data underline and give support to the following proposition about race in Brazil: (1) *Socially, color or race is a continuum running from black to white and so perceived by members of Brazilian society and, while the continuum is firmly anchored at either extreme, the intermediate categories are flexible in that they are variously defined by different persons and may be variously applied by different persons to the same person. Thus, evaluation of color in the intermediate categories is partly idiosyncratic and personal.*

Stereotyping

The negative stereotyping of blacks and implicit or explicit positive stereotyping of whites is an inescapable aspect of racial attitudes in Brazil. Pierson, while maintaining his thesis that discrimination against persons of color is based on their social class rather than on their racial ancestry (1951b:309; 1942:336, 348-349), lists such stereotyping statements as "The Negro, if he doesn't soil things on entering, soils them before he leaves" (1942:363). Harris (1956:117-118) found the following stereotyping statements, among others, in a small community in the State of Bahia: "The *negro* isn't human. God has nothing to do with him. The *negro* has an ugly face. He spends the day sleeping and the night robbing farms. If you've seen a buzzard you've seen a *negro*. He hasn't got lips, they're rubber tires." Hutchinson (1957:122) records the following, among others: "Negro's intelligence is the same size as his hair." "Negro at a white man's party is the first to grab and the last to eat." "Negro doesn't marry, he gets together."

Negative stereotyping of the Negro is not limited to the Northeast. Fernandes (1969:176) reports on the results of a study done in São Paulo:

We gathered large quantities of data, which unfortunately could not be listed here, on the new stereotypes which refer in a derogatory way to a Negro's color. In these stereotypes the Negro [is] associated with the personality status which can be inferred from the crudest manual labor, but classification of the Negro's characteristics suddenly points in a different direction. His disorganized social life has provided the point of reference for this process of re-evaluation. The word *Negro* becomes interchangeable with words such as *drunkard* or *boozer, bum, carouser,* and *thief;* and *Negro woman* becomes interchangeable with *streetwalker.*

Ianni (1958:359) found that, in the southern state capital of Florianópolis, his respondents attributed more negative characteristics to Negroes than to whites and more positive characteristics to whites than to Negroes. Costa Pinto (1952:221) found negative stereotypes in Rio de Janeiro not only by whites in regard to blacks but by blacks in regard to other blacks who were striving for upward social mobility. Whiteness is associated generally with positive traits such as goodness, generosity, trust, and so on, and blackness with negative traits. The attributes of whiteness are assigned to whites and of blackness to blacks. Russell-Wood (1968:190-191) reports two typical instances: "A colored witness in a murder case, testifying to the innocence of the accused, a negress, commented that 'although she (the accused) is black by color her attitude is that of a white person.'" Similarly, at a memorial service for Martin Luther King, the white priest referred to him as "This man of a dark race but with a white heart."

Stereotyping finds expression in many occupational roles. The stereotype of the Negro as shiftless, fun-loving, musical and irresponsible justified hiring Negroes as performers on São Paulo radio stations but prevents them from assuming managerial positions (Pereira, 1967:175-181). One of Pereira's informants (1967:177) stated that Negroes cannot be good speakers but are good at music, for this is a quality they inherit through their "flesh": "As a speaker, I repeat, a Negro is no good. First, because they never know how to read and, furthermore, the job requires a sense of responsibility, requires intelligence, and it is prudent not to take risks." Thus, stereotyping, which is a particular form of prejudice, justifies attitudes upon which, in turn, behavior is based.

Not all stereotyping is negative. Negroes are typed as being good workers at manual labors. They are purported to have greater endurance than whites, be able to withstand physical hardships, and to possess other qualities as workers, which are cultural survivals of the slave status. Likewise, the Negro may be typed as the faithful and humble servant of the white man in the role of the "old darkie" or the black mother. Such stereotypes, however, refer to qualities which are not valued in Brazilian society, that hearken back to the Negro's servile condition and simply serve as a reminder of his subordinate role in society, which stereotyping serves to maintain and reinforce.

Pereira (1967:181-184) transcribes verbatim the script of a television program, shown in São Paulo circa 1966, that embodies virtually every contemporary negative stereotype of the Negro and that would be unthinkable on U.S. television at the present time. A party at which colored couples are dancing the samba, *gafieira* or low-class style, is interrupted by a black who announces he has come to give them very sad news: "A *crioulo* (mildly derogatory synonym for Negro) has died." Two blacks enter carrying a covered body on an improvised stretcher. The partygoers surround the deceased, uncover his face and the following dialogue ensues:

"Poor thing, he was good-looking in spite of his monkey face."

"I'll go tell his wife."

"A married *crioulo*? That's a good one. A married *crioulo*. How about that!"

"Then notify his five wives."

"What? This *crioulo* had five wives?"

"Five, not counting the ones thrown in."

"Did he leave something for his family?"

"Yes. Two hundred cruzeiros in debts at the corner bar where he drank *cachaça* (cheap rumlike liquor)."

"Poor thing! He was so good-hearted! . . . He could not pass up a blind beggar's hat."

"That's right, he couldn't see a beggar's hat raking it in. He'd put in ten bucks and take out twenty."

"And he left eighteen children for his friends to look after."

"Did he make a request before dying?"

"Yes. He asked for eighty candles on his coffin because otherwise no one up there will be able to see him blended in with the darkness."

"Let me, the lawyer of the neighborhood, conduct the wake. I shall speak."

"Hurry up, because a Negro's wake without *cachaça* isn't a wake."

"Your attention: *aqui jaz* (here lies) . . . "

"*Jaz*? A Brazilian Negro doesn't have jazz, he has samba."

"He liked everyone."

"He liked his neighbor's chickens."

A white policeman enters, looking for a chicken thief. No one tells him a thing. The policeman leaves and the "deceased" gets up. The dialogue proceeds:

"What's this, *negro*? You steal chickens and run over here making like you're dead and scaring us half to death?"

"It's not thieving, it's a hobby."

"Stealing chickens is a black's hobby."

The dance resumes. The messenger ends the scene, saying: "Attention, *crioulos*; attention, you monkeys dressed like people; let's go, before the police come back."

This script is not the product of a propaganda machine dedicated to creating unfavorable images of the Negro, nor are the stereotypes it contains the creation of the television station. Rather, the mass media, including the lyrics to popular songs, reflect in their presentations the attitudes and stereotypes which are shared by large numbers of whites and by many persons of color as well.

Harris (1956:118), on examining stereotypes of the Negro in the community he studied in Bahia, concluded that the following features "emerge as fixed and immutable principles which form the core of the urban white's attitude. . . . 1. The Negro race is subhuman and inferior to the white race. 2. The Negro does and ought to play a subservient role to the white. 3. The Negro's physical features, including physique, physiognomy, skin color, and body odor, are irredeemably displeasing." Persons of mixed blood being intermediate on the color continuum tend to be intermediate as well with regard to stereotyping attitudes. In particular, stereotypes referring to physical appearance which do not have the same applicability to them as to Negroes are milder. On the other hand, since the mulatto has striven for and experienced greater upward social mobility than the Negro, he has been stereotyped as pretentious, conceited, uppity, pushy, supercilious, and untrustworthy (cf. Costa Pinto, 1951:212-213).

Although Harris's statement quoted just above seems extreme for application to Brazil in a national context, the available evidence supports a second proposition about race in Brazil: (2) *Negative stereotyping of the Negro is common among white Brazilians. The stereotypes relate to physical appearance and characterize Negroes as inferior in a variety of respects.*

The Many Faces of Prejudice

Negro Ruim

Since the existence of prejudice in Brazil is generally denied by white Brazilians and, not infrequently, by Brazilians of color, it is well to begin this section with a brief discussion of one of the most widespread and palpable manifestations of it. From north to south, from the Amazon to the Southern Region, to call a man a Negro is insulting. Wagley (1953:130) reports that in the Amazonian community which he studied "As in most of Brazil, the term *Negro* is seldom heard, and then only in anger. Against anyone who has physical traits suggesting Negroid ancestry, the label *Negro ruim* (bad Negro) is a powerful insult." Nogueira (1959:173) says that "As a rule, in Brazil, the nonwhite is submitted to sharp consciousness of his color in conflict situations, when his opponent tries to humiliate him by referring to his racial appearance." Ianni (1958:358) notes the same phenomenon in Florianópolis in Santa Catarina, in southern Brazil. He further notes that the lighter the persons against whom the epithet *Negro* is hurled, the greater the insult intended and felt. Essentially the same behavior is reported in two São Paulo communities by Pierson (1951a: 190) and Trujillo Ferrari (1960:193).

The fact that the term *Negro* is so widely regarded as pejorative clearly reflects the inferior servile status and innate inferiority associated with negritude. The term derives its punch from the stereotypes of the Negro discussed above. Consequently, in polite conversations between a white person and one of color, synonyms and euphemisms for Negro must be used.

Awareness of Prejudice

It is apparent that prejudiced behavior is directed by the white person against the person of color. For this simple and self-evident reason, the perception and awareness of prejudice is much greater and more generally acknowledged by persons of color than by whites. Racial self-awareness and the recognition of common problems associated with race or color have given rise to numerous attempts to organize Brazilian Negroes into associations for the betterment of their condition. Blair (1965:98-100) and Fernandes (1969:187-233) list many of these, some of which achieved considerable strength. The Brazilian Negro Front became sufficiently important as a political force to merit the special attention of then dictator Getulio Vargas, who interdicted it. That most of the members of these organizations and groups were acutely aware of racially based prejudice and discrimination is, perhaps, best illustrated by the following account (Costa Pinto, 1952: 225):

> The author will never forget the night when, by invitation, he presided at one of the memorable sessions of the first Brazilian Congress of the Negro, during which a black member of the congress affirmed that "in Brazil racial prejudice does not exist." The wave of protests that rose from the audience transformed the session into a tempest. There were boos and protests, proposals that the speaker be denied the floor, shouts and whistles that the president of the session quieted with great difficulty. . . . Then there were speeches of protest spoken in every tone from revolt to pity that implied that the speaker was simply insane.

The speaker, in his defense, stated that there should be harmony among men of color so that they might solve their problem. " 'What problem,' someone shouted from the floor, 'since you just now said that in Brazil the racial problem does not exist?' The question went unanswered."

The awareness of prejudice is not universal even among blacks, as the foregoing quotation also demonstrates, because national racial ideology denies its existence and imposes upon all persons norms for the avoidance of overt manifestations of prejudice. Discrimination in public accommodations is rare, and usually limited when it occurs to establishments that serve the white elite. Thus, a person of color, particularly if he is lower class, can go about his daily business for long periods of time without encountering overt manifestations of prejudice or without recognizing those that do occur.

There is great variation among individuals in their awareness of prejudice. Whites are less likely to develop an awareness of prejudice than blacks, and among whites it is common for persons to profess a complete and sincere belief in racial democracy while at the same time manifesting prejudiced attitudes without perceiving their nature or the contradiction (Fernandes, 1969:404-405). Persons of color are most likely to be the object of prejudice and develop an awareness thereof when they experience upward social mobility and leave a highly heterochromatic lower class and enter the much more uniformly white middle class. In this situation, particularly, the more negroid the person, the more likely it is that prejudice against him will be felt by others. The limited materials dealing with awareness of prejudice suggest the following, third proposition: (3) *The awareness of prejudice tends to increase as negritude increases.*

Some Other Manifestations of Prejudice

Probably many if not most white Brazilians are bearers of color prejudice in latent form which goes generally unnoticed and unrecognized when manifested. The stereotyping and the pejorative use of *Negro* documented above are evidence of this. Harris, for instance (1956:114) reports that the people of Minas Velhas, a Bahian community, generally consider the inferiority of the Negro to be a scientific fact and that the six white schoolteachers in the town all agreed with this viewpoint and further stated that an intelligent Negro is a rarity. Yet, although this datum is not provided by Harris, it is virtually certain that none of these persons considers these viewpoints to be prejudiced. Harris quotes from a textbook used in the schools of that community: " 'Of all races the white race is the most intelligent, persevering and the most enterprising. . . . The Negro race is much more retarded than the others.' " Cardoso (1965:121), in reviewing the evidence, states his agreement with Fernandes and Bastide in that "it appears that *color prejudice* exists in the several regions of Brazil and that it penetrates . . . all the social classes."

An important point, however, that has not been sufficiently stressed, is that prejudice in Brazil does not, generally, imply hostility. There is no sense of threat, no hatred, no desire to suppress. Hence, barring conflict situations of an *interpersonal* kind, relations between persons of color and whites in general are cordial and friendly. Friendliness does not denote the absence of prejudice. Rather it may simply reflect conformity to the prevailing norms of racial etiquette. It is the equation of hostility with prejudice, and its absence with the lack of prejudice that has often given birth to the conclusion that prejudice does not exist because hostility is absent (cf. Fernandes, 1969:164). Another factor causing prejudice and discrimination to seem absent is the upward social mobility achieved by mulattoes and, occasionally, by Negroes. These individuals are presented as proof of the existence of Brazilian racial democracy. Yet this circumstance itself can be the matrix for the revelation of prejudice, since when a black or a mulatto is singled out and pointed to as acceptable and an exception, he, essentially, possesses attributes that are considered to be those of whites (cf. Costa Pinto, 1952:218-219).

The coexistence in the same persons of the racial democracy ideal and of prejudice is well documented by Costa Pinto (1952:192). When white schoolchildren, asked to pick a study companion to take home to prepare for a test, chose between a white and a mulatto, 216 picked the former and 28 the latter; when choosing between a mulatto and a Negro, 128 picked the former and 111 the latter; when choosing between a white and a Negro, 206 picked the former, 35 the latter. About 73 students declared indifference. While the preference for white companions is clear, it is difficult to interpret the meaning of the choices made of persons of color or the declared indifference in this and in other studies, since respondents may be reacting to specific individuals or may be expressing conformity to the prevailing racial ideology. Ginsberg (1955:317-322) found that white and black elementary school children in São Paulo when presented with a variety of choices between white and black dolls overwhelmingly favored the white doll.

Discriminatory behavior is also reported in the literature. Bicudo (1947:209, 213) states, on the basis of a survey, that Negroes encounter resistance to upward social mobility because they are Negroes and feel discriminated against in social situations. Pereira (1967:111-112) reports several instances of harassment of Negroes by police in São Paulo. In analyzing the occupational position of Negroes in radio broadcasting, he concludes that they are highly under-represented in managerial, executive, and public relations spheres in which radio stations are linked to the business and economic institutions of the city, in which "good" appearance, manners, and savoir faire are considered important; they are not well represented in positions involving control and manipulations of others (" ' . . . Blacks do not direct, do not choose, do not "program." They are directed, are chosen, are programmed' "). Nor are Negroes well represented in positions which are springboards to the higher echelons of management. This behavior relates directly to the stereotype of the Negro and is most explicit with regard to positions which involve dealing with the public where it is felt that the presence of a Negro would be "inconvenient." Although Pereira's study deals with radio broadcasting, the same patterns almost certainly prevail in other types of enterprises in São Paulo, and probably in most of the nation with the possible exception of the "darker" spots on the map such as Bahia (cf. Garcia-Zamor, 1970: 249-250).

The ambivalence of Brazilian society regarding attitudes toward race or color typically produces a variety of responses when evidence of prejudice or discrimination is presented. Frequently, the evidence is simply denied and disbelief is expressed. If the evidence is accepted as true, the behavior involved is attributed to the idiosyncracies of the persons involved or to some sort of foreign influence such as inferring that the person is not truly Brazilian (for instance, being the child of immigrants). When discrimination occurs in public accommodations, as occurred when American Negro celebrities were denied rooms at the Copacabana Palace Hotel in Rio, the action is attributed to the prejudices of others, i.e., the foreign guests at the hotel who would object to the presence of the Negro. The most sophisticated response is to argue that the actions only seemingly reflect color prejudice, that it is really class prejudice directed against lower-class persons who coincidentally happen to be of color. The latter assertion has an element of truth in that the lower-class person of color experiences prejudice on both counts, its intensity increasing as class drops and negritude rises. But the middle-class man of color, the professional, usually mulatto, experiences prejudice from his white peers. This prejudice and its accompanying discrimination is, to be sure, mild. The person of color is suitable as a colleague on the job, a co-worker, a co-participant in the same work world. In this context, great camaraderie and goodwill may exist. One may be prejudiced against colored persons in general while being a friend and admirer of a nonwhite person without feeling inconsistent (Nogueira, 1959:171). The white does not, however, ordinarily select such persons as intimate friends or include them in family gatherings. Contact tends to be restricted to the relatively formal, established work situation and subtle barriers are raised to more intimate relations implying less social distance. Pereira, for instance (1967:251), relates the case of a black performer who was invited to a party at the home of a white colleague and friend of many years. On arriving, he discovered that he was not a bona fide guest, but was expected to entertain the guests. The middle-class mulatto typically is aware of these fine distinctions and avoids situations in which he might be unwelcome and feel embarrassed even though invited and received with a show of friendliness. The same rules apply to camaraderie among school children which can outwardly give the appearance of the complete absence of prejudice or discrimination (cf. Pereira, 1967:250-254).

Because of the complexity of the factors that contribute to an individual's attitudes about color and his behavior toward persons of color, discrimination has low predictability and individuals susceptible to it are kept in suspense. A person may go for long periods of time without being its victim, particularly if he consciously avoids situations where he may experience discrimination. Yet, the fact that this type of avoidance is being practiced, even though successfully, makes him a victim (cf. Costa Pinto, 1952:328).

Although reactions to prejudice have not received much attention from researchers, the available evidence indicates that it produces inner resentment against whites which is outwardly repressed. One author suggested that this accounts for the results of a study which showed that an assassin complex was a common element in the dreams of Negroes (Oberg, 1958:346). Bicudo (1947:213) also reports a suppression of feelings of hostility toward whites. Urban middle-income and middle-status colored persons tend to accept color prejudice and are preoccupied with avoiding conflict with whites. To protect their social status, they avoid identification with blacks. Since their association with whites is mainly limited to work relationships, they suffer from psycho-social isolation and must depend upon others like themselves for intimate companionship and social life (cf. Oberg, 1958: 348; Cardoso, 1965:126-127, 1960:596; Pereira, 1967:254).

From the foregoing, the following (fourth) proposition can be formulated: (4) *Both color and prejudice tend to slide along a continuum. Prejudice and discrimination are functions of the perception of the degree of negritude of the individual and of the situational factors in which interpersonal relations occur.*

Prejudice and Social Distance

Several studies have obtained data on the rejection of Negroes and mulattoes based on a social distance scale of the Bogardus type. One of the more complete analyses of this type, based on data collected in Florianópolis, Santa Catarina, through interviews with white high school students, was made by Cardoso and Ianni (1960:155-190). The following table is reproduced with slight modifications as illustrative of the findings that were obtained by other investigators as well.

PLACES WHERE RESPONDENTS WOULD NOT LIKE TO FIND
NEGROES OR MULATTOES, BY SOCIAL CLASS OF RESPONDENT

Situation	% Rejection Negroes			% Rejection Mulattoes		
	Lower	Middle	High	Lower	Middle	High
School	14	21	19	10	16	15
Neighborhood	28	33	37	19	26	30
Movie	26	36	31	21	26	22
Ball (dance)	66	74	83	55	63	70
Family	86	91	89	80	90	88

SOURCE: Fernando Henrique Cardoso and Octavio Ianni, Côr e Mobilidade Social em Florianópolis, Brasiliana, 307:177 (São Paulo: Companhia Editôra Nacional, 1960).

While other studies conducted in other Brazilian cities have revealed differing degrees of rejection of Negroes and mulattoes, the general pattern observed above holds true: increasing rejection with decreasing social distance and generally higher levels of rejection among the upper and middle classes than among the lower classes (cf. Costa Pinto, 1952:177-193; Zimmerman, 1952:105). Garcia-Zamor reports (1970:251) that "In 1962 a poll of 2,000 white college students in Recife and São Paulo showed that only 54 percent of them would accept Negroes as fellow club members, 64 percent as neighbors, 58 percent as members of the same profession, and 62 percent as fellow citizens. Eight out of one hundred questioned felt that Negroes should be thrown out of the country." Virtually identical results were obtained in interviews with more than 1000 students in Recife about ten years earlier (Ribeiro, 1955:159).

Community studies and other intensive studies done in widely divergent sections of the country reveal a rejection of persons of color in the two situations involving the greatest intimacy and least social distance. These are the family and the social club. The social club is relevant because in many Brazilian communities the social club is the main place, outside of one's home or outside of the supervised atmosphere of the school, where contact between young people of opposite sexes can take place. In the nearly complete absence of informal, relatively free dating such as occurs in the United States, in many communities the social club and its dances are a major ground for encounters between boys and girls. The club in this sense is a kind of extension of the family, permitting contact with a wider range of persons than would be found in the home, all of whom are presumably acceptable. When there is more than one social club, they tend to be stratified by class and color and to function as a sort of social sieve. Cardoso and Ianni (1960:180-181) report separate clubs of whites, mulattoes, and Negroes in Florianópolis, noting that they rarely have mixed membership or mixed attendance at dances.

Similar findings are reported by Willems in São Paulo (1961:94); by Harris (1956:129) in Bahia, who adds, however, that "Those who are not [white] have an excess of money or some other prestige factor in a ratio inversely proportional to their racial 'deficiency' "; and by Azevedo (1963:45), who states: "The social clubs, religious brotherhoods, banks, business organizations controlled by the elite [in Bahia] are the most resistant to access by colored persons, which does not exclude the existence within them of successful presumed whites."

With regard to club membership, the critical factor is the intimacy of dancing. Although persons of color may sometimes belong to white social clubs and participate in many of their activities, the line is generally drawn on the dance floor. Harris notes (1956:128-129) "During the scores of dances which were observed at the Club only one Negro was ever seen on the dance floor. He was the son of Waldemar, the councilman. His partner, moreover, was always one of his white sisters-in-law. The rest of the dancers were white or mulatto." Willems's informants (1961:94) explained that blacks were not accepted in the social club because, although there was nothing against them personally, they are "rejected by society" and the girls would not wish to dance with them. The one mulatto who belongs to the club does not attend the dances. Cardoso and Ianni (1960:182) discuss this matter in some detail. They state that white women systematically reject a Negro or a mulatto partner when they are asked to dance, because any white woman dancing with a Negro or a mulatto would immediately stand out and be noticed by the white men and the other white women present who would think less of her for it, for she would be dancing with a person considered to have undesirable attributes. Furthermore, in the eyes of the white males, she becomes the object of the desire of a Negro, a candidate for miscegenation, and so loses face with her own group.

The difficulties with heterochromatic marriages are, of course, even greater. Such marriages are legal and can be freely entered into, but the considerable barriers are a function of the social class and chromatic differences between the partners. Azevedo (1965:96-97) points out that various degrees of prejudice against heterochromatic marriages are to be found in different regions of Brazil and that research has confirmed the relationship of social class to these prejudices. Yet, he states that color among white upper-class families is a more important barrier than social class. Color, however, it should be remembered, is based on subjective and imprecise definitions. In the upper classes of Recife (Ribeiro, 1965:108) marriages with persons at the black end of the scale may occur when the superiority of the dark man is unquestionable or the inferiority of the white woman (a crippling physical defect, for instance) undeniable, but even so, they are rare. Heterochromatic unions do occur occasionally in the upper classes, therefore, and are formally sanctioned. They are most common, however, among the lower classes and, within those, particularly in consensual unions. It is this social stratum and within it the consensual unions that account for the bulk of mixed racial types to be found in the Brazilian population.

Unions in which the male partner is darker than the female are more common than those in which this condition is reversed. This is due to the following factors. Given the association of light color with high social class, a dark man gains in prestige by marrying a light woman, whereas a light man would tend to lose prestige by marrying a dark woman. Since the man is the initiator in courtship, he can more easily select than can the woman. Since it is virtually axiomatic that the dark man wishing to marry a light-skinned upper-class woman comes from a lower socioeconomic background than she, this double handicap of origin, social and genetic, must be overcome by wealth, accomplishments, political power, professional repute, and the like. Thus, in exchange for their whiteness, the girl's family receives the symbols of prestige brought by the dark partner. If the dark partner is female, this does not happen, and she does not have the same power to compensate for her dark color as does the man. Furthermore, the lesser the chromatic difference between the couple, the easier it is to compensate for the innate deficiencies of color (cf. Azevedo, 1965:93). Whites, in Bahia at least, according to Azevedo (1953:45), justify their opposition to marriage with Negroes on the basis of their innate mental and moral inferiority and also on the basis of what they consider to be an "instinctive" revulsion, pointing to physical characteristics such as body odor which they consider to be a genetically inherited trait and therefore unsusceptible to amelioration. Pierson (1955:443) implicitly acknowledges that marriages between whites qua whites and blacks qua blacks are rare and frowned upon.

A number of community studies done in different parts of the nation have revealed strong opposition by whites, particularly those of the upper class, to heterochromatic marriages. Opposition is strongest in the case of a completely black partner. Hutchinson's findings in a Bahia community (1957:125-126) are typical. "The one impassable gap between the upper class 'aristocratic' whites and those below them is marriage. The white of the second class may be acceptable to the upper class because he is white. But the chances are heavy against the marriage of a member of Class A [white rural landowners] with a 'man of color.' " Willems (1961:59) collected data in a São Paulo community which revealed that out of 1,005 marriages, seven were between whites and blacks, 158 were between black and brown, or brown and white, while the remaining 840 were chromatically homogeneous. It is also worthy of note that in 103 of the mixed marriages, or about two thirds, the darker partner was the male. Cardoso (1965:128) interviewed 4,000 secondary school students in Pôrto Alegre and found that nearly 100 percent rejected Negroes as marriage partners. Pierson (1951a:191-192) states of a São Paulo community: "If discrimination on the basis of color exists in the community, it is in the final and ultimate realm of personal relations; that is, with reference to marriage and incorporation into the family." Altenfelder Silva (1961:153) studying a community in the São Francisco River Valley concluded that the local upper class would rather marry first cousins than risk "contamination" through marriage with nonwhites. In São Paulo, at least, discrimination against persons of color in heterosexual situations such as dating or school dances, tends to limit opportunity for the courtship of persons of different color (cf. case studies in Fernandes, 1969:146-150). It is interesting to note, apropos of the foreign influence theory, that in Pôrto Alegre (where immigrants and their descendants are a substantial element) Cardoso (1960:587) did not find significant differences between respondents who were descended from immigrants and those who were descended from native-born parents, with regard to the degree of prejudice revealed by his data. The available evidence tends to indicate, rather, that immigrants learned their prejudices, such as they are, after arrival.

The foregoing leads to the statement of another proposition: (5) *Color prejudice is in direct relation to the intimacy of interpersonal relations and is most accentuated in primary group situations involving intimacy between the sexes. It tends to increase as social distance decreases.*

Prejudice and Social Mobility

The fact that in Brazil the upper classes are almost completely white while the lower classes contain a disproportionate share of persons of color is generally recognized. Persons of color are virtually nonexistent in the national upper class although they may occasionally be found in local upper classes, particularly in those parts of the nation with the highest percentages of persons of color. This fact finds reflection in the under-representation of persons of color in the professions, in managerial positions, and in the ranks of employers. Nogueira (1955:478) found that in a community in the state of São Paulo the lower class was 75 percent white, 15 percent mixed, and 10 percent black; the middle class, 98 percent white and 2 percent divided among blacks and mixed with an almost absolute predominance of the latter; and that the upper class was 99 percent white, the remaining one percent being completely made up of mixed-bloods. Costa Pinto (1952: 65-111) documents extensively the lower educational, occupational, and income levels of the colored population in Rio de Janeiro as compared with the white; and Fernandes (1968:144-145) presents data documenting the disadvantaged position of persons of color in São Paulo with regard to occupational status and educational achievement (cf. also Garcia-Zamor, 1970:251).

These data reflect limited access to the principal avenue of upward mobility, the school, particularly the secondary school system, and the existence of barriers placed in the way of colored persons once formal requirements for a position have been met. Limited access to schools, although discrimination has been observed in private schools with a white clientele, is mainly an economic limitation that applies generally to the population of reduced means, both white and black. Even though primary instruction is tuition-free and generally available, costs are involved in sending a child to school. At the secondary level, the situation is more serious, for over half of the secondary school enrollments are in private schools (Saunders, 1969:121), which the poor and, therefore, a substantial majority of the colored, cannot afford. Admission to public secondary schools is difficult and attendance even more costly in terms of books, supplies, clothing, and so on, than at the primary level. Low income is both cause and effect of low educational status. Torres (1965:216) argues that limitation of educational opportunity was used by the elite as a mechanism for maintaining the status quo following abolition. Harris, in his study of a Bahia community (1956:139) notes that schools "were created in almost all of the village satellites with the exception of Baixa do Gamba—the predominantly Negro group." Eventually, when the residents of Baixa do Gamba demanded a school, they got it, but it was a long time before it was staffed, and Harris maintained (1956:140) that in the community "the tendency of the white to resist Negro rank pertains to every level of society."

The low profile of black and colored in the economic and occupational structure of society, which reflects disparities in the opportunity structure, is popularly explained in terms of innate dysfunctional qualities of persons of color which make them unable to compete on an equal footing with whites. Their inferior position is thus accounted for by factors outside the realm of the control of the whites (cf. Cardoso and Ianni, 1960:231). Frequently, their presumed "inferiority complex," which is not perceived by whites as being, if true, a consequence of the limitations experienced by persons of color resulting from a white-dominated social structure, is given as the reason for their inferior status.

Blacks and mixed-bloods are, however, experiencing upward social mobility. The greater opportunities for upward mobility of persons of color (as well as whites) in the southern region may account for the apparent higher prevalence and intensity of prejudice in that region, through the increasing competition of colored persons for high-status social roles heretofore performed by whites. This mobility has tended in the past to be intergenerational through the device of marrying "light" so as to produce offspring which more nearly approached the white phenotype, but with the expansion of the opportunity structure, particularly in the service sector of the industrializing regions of Brazil, it is now occurring in one generation; and, according to some observers, it is changing from the individual mobility of exceptional cases to group mobility (cf. Costa Pinto, 1952:332, 336; Azevedo, 1963:53-54), thus creating a colored elite that does not repudiate its racial origins while heightening white middle-class prejudice. This colored elite suffers social-psychological isolation in social (as opposed to professional) contacts, being unable to fraternize with other colored for social-class reasons or with whites of its own social class by virtue of its race, and consequently tends to create institutions of its own in which intimate social interaction can occur (cf. Cardoso, 1965:126-127; 1960:596; Pereira, 1967:255-256; Costa Pinto, 1952:223-224). The colored elite, overwhelmingly composed of mulattoes, has the economic means to maintain a middle-class life style. Not wishing to be identified with blacks, its members avoid contacts with lower-class colored whom they criticize severely and blame for the low status of colored persons generally (cf. Oberg, 1958:348). It is this attitude which has made it difficult for Negro movements to obtain the support of middle-class blacks (cf. Morse, 1953:303).

The achievement of middle-class status by persons of color remains difficult; and the greater the negritude, the more difficult the upward path. Discrimination is subtle and covert; but in competitive situations, when equality of qualifications exists between a white and a person of color, the latter is frequently handicapped. Cardoso and Ianni report (1960:174) that the totality of the Negroes and mulattoes they interviewed in Florianópolis stated that unless a job was open to public competition through examination, that is, unless the award of the position was based on objective criteria, color was a limitation. Yet, the competition only increases the opportunities available to colored persons when the job to be performed is "compatible," that is, when no representation is involved. Similar findings, although not so extreme, are reported by Fernandes (1969:246). Sixty-six percent of his male respondents and 68 percent of the female respondents reported that race prejudice limits a person's occupational opportunities. White employers were found to reject Negroes as employees, offering as their reasons stereotyping statements of the type already mentioned (Fernandes, 1969:249-253). One of Pereira's informants (1967:178) further stated that neither blacks nor whites like to take orders from blacks.

Nonetheless, the fact that persons of color are in a position to be affected by the prejudice of others in an occupational context reveals the fact that educational opportunities are broadening and that upward social mobility is becoming a possibility for increasing numbers of colored persons. The formation of a colored elite in Brazilian society is slow but is possible within the existing social structure. It also appears that discrimination in the occupational sphere is more pronounced in the more modernized, industrialized, and white southern region than in the northeast, and, in particular traditional plantation areas of the northeast located in the humid coastal lowlands. The data support Oberg's conclusion (1958:346) that "In general, prejudice is less in the lower class than in the middle and upper classes; less in the north of Brazil than in the center and south; less in the rural areas than in the cities." Another proposition seems justified at this point: (6) *Occupational mobility is hindered by color and the degree of hindrance is related to the degree of negritude. Barriers to occupational mobility tend to be least in the less developed, "darker" sections of the nation and greatest in the more developed, "whiter" sections which, however, paradoxically, have a broader opportunity structure, by virtue of greater development, for both whites and colored.* Furthermore, the foregoing materials suggest an extension of proposition (3) to read:

Awareness of prejudice increases as negritude increases and social status rises.

The Racial Democracy Ideal

The work of Freyre and Pierson, in particular, has contributed to the care and feeding of the racial democracy myth: the former, by laying the foundations for it in social history; the latter, by providing contemporary social science analyses which support it through the proposition that apparent manifestations of prejudice and discrimination are but manifestation of social-class differences and the prejudices associated with them. Yet, Pierson's pioneering work is not in question here so much as is the generalization of his Bahia findings (1942:349) to Brazilian society as a whole—an almost irresistible temptation, given the strength of the racial democracy ideal in Brazil, and the widespread belief that in that nation there is no prejudice or discrimination. The racial democracy myth serves several purposes. Like stereotypes of the Negro (in a sense, the racial democracy myth is itself a stereotype), it assigned to the Negro responsibility for his condition (since society did not place any barriers in his path by virtue of his race) and concurrently exonerated upper- and middle-class whites from the need to be concerned about problems over which they could have no control. Also, the belief in racial democracy has made the study of race relations difficult and sometimes impossible (cf. Ianni, 1970:275). To question the existence of racial democracy is somehow un-Brazilian and threatening to the national self-image, as well as to that of the individual.

Nevertheless, it should be remembered that racial democracy is a widely shared ideal of long standing in Brazilian society, to which Brazilians with rare exception subscribe. Its strength was, in good measure, responsible for the peaceful abolition of slavery. Legislative repression of persons of color has not existed since abolition; relations between persons of all hues are guided by norms of courtesy and consideration; race conflict as it is widely known elsewhere is impossible; segregation and discrimination, particularly as compared with other multi-racial societies, are very mild. Thus, although racial democracy is a myth, it must also be noted that it is an ideal which itself is largely responsible for the creation of the myth. That the racial democracy ideal coexists with segregation at the intimate level of interpersonal relations, negative stereotyping and endogamy (cf. Bastide and van den Berghe, 1957:605) does not deny the essentially courteous, harmonious, interracial behavior which prevails in Brazil, best expressed per-

haps in the chromatic "promotion" to "white" from mulatto, or to
"moreno" (dusky) from Negro accorded to persons who have
achieved high social rank. This shift in color typing does not reflect
changed sensory perceptions of the persons engaging in it, but is,
rather, a recognition of social merit reflected in the more courteous
designation (cf. Wagley, 1963:143).

A Final Word

Finally, we should not fall into the trap of over-generalizing
again. The studies of race relations in Brazil conducted so far have
been carried out at the community level, or have relied on interviews
with groups such as secondary school students that are hardly representative of the population at large. The more recent studies, in particular, have pertained to Southern Brazil. While they provide valuable insights, they obviously do not reveal all of social reality. While
they are probably generalizable to the particular populations included
in the respective research designs, they are not necessarily generalizable to larger universes. Thus, although data can be found to support
the propositions I have listed here, and although some propositions
(stereotyping, for example) seem amply supported, they must be
regarded as tentative and subject to the need for further verification.

REFERENCES

Altenfelder Silva, Fernando.
  1961   Xique-Xique e Marrecas. Duas Comunidades do Médio São Fran-
         cisco. Rio: Comissão do Vale do São Francisco.
Azevedo, Thales de.
  1953   Les Èlites de Couleur dans une Ville Brésilienne. Paris: UNESCO.
  1963   Social Change in Brazil. Gainesville: University of Florida Press,
         Latin American Monograph Series, no. 22.
  1965   "Mestiçagem e Status no Brasil." In Actas, V Coloquio Interna-
         cional de Estudos Luso-Brasileiros 1:87-112. Coimbra: Gráfica de
         Coimbra.
Bastide, Roger, and Pierre van den Berghe.
  1957   "Stereotypes, Norms and Interracial Behavior in São Paulo, Bra-
         zil." American Sociological Review 22, no. 6 (December):689-
         694.
Bastide, Roger, and Florestan Fernandes, editors.
  1955   Relacces Raciais Entre Negros e Brancos em São Paulo. São Paulo:
         Editôra Anhembi.

Bicudo, Virginia L.
   1947   "Atitudes Raciais de Pretos e Mulatos em São Paulo." Sociologia
          IX, no. 3:195-219.
Blair, Thomas.
   1965   "Mouvements Afro-Brésiliens de Liberation, de la Periode Es-
          clavagiste à nos Jours." Présence Africaine, no. 53, 1ᵉʳ Trimestre,
          p. 96-101.
Boxer, C. R.
   1963   Race Relations in the Portuguese Colonial Empire, 1415-1825.
          Oxford: Clarendon Press.
Cardoso, Fernando Henrique.
   1960   "Os Brancos e a Ascenção Social dos Negros em Pôrto Alegre."
          Anhembi XXXIX. no. 117 (agosto):583:596.
   1965   "Le Préjugé de Couleur au Brésil," Présence Africaine, no. 53, 1ᵉʳ
          Trimestre, p. 120-128.
Cardoso, Fernando Henrique, and Octavio Ianni.
   1960   Côr e Mobilidade Social em Florianópolis. São Paulo: Companhia
          Editôra Nacional, Brasiliana, v. 307.
Costa Pinto, L. A.
   1952   O Negro no Rio de Janeiro. São Paulo: Companhia Editôra Na-
          cional, Brasiliana, 276.
Fernandes, Florestan.
   1968   "O Negro em São Paulo." In São Paulo: Espírito, Povo, Insti-
          tuições, edited by J. V. Freitas Marcondes and Osmar Pimentel.
          São Paulo: Livraria Pioneira Editôra.
   1969   The Negro in Brazilian Society. New York: Columbia University
          Press.
Freyre, Gilberto.
   1959   New World in the Tropics, The Culture of Modern Brazil. New
          York: Alfred A. Knopf.
Garcia-Zamor, Jean-Claude.
   1970   "Social Mobility of Negroes in Brazil." Journal of Inter-american
          Studies XII, no. 2 (April):242-254.
Ginsberg, Anicia Meyer.
   1955   "Pesquisas Sobre as Atitudes de Um Grupo de Escolares de São
          Paulo em Relação Com as Criancas de Côr." In Relações Raciais
          Entre Negros e Brancos em Sao Paulo, edited by Roger Bastide
          and Florestan Fernandes. São Paulo: Editora Anhembi.
Harris, Marvin.
   1956   Town and Country in Brazil. New York: Columbia University
          Press.
   1964a Patterns of Race in the Americas. New York: Walker and Com-
          pany.
   1964b "Racial Identity in Brazil," Luso-Brazilian Review 1, no. 2 (De-
          cember):21-28.

Harris, Marvin, and Conrad Kottak.
 1963 "The Structural Significance of Brazilian Racial Categories." Sociologia XXV, no. 3 (setembro):203-208.
Hutchinson, Harry William.
 1957 Village and Plantation Life in Northeastern Brazil. Seattle: University of Washington Press.
Ianni, Octavio.
 1958 "A Ideologia Racial do Negro e do Mulato em Florianópolis." Sociologia XX, no. 3:352-365.
 1970 "Research on Race Relations in Brazil." Pages 256-278 in Race and Class in Latin America, edited by Magnus Morner. New York: Columbia University Press.
Kottak, Conrad Phillip.
 1967 "Race Relations in a Bahian Fishing Village." Luso-Brazilian Review IV, no. 2 (December):35-52.
Morse, Richard F.
 1953 "The Negro in São Paulo, Brazil." The Journal of Negro History XXXVIII, no. 3 (July):290-306.
Nogueira, Oracy.
 1955 "Relações Raciais no Município de Itapeteninga." Pages 362-554 in Relações Raciais Entre Negros e Brancos em São Paulo, edited by Roger Bastide and Florestan Fernandes. São Paulo: Editora Anhembi.
 1959 "Skin Color and Social Class." Pages 164-179 in Plantation Systems of the New World, edited by Vera Rubin. Washington: Pan American Union, Social Science Monographs, no. VII.
Oberg, Kalervo.
 1958 "Race Relations in Brazil." Sociologia XX, no. 3 (agosto):340-351.
Pereira, João Baptista Borges.
 1967 Côr Profissão e Mobilidade, o Negro e o Radio de São Paulo. São Paulo: Livraria Pioneira Editôra.
Pierson, Donald.
 1942 Negroes in Brazil. Chicago: University of Chicago Press.
 1951a Cruz das Almas, a Brazilian Village. Washington: Smithsonian Institution, Institute of Social Anthropology, Publication no. 12.
 1951b "Preconceito Racial Segundo o Estudo de 'Situações Raciais.'" Sociologia XIII, no. 4:305-324.
 1955 "Race Relations in Portuguese America." Pages 433-462 in Race Relations in World Perspective, edited by Andrew W. Lind. Honolulu: University of Hawaii Press.
Ribeiro, René.
 1956 Religião e Relações Raciais. Rio: Ministério da Educação e Cultura, Serviço de Documentação.

Russell-Wood, A. J. R.
1968 "Race and Class in Brazil, 1937-1967, A Re-Assessment: A Review." Race 10, no. 2 (October):185-191.
Saunders, John.
1969 "Education and Modernization in Brazil." In The Shaping of Modern Brazil, edited by Eric N. Baklanoff. Baton Rouge: Louisiana State University Press.
Torres, João Camillo de Oliveira.
1965 Estratificação Social no Brasil. São Paulo: Difusão Européia do Livro.
Trujillo Ferrari, Alfonso.
1960 Potengi, Encruzilhada no Vale do São Francisco. São Paulo: Editôra Sociologia e Política.
Wagley, Charles.
1953 Amazon Town, a Study of Man in the Tropics. New York: Macmillan.
1963 An Introduction to Brazil. New York: Columbia University Press.
Wagley, Charles, editor.
1952 Race and Class in Rural Brazil. New York: UNESCO-Columbia University Press.
Willems, Emilio.
1961 Uema Vila Brasileira, Tradição e Transição. São Paulo: Difusão Européia do Livro.
Zimmerman, Ben.
1952 "Race Relations in the Arid Sertão." In Race and Class in Rural Brazil, edited by Charles Wagley. New York: UNESCO-Columbia University Press.

❖ *Comment* WERNER BAER

Prejudice, Tension, and Questions
For Further Research

PROFESSOR SAUNDERS has written an admirable survey of the work which has been done to date on racial prejudice in Brazil. I shall limit my comments to a few marginal remarks and suggestions for further research.

The evidence Professor Saunders presents is based on case studies or small community studies. I would be curious to know how representative of whole areas of this huge country are the studies of communities in Santa Catarina or Bahia or the interior of Pernambuco. Are there ways to do this type of checking, or are we forced to rely principally on scientific community studies complemented by more journalistic evidence (for example, TV programs, some newspaper coverage) and casual observation?[1]

I was fascinated by the findings of various studies to the effect that there was "increasing rejection with decreasing social distance and generally higher levels of rejection among the upper and middle classes than among the lower classes." This seems to be an interesting contrast to the situation in the United States where racial an-

---

1. A complementary study to this paper is that of Thomas E. Skidmore, "Brazilian Intellectuals and the Problem of Race, 1870-1930," *Occasional Paper No. 6*, the Graduate Center for Latin American Studies, Vanderbilt University, Nashville, Tennessee. 1969. Also see "Existe Preconceito de Cor no Brasil," *Realidade*, October 1967, on current race prejudice in Brazil.

tagonism seems much stronger among the lower classes than among the elites. What is the explanation of this? Is it due to the psychological problems which result from the uncertainty over the racial origins of some of the elites? Is it the fear of some elites of social rejections by their "social peers" in more advanced countries? Is employment in blue collar and government jobs based less on racial background, which would explain the lesser antagonism among the working classes? This would certainly be a most interesting phenomenon to study.

I have some doubts about the statement that upward mobility "has tended in the past to be intergenerational through the device of marrying 'light' so as to produce offspring which more nearly approached the white phenotype, but, with the expansion of the opportunity structure, particularly in the industrializing regions of Brazil, it is now occurring in one generation; and, according to some observers it is changing from the individual mobility of exceptional cases to group mobility." One grave contemporary socio-economic problem of Brazil is the small numbers of jobs which are being created in the industrial sector. The annual rate of growth of Brazil's urban population has been about 5.5 percent, while the annual growth rate of industrial employment has been 2.5 percent a year. Thus a large proportion of the growing urban population has been forced into the service sector, which often means very marginal types of activities. One would expect under such circumstances to have increased social tensions and, perhaps, even racial tensions. Why has this not occurred until now?

I am also struck by the assertion, based on the work of Oberg, that occupational discrimination is more pronounced in the modernized, industrialized South than in the Northeast. What is the evidence? What is being compared—similar industries in the regions? Since occupational discrimination is not at all obvious to those who have done research in the industrial sector, I would be most interested in seeing the evidence which has led to this generalization.

Since the government bureaucracy is a large employer in Brazil, and since I have encountered a great racial variety in various levels of this bureaucracy, I would be interested to see more studies done in that area. Since a vast number of jobs in government bureaucracy are filled by competitive examinations, is there a racial barrier beyond the educational one—i.e., more colored and black Brazilians failing the exams or not taking them for lack of educational facilities to prepare them for the examination? How does the promotion system work in the bureaucratic system?

I suppose the most interesting question which arises is why racial prejudice, which does exist in Brazil and which has been well documented, has not to date created the type of racial tension and strife which we have undergone in the United States. Is there enough mobility for ambitious blacks and mulattoes in Brazil, which lessens the frustrations and potential activism of such people? Is the myth of racial democracy entrenched enough in all Brazilian social levels to contain the issue or problem? Or will faster economic development and increased literacy and the accompanying revolution of rising expectations ultimately create a situation similar to our own? I hope that Professor Saunders and his fellow Brazilianists will soon answer some of these queries.

6 AUSTIN T. TURK

The Limits of Coercive Legalism In Conflict Regulation: South Africa

ELSEWHERE I have argued that the most probable outcome of South Africa's racial conflict—viewed as a fundamentally political, "realistic" struggle more over *how* than over *whether* the authority structure of the polity shall be changed—is an accommodation of contending group interests in "a federation of *primarily* white-controlled and *primarily* nonwhite-controlled sectors" (Turk, 1967). Though I still believe that the available evidence supports that view, I am increasingly concerned with the theoretical and humanitarian problem of how to minimize the human costs of the conflict out of which South Africa's future is emerging. It is clear to me that South Africa's authorities are operating in terms of an archaic and misleading conception of the nature and province of law (Turk, 1970), and that they are consequently likely to make, and are making, "conflict moves" that reduce the chance of reaching a viable accommodation with their political adversaries. My objective in this paper is to spell out the incompatibility between their goals and their means, specifically by indicating the uses and limits of coercive legalism in regulating social conflict, then applying the ideas thus developed to an examination of available data on the degree and effectiveness of coercive legalism in South Africa.

A faculty research grant by the Social Science Research Council greatly facilitated the 1968-69 research in South Africa on which this paper is largely based.

171

Conditions of Legal Order

Though all legal orders are "legalistic" in that they are based on the assumption that right behavior is to be defined in reference to rules (Shklar, 1964), and though all are coercive in that they are based ultimately—and directly or indirectly—on the use of force to prevent sudden and radical changes in the hierarchical structuring of social authority and advantage (Turk, 1969:30-52), it is obvious that legalism and coerciveness are variable both separately and conjointly. Having borrowed much from jurisprudence, the sociology of law has long since incorporated an awareness of the variability of legalism —as in, for example, the distinction between the more legalistic civil law tradition relative to the common law tradition (Merryman, 1969). However, coerciveness has been treated more as a deviation from than a characteristic of legal ordering, so that coercion is admitted only grudgingly by such pioneers as Ehrlich (1962:3-82) and such contemporaries as Selznick (1968; 1969:3-34), to be even ultimately and occasionally a component of legal reality. Moreover, the range of variability allowed is severely restricted, and a relatively coercive legal order is likely to be redefined as something else than legal. Redefinition is accomplished by arbitrarily reserving the term *legal* for presumably just orders, where the exercise of power is in accord with properly created procedural rules and in reference to explicit and specific substantive norms, and by requiring that the law in word and action conform to some conception of natural justice (Selznick, 1961, on which see Stone, 1965:336-338). This way of defining the legal has the unfortunate consequence of inhibiting and obscuring analysis of the increasingly crucial linkage between legalism and coerciveness, especially insofar as it encourages us to *assume* (1) that the legal is or can be really independent of the political, (2) that legal power is, from the standpoint of individuals and minorities, necessarily less overwhelming and arbitrary than other forms of power, (3) that legalism and coercion are somehow mutually exclusive, or at least incompatible, and (4) that coercion is actually a negligible and generally ineffectual resource whose use virtually precludes the regulation and resolution of social conflicts. While in principle I leave all these assumptions open to testing, in practice I have concluded that the evidence amply justifies assuming the negative in each instance.

"Assuming the negative" has led me to the view that a legal order is an established distribution of power—a social order in which the differentiation of authorities and subjects has been achieved and in which both authorities and subjects have learned to interact in terms of social norms of domination and of deference, respectively (Turk, 1969:30-52). This severely objective model of legal order postulates that the authority of legal authorities, indeed the basis of their legitimacy, is solely the product of a history of struggle in the course of which both authorities and those subject to them have been conditioned to interact within the framework of their superordination and subordination. To the degree that the question of relative power has been settled and people have forgotten that there ever was a question, a legal order rests upon conditioning. To the degree that the settlement has been, in some version, articulated and justified in the common culture of authorities and subjects, a legal order rests upon consensus. To the degree that neither conditioning nor consensus is fully successful, a legal order rests upon coercion. Therefore, empirical approximations of legal orders are most secure when based primarily upon conditioning (hardly any questions arise regarding the power structure), partly upon consensus (such questions as do arise are made innocuous by being asked and answered in the terms set by the sacred assumptions of the culture), and ultimately by coercion (persistent and profane questions and questioners are neutralized by coercive persuasion and force).

It follows that the establishing and maintaining of a legal order is a process moving toward creation of the following conditions:

(1) The most elementary form of the struggle for control is ended by the demonstrated military superiority of one party, including coalitions, over all others in the arena. At this level of conflict the arena is always territorial, whatever other features it may have. The dominance thus achieved is used to eliminate the remaining military potential of the conquered; monopoly of the means of violence removes the possibility of reversing the military decision.

(2) Jurisdiction is established, i.e., the territorial and social boundaries of the polity are asserted. Both egress and ingress are controlled, so that neither outsiders nor insiders can operate with impunity within the bounds established. Because such boundaries are functions of both the social realities of power and the cultural realities of legal conventions and definitions (e.g., international law, constitutional law) they shift in response to changes in the relative power of those asserting polity boundaries and to changes in legal conceptualizations. Between and within polities the official boundaries, as legally defined, will to some extent be discrepant with the actual limits in regard to effective control. Hence arise such distinctions as those

between "nations" and "spheres of influence" and between "legal technicalities" and "practical politics."

(3) Effective control within polities is demonstrated by defining, detecting, and punishing "crime," especially "political crime," which is any deviation seen by the authorities as a challenge to the social and cultural foundations of their authority. To maintain a polity an effective police is required, i.e., a reliable *ergo* controlled apparatus for neutralizing challenges to legal authority. The requirement that the police be under control is essential because a crucial problem for authorities is to distinguish among situations where coercion is needed, situations where police action is unnecessary (given limits upon the resources which can be invested in policing), and situations where coercion is self-defeating in that the net result of the police effort is to increase, rather than decrease, the need for coercion—which implies an increase in the threat to the legal order.

(4) Effective control is maintained through two or more generations, so that the control task becomes decreasingly that of military occupation of a conquered set of specific persons and increasingly that of tranquilizing and socializing people who themselves have never lived outside the power settlement reached by the wars of their ancestors. The point is that there must be time for the power structure to become the fundamental factor in the learning situation. Later generations grow up within the limits and under the conditions set by the outcome of their ancestors' struggle to answer the power question. They start learning their places, acquiring identities, statuses, roles, from birth in a system whose main features are already set by the terms of the power settlement. The very idea that things were different and could be different becomes more and more just an idea, having no grounding in the actual experience of living people. It becomes, because of the increasing detachment of such ideas from the experiences of real people in real life, more and more difficult even for people to think about their situation in terms other than those set by a culture part of whose bedrock is the explanation and justification of the power structure. This anticipates the last condition:

(5) Deliberately and inadvertently, and helped by the impact of collective experience on language, the producers, disseminators, and consumers of knowledge and opinion (from the most specialized scholars to the most commonsensical laymen) eliminate the original cultural expressions, the "real reasons," that gave meaning to the raw struggle to win and that stated baldly the fierce hope and joy of victory and the hopelessness of defeat. The historical and current social

realities of power and coercion are overlaid and buttressed, and thus softened, by the emergence of a cultural consensus. Even though the softening may be real, the key feature of the consensus is that it includes a palatable version of what was at stake in the original and early conflicts, and of what was fortunately lost and fortunately gained by the providential outcomes of those conflicts—i.e., a version proving that the unfortunate clashes of the ancestors nevertheless led to the triumph of right, so that their descendants are occupying their appropriate positions in a social structure that not only *is* but *ought to be,* that is at least moving along as fast as possible to the good society, in which each receives his needed and proper share of the common fund of good things.

To summarize briefly, the conditions present in a fully realized legal order would be that the people of a polity do not question the *fact* of the power structure and that they accept explanations and justifications of social stratification (itself a relatively harmless conceptualization of power relations and their implications) that limit such questions as may arise and supply palatable answers. Indeed, it would be psychically and socially impossible for them to engage in political crime, or even radical dissent (assuming in principle a difference)—a challenge to authority that disturbs its roots, conditioned acceptance of the power structure, especially, and secondarily the consensus implicit in the language of respectable questions and answers about the origins and workings of the society.

Conditionals of Legal Order

That historically no fully realized legal order has existed and that, despite the formidable development of control technology (London, 1969) none are likely to appear in future is a problem of fit to which a methodological response would be a cop-out. It is irresponsible theorizing to take the position that such problems arise merely because of phenomenological complexities, or the limitations of language, or the restricted computer capacities of human minds, or the difficulty or impossibility of measurement. This particular problem of fit is to me a theoretical problem, that of finding what it is that limits the process of legal ordering.

An obvious possibility is to adopt the perspective of the experimental psychologist, defining the problem as one of defective socialization. The failure of authorities and subjects to learn appropriately complementary behavior patterns, is, then, attributable to the crudities of "real world" legal and other social organization in contrast to, say, a Skinner box for the purposes of reinforcement scheduling. Residual variance is explained by the idiosyncratic sources (e.g., genetics, disease, injuries) of variation in the conditionability of individuals. The weakness of this line of explanation is that the major explanatory factor, the ineffectiveness of legal structures and processes, is precisely what we are trying to explain. As for variable conditionability, the fact is incontestable; but we have still to account for the assumed failure of control technology (so far, at least, and despite the enormous attention given by rulers to its development) to neutralize the impact of variable conditionability upon legal ordering. Actually, it is pointless to debate the issue since the very presence of cultural and social structures—the regularities of communication, interaction, and functional interdependence—imply considerable success in neutralizing the impact of individual variability whatever its sources.

A more sociologically congenial, and I think more viable, approach is to pursue the implications of the fact that the establishment of polity boundaries does not imply control over environmental variability. Here is one place where the distinction between the problems of legal order and the larger ones of political order can be usefully made, i.e., without assuming either the independence or the identity of the legal and the political. The statement of the conditions of legal order presupposes that the realization of legal order amounts to settling the issue of "internal" power, a matter of relative deprivation. If the currently fashionable, though nonetheless serious, ecological problem were solved and if the polity boundary was either all-inclusive or, equivalently, completely impermeable, then the theory of legal ordering would be conceptually sufficient, limited in application only by measurement error. These two big "if's" are, in fact, those larger problems of political ordering, larger in the sense that working solutions to both must be found before the process of legal, "internal" ordering can even begin.

The ecological problem is fundamentally one of absolute deprivation, in that nature does not compromise: eventually men survive or they do not. This clearly is not a problem of social control, but one requiring decision by authorities *to the effect that* the technical ability to *live* be developed and applied. There must be found solutions to the problems of satisfying organismic needs on a scale sufficient for collective survival. The distribution of power, the rank ordering of contending parties in terms of their relative ability to get their way despite resistance from others, is irrelevant to the technical business of surviving and using the play of natural forces. Contrary to the mythology of exploitation, man does not master nature: nature poses questions, and man tries to answer them. If politics (which is residual conflict over the organizing of power), or the exigencies of foreign relations (forming and preserving polity boundaries), or ignorance in high places, or sheer technological impossibilities prevent men from answering nature's questions, the operation of natural forces will insure that the cost be paid.

A significant part of the cost will be the diminution of men's capacity to be deprived of things valued—including most importantly the hope of survival at least, and perhaps even a better life for them or their progeny. Destitute men can be incorporated into grossly inegalitarian legal orders. But men utterly without hope even of survival can only be forced or killed in the immediate encounter; they cannot be conditioned to perform either authority or subject roles, since "aversive stimulation" cannot be complemented by *subjectively meaningful*, as well as *objective*, negative and/or positive reinforcement (Bandura and Walters, 1964; Burgess and Akers, 1966). Where coercion is not meaningful because there is no anticipation of a future the more powerful can learn only to take advantage of the weaker when they can catch them, while the weaker can learn only to avoid capture. Viable social, including legal, interaction is thus precluded.

The loss of all hope is, of course, the limiting case. It is more probable that failures to solve the ecological problem will be felt as partial instead of total, especially since it is likely that an ecological crisis will take a long time to be felt and for the implications to disturb the universal cultural assumption that we will survive. Short of the extreme, such failures become variables in terms of which we measure the differential life chances of populations and subpopulations, along with the cultural consequences and concomitants (e.g., alienation, anomie, *embourgeoisement*, elitism) of such differentials. To the extent that a population or any part of it approaches the point of concluding that the authorities will not or cannot solve the problems of survival, it becomes increasingly difficult for them to believe that the fate of the polity really concerns them and that, more specifically, their interests really do lie in the preservation of law and order.

Social-economic inequality alone is insufficient to prevent legal ordering; but where deprivation—especially absolute deprivation—is coupled with hopelessness[1] the authorities will be forced to the con-

---

1. Gurr's provocative study (1970) of the sources and dynamics of political violence is weakened by his overemphasis upon relative deprivation and his consequent neglect of absolute deprivation and of the conditions under which people perceive even relative deprivation as violating a "just" order.

clusion that there exists an unreachable, intractable "dangerous class" who understand only force. And in fact little more than force will have an impact as the authorities try to assert and maintain their jurisdiction over such subjects. Though the authorities will—because of their own conditioning, for the sake of principle, and perhaps for strategic reasons—expend resources to maintain their power over these people, neither they nor their ostensible subjects can long hold illusions that the military order thus imposed is legal, i.e., accepted. At some point the cost of occupation is quite likely to exceed the ability of the collectivity, as well as the will of the authorities, to meet it. The classic solution tried, with varying success, by authorities faced with this problem is the "final solution" of exterminating or otherwise removing the troublemakers.[2] Resort to the final solution marks the failure of legal ordering. Even though remaining subjects may be intimidated by the object lesson, such a blatant reminder of the power core of the legal authority relationship is likely to be negative in its net effect because it erodes the conditioned acceptance of the relationship by stimulating *awareness* and by implying the irrelevance of anything but force to the preservation of that relationship (Turk, 1969:44-46). As authority declines, legal conflict and the more restrained forms of politics give way to more deadly modes of conflict: the fundamental issue of power supersedes all else—most notably the legalistic issues regarding the legal validity, meaning, and applicability of substantive and procedural rules.

The other basic problem of political ordering—that of asserting and maintaining the polity's boundaries—is, short of the all-inclusive state of which rulers have long dreamed, the problem of foreign relations. The authorities must deal with outsiders (usually other authorities but often also bandits, guerrillas, and other outlaws) so as to survive and prosper in their company. Warfare, subversion, diplomacy, and international law are invented and developed out of the efforts of authorities to insure the survival of their respective polities. Conceptions of strategy grow in subtlety and complexity as authorities gain experience in the arena of foreign relations, but one principle of special interest here is maintained with ferocity: that the authorities of a polity are masters in their own house. Specifically, the authorities of *all* political communities, whatever else they may do,

2. One obvious tactical possibility here is political scapegoating, in which control problems with a population are at least temporarily handled by enlisting them in the business of detecting and punishing some "minority" who are supposedly the villains causing everybody's troubles.

reserve to themselves the prerogative of defining and dealing with "crime." Though they may have frequently or usually to accept the advice, decisions, and resources of more powerful sets of authorities from the outside, they are and must be extremely jealous of their right to make the decisions when it comes to the matter of internal control.

To allow parties external to the political community to define and deal with crime is to abdicate as legal authorities and to allow the erstwhile polity to be incorporated into some other political community. Similarly, efforts by outside parties to intervene in the legal ordering process have to be resisted, since such efforts imply the same loss of autonomy. Subversion (efforts aimed at undermining authority or else preventing the conditions for legal order from being realized) is always strongly resisted, because it implies the replacement of the incumbents by new authorities—with or without radical changes in the structure of authority. Aid (efforts aimed at supporting authority and helping the authorities to achieve the conditions for legal order) is sought only in dire need and is never welcomed by astute authorities, because it implies at least temporary dilution or forfeiture of decision-making power, signals the weakness of the incumbents (who can expect trouble when their powerful friends leave, unless these friends have managed the most unlikely feat of restoring the authorities to their former clear-cut position of relative power), stamps them as inferior failures as authorities, and may even be the prelude to a take-over by the ally or to his continued interference in the heretofore private matter of internal control. In short, foreign aid implies that the authorities who have thus admitted weakness will have great difficulty retrieving their lost autonomy and privacy.

To summarize, the problem of legal ordering is that of *internal* control, the establishment and maintenance of a distribution of power within the boundaries of a polity. The problem of political ordering is to solve the problems presented by nature and by foreign relations so that the legal ordering problem *is* purely that of internal control, i.e., the problem of relative deprivation implied by any differential distribution of power. Given a static environment, successful handling of the political ordering problem would mean that absolute deprivation and external social forces were eliminated as factors in the control problem (the situation which Gurr, 1970, appears to take as the starting point for his stimulating analysis of revolutionary violence). However, the environment is not static but ever shifting; thus, solutions to the ecological and the foreign relations problems are never final, and therefore never entirely adequate. The extent of failure to achieve a polity impervious to natural and external social forces is the extent of failure to realize the conditions of legal ordering. Political failure implies the failure of legal ordering regardless of the legal control policies and practices of the authorities. Neither more nor fewer laws, stiffer nor lighter penalties, greater nor lesser coerciveness, relaxed nor tightened adherence to the rules restraining the use of legal coercion, more threatening nor more conciliatory gestures will preserve a legal authority structure undermined by political failure.

To argue that legal ordering is contingent upon political ordering is to assert only the priority and decisive impact of political relative to legal structures and processes, and especially of political relative to legal decision-making by authorities. Given that the political problems have been at least survived to the point where a polity-in-the-making is identifiable—i.e., where polity boundaries and therefore boundary problems are appearing—it becomes possible to conceptualize the problem of legal ordering. Without a boundary, the notion of internal order is meaningless. It then becomes logically possible, as empirically necessary, to consider the question of "feedback" effects of the legal upon the political. The legal most clearly affects the political via the consequences of (1) the attention and resources commanded by the legal ordering problem at the expense of the ecological and foreign relations problems; (2) the fear of technological and other innovation where the authorities are insecure; (3) the largely ideological significance of particular legal cultural and social structures in the international arena; and (4) the organization of authorities, particularly in terms of divisions of labor among administrative, legislative, and judicial officials; between those primarily concerned with the political and those primarily concerned with the legal ordering problems; among those concerned with different facets of the legal ordering problem; and between those concerned with the lower-level and those concerned with the higher-level problems of law enforcement.

It is time now to see whether the notions of *conditions, conditionals,* and *feedback effects* of legal ordering increase our understanding of South Africa, possibly to the point where we can offer not only justifiable criticism but also usable policy implications to those who make the strategic decisions in the South African polity, for better or worse.

Coercive Legalism in South Africa

It is easier to offer questions than to come up with the answers.

Nonetheless, I believe that the potential theoretical and practical worth of my inquiry is increased by trying to answer the following questions:

1. To what extent have the *conditions* of legal order been realized in South Africa?

2. To what extent can the failure to realize fully the *conditions* of legal order be explained by failure to satisfy the political *conditionals* of legal order?

3. To what extent can the failure to satisfy the political *conditionals* be attributed to the feedback effects of legal ordering efforts upon political ordering efforts? More specifically, in what ways and to what extent is the increasing coerciveness and legalism of South African law self-defeating?

Conditions of legal order

Even though abortive rebellions, massive labor violence, faction-fighting, riots, and other direct and implied challenges to authority have occurred since the Boer War, the end of that war in 1902 and the political unification of South Africa in 1910 mark the establishment of South Africa as a polity. There has been no significant change in official polity boundaries since 1910 except for the international recognition of the de facto control of South West Africa resulting from World War I campaigns against the Germans; efforts to rescind that recognition of South African jurisdiction over South West have repeatedly failed, most notably in the 1966 conclusion of the case brought by Ethiopia and Liberia before the International Court of Justice in The Hague (South African Department of Information, 1966). During the past sixty years South Africa's authorities have successfully asserted and defended their jurisdictional claims against many external and internal challenges. Currently, the possibility of an internal military challenge is nil, while South Africa's military defense forces have yet to be seriously tested. Backed by a formidable array of combat-ready armed forces—air, ground, and naval, and with tactical nuclear weaponry well within reach—a small number of South African police have had relatively little trouble containing guerrilla incursions in South West Africa, and, supporting Rhodesian forces, in the Zambezi valley. For the present, in short, the South African republic stands as testimony to the presence of at least two of the five conditions of legal order: military dominance has been established within perforce recognized polity boundaries.

Equally apparent as a fact of life for South Africans is the effective police control, as distinct from sheer military domination, of the country. As we shall see later, South Africa's "known crimes" rates are high and rising; however, the situation is very far from being out of control, in terms of the demonstrated ability of the police and other legal control agencies to detect and punish law violators. (Indeed, the continued detailed reporting of crime statistics and other data on the routine operations of police, courts, and prisons is itself evidence of effective internal control.) Moreover, the authorities have shown themselves to be anything but reluctant to increase their investment of resources in at least the more coercive aspects of legal ordering. Apart from a 1969-70 military budget seven times larger than that of ten years ago and now representing 2.5 percent of the GNP (Horrell, 1970:31), by 1967 expenditure on justice, police, prisons, and—beginning in 1966-67—"emergency planning" amounted to some 97 million *rand* (roughly $135 million), more than a one-third increase in five years *(South African Statistics, 1968,* Table T-6.) In 1969 an additional expenditure was begun with a vote of over 4 million *rand* for the newly established Bureau for State Security, a secret service reporting only to the Prime Minister and having prime though vaguely defined responsibility for both external and internal security activities (Horrell, 1970:34). Based on information from varied public and private sources, my estimate is that 3.5 to 4.0 percent of South Africa's male population 15 years old and older is engaged full-time or part-time in control, or constitutes a trained force which can be mobilized rapidly if needed. This estimated total includes both military and police forces —which appears reasonable, since there is a unified command structure and since the military have been used during the past quarter-century only to help quell internal disorders. The police forces proper include some 31,000 national police, 20,000 police reservists on active duty, and several thousand special (e.g., railway and harbour), provincial, and municipal police. The existence and demonstrated effectiveness of such a formidable organization of force realizes the third condition of legal order: crime control.

It is in regard to the fourth condition of legal order that South Africa is falling short and in regard to the fifth that virtually no success has been achieved. Although the gross features of the South African power structure—especially white dominance—have long been established, it can hardly be claimed that that structure has been unambiguous and substantially unchanged through two or more generations, or even one generation. Apart from the continuing intra- and inter-racial conflicts over the desirability, necessity, and possibility of prolonging white dominance through the metamorphosing pattern of racial separation and discrimination—the keystone of the power structure—the distribution of power within the dominant white population still exhibits many discrepancies, ambiguities, and gaps. No serious and informed white or nonwhite in South Africa, including the authorities, believes that the distribution of power has been settled to the point where it is "the fundamental factor in the learning situation" (despite much brave talk by the state-controlled South African Broadcasting Corporation on the tranquility of South Africa in contrast to the turmoil of virtually all the rest of the world, including the United States). Indeed, perhaps the one point of agreement between pro- and anti-government, official and unofficial, public and private views held by all but the most reactionary Hertzogites is that the present structure of power *must* be changed if the South African polity is to survive (Pienaar and Sampson, 1960; Ngubane, 1963; United Nations, 1966; Scheepers Strydom, 1967; N. J. Rhoodie, 1969). Until a more viable power distribution is reached, the task of South Africa's control agencies will continue to be in large part that of military occupation of a population, particularly the nonwhites, impressed by proximate and explicit legal power at least as much as by ultimate and implicit power.

Historical social and cultural conflicts are anything but forgotten by South Africa's peoples. Despite political rhetoric, "Christian National" and "Bantu" education, fairly strict censorship, banning, and other deliberate attempts to eliminate "liberalistic" and other dissenting and distracting views on South Africa's past and present realities, South Africans still speak with many and conflicting voices. The diversity of major themes in interpreting South African history (Wilson and Thompson, 1969: preface) is indicative of culturally unresolved clashes: the Afrikaner's heroic struggle against enormous odds (van Jaarsveld, 1964); the long and sacrificial effort by Britain's statesmen, generals, colonial administrators, missionaries, educators, financiers, engineers, and settlers to civilize and develop the country (Walker, 1957); the oppression and exploitation of the African and other nonwhite peoples seeking freedom and justice for all (Roux, 1964). From basic premises to the technical lore of practical politics, no generally accepted political culture is to be found in South Africa. In Munger's words, "There are no universal symbols of even a tenuous South African nationalism" (Munger, 1967:9).

The military, political, and legal reality of the South African polity is clearly yet a long way from being transformed from a structure of power into a structure of authority. Coercion and expedience, as much as conditioned acceptance and far more than consensus, hold South Africa together.

Conditionals of legal order

The pace of South African economic development since World War II is impressive *(South African Statistics, 1968:7-21)*. Unfortunately, the ostensible affluence of South Africa is due far less to success in solving the ecological problem than to the exploitation of the many by the few. Despite some progress in raising levels of living and despite some evidences of growing realism in regard to job reservation and differential wage scales,[3] it does not appear that South Africa's authorities—still less the white electorate (Hudson, Jacobs, and Biesheuvel, 1966:27-30)—have yet given up the belief that they, in Spooner's words of a decade ago, "can enjoy the fruits of twentieth-century mechanization without the obligation of lifting the real earnings of the mass of the workers to effective twentieth-century consumer levels" (Spooner, 1960:216). Though magnificent regional development schemes are envisioned for southern Africa (Rhoodie, Eschel, 1968), the reality present and projected for most South Africans is a miserable life and an early death. They have little or no share in the fruits of the "spreading green bay tree," as the booming South African economy has been described. South Africa is a *developing* country confronted with all the problems the term implies. The glitter of her "white" cities, the excitement of financial speculation, the pleasures of travel by car and air at home and of trips abroad, the joys of moneyed leisure, the security of excellent medical and other social

---

3. Privately, virtually everyone I have talked with in South Africa—including many Nationalists, officials, and businessmen—professes to accept the principles of "anyone who can do the job" and "equal pay for equal work." However, Hudson, Jacobs, and Biesheuvel (1966) found a majority of their sample of white South Africans favored job reservation. And in perhaps the most important public test in recent years of the differential wage scales, "work-to-rule" protests by nonwhite doctors in Durban against 1968 salary raises for only the already better-paid white doctors—a stand for "equal pay for equal work" which was strongly supported by the council of the South African Medical Association and by numerous individual white doctors and officials, as well as other agencies and individuals—ended in increases for the nonwhites that left them still far short of the white levels, and in the refusal by the Natal Provincial Administration to reinstate nine "ringleaders" of the protest (after all 156 nonwhite doctors employed in the Durban and Pietermaritzburg hospital facilities for nonwhites had submitted their resignations). On this case, see Horrell's annual surveys for 1968, pages 278-279, and 1969, pages 235-236.

services—all this and all else comprising the good life enjoyed by the few (mostly white) has been and is being made possible only by the gross and deliberately enforced discrepancy between the labors and the rewards of the many (mostly nonwhite).

No one can say confidently what proportion of South Africa's population have concluded that the authorities "will not or cannot solve the problems of survival"—Limehill stories are matched against Daveyton stories—but it is certain that enough have given up hope for the authorities still to fear the voices of such as Robert Sobukwe and Nelson Mandela. Moreover, the ideology of separate development is premised on the belief that Bantu rejection of white political domination has passed the point of no return. Thus, separate development is for the moment a not-quite-final solution to the problem of what to do with a potentially very "dangerous class." Political separation to the extent that it has been achieved in the Transkei has not been matched by significant improvements in the wretched conditions under which the great majority of the area's inhabitants live (Carter, Karis, and Stulty, 1967); and the area is still under very tight police control. Even the concession of political independence to such incipient polities as the Transkei would only exacerbate the white-nonwhite conflict so long as such moves were perceived as abdication of moral and political responsibility and repudiation of moral and economic debts. South Africa's failure to solve the ecological problem for most of her people cannot be turned into success by redefining official polity boundaries to exclude those for whom she has failed—especially when these people must necessarily stay well within the de facto boundaries of South Africa's military and economic power.

Far from being guaranteed even formally, South Africa's boundaries are continually and seriously threatened by a wide variety of external forces. Ecclesiastical condemnation, formal and repeated censure and rejection by the United Nations and other international organizations, diplomatic protests, law suits, economic sanctions, and externally supported violence have all been directed against the South African polity. South Africa's unenviable position in the international arena is largely attributable to her symbolic and strategic importance in the conflicts of East and West, of poor ex-colonial nations and rich ex-colonialist nations, and of "black" and "white" Africa. Historically, South Africa has been anything but an imperialist threat beyond her borders; rather, her characteristic deficiency in foreign relations has been to seek as few as possible. Indeed, South African isolationism has for many years played into the hands of those who,

out of varying mixtures of good and bad intentions, encourage the
rest of the world to isolate South Africa. The real and generally quite
explicit target of and excuse for the attack upon South Africa is not
her *foreign* policies but her *domestic* policies—and especially her legal
ordering efforts, the decisional area in which the authorities of any
polity will, I have suggested, defend their prerogative with special
ferocity.

Not only have South Africa's enemies sought to subvert the polity, but her friends have tried to influence the formulation and implementation of internal control programs—with similar lack of success.
Sure of their own lessons of history and suspicious of any attempt to
apply the experiences (including the social sciences) of other peoples
and polities to their unique situation, South Africa's authorities have
pursued their stern and terrible course. They have survived, and they
have been learning some things about the business of surviving. One
extremely important lesson has been that it is not enough merely to
denounce "illegal interference" in one's domestic affairs as did Eric
Louw (1963) again and again at the United Nations. One must also
move outward to press one's own case in the once-despised "court
of world opinion." Thus, diplomatic, trade, and propaganda initiatives have been undertaken; technological assistance and other forms
of aid have been offered to other African states (and sometimes accepted, overtly and covertly); and conservative politicians, businessmen, scholars, and journalists have been cultivated.

The result is clearly an improvement in the sorry mess of South
Africa's foreign relations; perhaps the most significant public response is the manifesto adopted by fourteen east and central African
states in Lusaka in April 1969. That statement asked in vague terms
for a commitment by South Africa, Rhodesia, and Portugal to the
principles of human equality and self-determination, given which,
policy decisions and the rate of progress will be purely domestic issues; furthermore, the participating governments are willing on these
terms to encourage "our brothers in the resistance movements to use
peaceful methods even at the cost of some compromise on the timing
of change" (Horrell, 1970:78). The manifesto was, of course, welcomed by the South African authorities as evidence of the success of
the outward movement in gaining increased external understanding
and sympathy. However, as John Barratt (1970) has pointed out, the
Lusaka manifesto does not promise or imply any relaxation of opposition to apartheid as it is currently being interpreted and enforced;
and it is equally clear that genuine improvement in South Africa's

foreign relations will result not really from better explanations of the problems and policies, but from actual development of the "home-lands" and reduction of racial discrimination. As he puts it, an "in-ward movement" is needed to complement the "outward movement." As I put it, the polity boundary problem will not be solved unless the ecological problem is also solved, and until the negative feedback ef-fects of coercive legalism in South Africa are eliminated.

Feedback effects of coercive legalism

Since 1948 the relatively liberal traditions and structures of an-glicized South African law have been increasingly subordinated to the more legalistic and authoritarian Roman-Dutch law (Turk, 1970). Guided largely by the nineteenth-century Boer republican experience with the pre-Napoleonic Dutch law of the eighteenth century, the Afrikaner Nationalists have introduced unprecedented clarity and for-mal rigor into the legalities of white domination of nonwhite in South Africa. However, during the past twenty years it has also become in-creasingly apparent that old-fashioned white supremacy is doomed. The authorities have, therefore, followed the late Verwoerd's lead in seeking a political solution to the legal ordering problem via a strictly controlled program of legal change: the separate-development policy. Fearing that any other course will be countered by a violent attempt to hasten and radicalize political and social changes, they have been ruthless in suppressing resisters and intimidating dissenters.

That South African legalism is accompanied by the ready resort to coercion to enforce compliance exemplifies what I take to be the sa-lient characteristics of legalism under intense political pressure: to spin out rules ever more frantically in the effort to control every con-tingency, and to rely increasingly upon coercion to insure their effi-cacy. As the pressure mounts, the reliance upon coercion tends to increase at the expense of the legalistic impulse; and the legalistic concern with rule formation and interpretation is skimped and sloughed in the haste to meet "the emergency." Despite the plethora of rules thrown into the breach there always seem to be unanticipated difficulties. As fast as the legalists find holes in the technical fabric of legal control, new rules are plugged in. Because no system of for-mulas ever allows for all possibilities, holes continue to be found. Such gaps in the defenses become more and more intolerable as "the emergency" persists; so the authorities take shortcuts by worrying less about the semantic details of urgent legislation and by evading, postponing, or otherwise negating the judicial function.

Table 1 indicates that South Africa's authorities have produced a
fairly steadily increasing volume of legislation, and provides evidence

TABLE 1. LEGALISM AND CONTROL IN SOUTH AFRICA, 1950-1968

	Number of Acts of Parliament	Percentage "Control"	Proportionate attention to "control" in *Annual Survey*
1950	49	6.1	18.9
1951	73	6.8	11.4
1952	67	6.0	15.5
1953	49	10.2	16.5
1954	57	19.3	15.6
1955	70	7.1	16.6
1956	73	15.1	13.9
1957	83	10.8	15.0
1958	49	20.4	11.3
1959	82	13.4	11.3
1960	69	2.9	11.5
1961	81	9.9	11.4
1962	93	19.4	17.5
1963	96	12.5	17.3
1964	91	13.2	16.0
1965	103	17.5	14.7
1966	63	7.9	18.0
1967	105	10.5	20.4
1968	88	17.0	15.8
Annual average	76	11.9	15.2

NOTES: Number of parliamentary acts as reported in the *Annual Survey of South
African Law* for the years 1967 and 1968. The percentage devoted to "control" is
based upon (a) acts mentioned in the *Annual Survey* chapters on criminal law and
criminal procedure, and (b) listed in *Statutes of the Republic of South Africa,* sections on *aliens and citizens; arms and ammunition; Asiatics; Bantu; censorship; colored persons; criminal law; group areas; intoxicating liquor; mental disorders; police;* and *prisons and reformatories.* For each year the larger of the two counts is
used as probably the most nearly complete tally of relevant legislative activity. The
proportionate attention by the *Annual Survey* to problems of legal control is calculated from the number of pages dealing with criminal law and procedure, citizen
and state, and the administration of justice in regard to the legal profession, police
force, crime statistics, and prisons and penology. It is interesting to note that on
this basis the first three annual surveys, for 1947, 1948, and 1949, dealt with control
in 7.1, 4.8, and 9.0 percent, respectively, of their pages.

—though the indicators are crude—of growing concern with the problems of legal control. The proportionate attention given to the passage and enforcement of control laws by the authors of the *Annual Survey of South African Law* appears to have risen in response to especially crucial developments in law—notably (a) the passage and implementation of the 1950 Suppression of Communism Act and related laws, and (b) the response of the authorities to the emergencies of 1960 (the year of Sharpeville) and subsequently. The titles of some of the most directly relevant legislative acts clearly point to the difficulties which the authorities have been having in their search for the completely adequate system of laws:

Suppression of Communism Act, No. 44 of 1950 (often amended)

Public Safety Act, No. 3 of 1953

Criminal Procedure Act, No. 56 of 1955 (amended at least two dozen times, including the 1965 addition of Section 215 *bis*, authorizing solitary detention of possible witnesses in security cases for periods of 180 days)

Riotous Assemblies Act, No. 17 of 1956

Police Act, No. 7 of 1958 (often amended)

Prisons Act, No. 8 of 1959

Unlawful Organizations Act, No. 34 of 1960

Section 21, General Law Amendment Act, No. 76 of 1962 ("Sabotage Act")

Section 17, General Law Amendment Act, No. 37 of 1963 ("90 Days Law" authorizing solitary detention of suspects; no longer used—obviously because it is superfluous, given sweeping powers under other laws)

Section 22(1), General Law Amendment Act, No. 62 of 1966 (authorizing solitary detentions for periods of 14 days of anyone possibly connected with or having information about cases involving security laws)

Terrorism Act, No. 83 of 1967

Dangerous Weapons Act, No. 71 of 1968 (Firearms and ammunition already being under strict control—though in fact thousands of firearms are stolen or lost in South Africa each year—this law authorizes the Minister of Justice to prohibit any person or class of persons from possessing "any object . . . which is likely to cause serious bodily injury if it were used to commit an assault.")

Security Services Special Account Act, No. 81 of 1969 (carte blanche funding of Bureau for State Security)

Public Service Amendment Act, No. 86 of 1969 (established Bureau for State Security, which coordinates all internal and external intelligence activities and is answerable only to the Prime Minister)

Sections 10 and 29, General Law Amendment Act, No. 101 of 1969 (security matters also covered under 1956 "official secrets" law as amended, regarding military and police matters; no one can be required to give testimony or evidence in court if the Prime Minister or another Minister certifies that state security is involved and that disclosure would not be in the best interests of the state).

Continuing the trend documented and strongly protested by Brookes and Macaulay in 1958 and by many others since as the "erosion of the rule of law" in South Africa,[4] such laws have steadily extended the discretionary powers of the executive and law enforcement authorities while defining ever more broadly and vaguely the offenses to be detected and penalized by use of those powers.

Tables 2, 3, and 4 together give a picture of South African law enforcement activity since 1949 that reflects the effort of the tumultuous 1950s to overcome political resistance and to bring the not unrelated general crime problem under control. By and large, the effort appears to have been successful, in that from about the mid-1950s the over-all prosecution and conviction rates for both whites and nonwhites declined, as did the rates for Class A and Subclass A-1 offenses (see Tables 3 and 4).

The same pattern is found in the over-all age-specific conviction rates (7 years and over, and 21 years and over) computed by the South African Bureau of the Census for the years 1949-1962 (Special Report No. 272, Table 4). However, as a consequence of the appearance and suppression of the organized violence of Poqo, Umkonto we Sizwe, and the African Resistance Movement in the 1960s, the nonwhite conviction rate for political crimes (Subclass A-1) did rise sharply in 1963-64 (Table 4). In addition to the thousands of nonwhites detained in the Transkei under the emergency proclamations of 1960

---

4. The issues and key arguments in regard to the existence, permanence, or degree of the "erosion" or "suspension" of the rule of law in South Africa are summarized in the publications of the International Commission of Justice (1961, 1968) and of the South African Department of Foreign Affairs (1968).

TABLE 2. PROSECUTION AND CONVICTION RATES BY RACE, 1949-1967

	Prosecutions/1,000		Convictions/1,000	
	Whites	Nonwhites	Whites	Nonwhites
1949	19.2	32.6	14.8	26.7
1950	20.7	33.2	15.7	27.1
1951	20.2	33.5	15.5	27.3
1952	20.7	33.0	15.8	26.7
1953	20.6	34.4	16.0	28.0
1954	21.1	36.5	16.3	29.9
1955	21.0	36.6	16.0	29.9
1956	21.7	37.2	16.4	29.8
1957	20.8	36.0	15.6	28.5
1958	20.6	34.8	14.9	27.3
1959	20.9	34.2	15.1	26.0
1960	20.0	33.6	14.1	24.9
1961	19.5	33.8	13.5	24.9
1962	19.7	33.0	13.7	24.2
1963-64	18.2	33.0	12.5	24.2
1964-65	—	—	12.5	23.6
1965-66	17.6	32.4	11.9	23.3
1966-67	19.4	35.1	13.1	25.3
Annual average	20.1	34.3	14.6	26.5

NOTES: For "offenses" only (see Table 5). No explanation for absence of 1964-65 prosecutions by race; the South African Police Commissioner's report for 1964-65 puts the total prosecutions for that year at 534,882 (which gives a rate of 29.9 for the total population, not out of line with the previous year rate of 30.2 and the 1965-66 rate of 29.6). Data sources are the statistical reports of the South African Bureau of the Census and the annual reports of the Commissioner of the South African Police (see references).

(most of which are still in effect)[5] there were 3,605 persons, including 113 whites, detained or arrested in 1963 and 1964 under the security laws in effect at that time,[6] of whom 1,604 had been convicted by February 2, 1965, and 199 were awaiting trial (Horrell, 1965 survey: 61). From July 1, 1964, to June 30, 1965, there were 1,267 convictions under the security laws; afterward, the numbers of convictions dropped in an abrupt decline: 1966, 188; 1967, 74; and 1968, 66 (Horrell, 1966-1969 surveys). Detentions under the generous provisions of South Africa's various security laws followed the same

5. Detentions under the provisions of Proclamation 400 of 1960 numbered 19 in 1967, 32 in 1968, and 7 up to May, 1969.
6. General Law Amendment Act of 1962, section 21; Suppression of Communism Act of 1950; Public Safety Act of 1953; and Unlawful Organizations Act of 1960.

TABLE 3. CLASS A PROSECUTION AND CONVICTION RATES BY RACE,
1949-1967

	Prosecutions/1,000		Convictions/1,000	
	Whites	Nonwhites	Whites	Nonwhites
1949	3.9	3.1	2.7	2.5
1950	4.3	2.9	2.9	2.4
1951	4.0	2.8	2.6	2.3
1952	4.0	2.5	2.7	2.1
1953	3.8	2.4	2.7	2.0
1954	3.6	2.5	2.5	2.0
1955	4.4	2.3	3.0	1.9
1956	4.4	2.5	3.1	2.0
1957	3.8	2.4	2.5	1.9
1958	4.1	2.4	2.5	1.9
1959	3.8	2.4	2.5	1.9
1960	3.6	2.3	2.3	1.7
1961	3.6	2.3	2.5	1.8
1962	3.5	2.2	2.4	1.7
1963-64	2.7	2.5	1.8	1.9
1964-65	—	—	1.5	1.9
1965-66	—	—	1.4	1.9
1966-67	—	—	1.6	2.0
Annual average	3.8	2.5	2.4	2.0

NOTES: Class A offenses include all those considered to affect the "safety of the state and good order." The major subclasses are entitled "public safety, order and peace" (i.e., the more specifically political offenses), "administration of justice and good order" (i.e., offenses involving obstructing or resisting law enforcement), and "public finance and revenue" (i.e., tax, customs, and counterfeiting offenses). Data sources are the statistical reports of the South African Bureau of the Census and the annual reports of the Commissioners of the South African Police (see references).

path. During the eighteen months in which it was used, in 1963-64, there were 1,095 persons detained under the "90 Days Law." Thereafter, the numbers detained dropped considerably: 1965 and 1966, 247; 1967, 124; 1968, 27; and up to May in 1969, 11 under the 1965 "180 Days Law." In addition, 91 persons were detained under the "Sabotage Act" between November 4, 1966, and the end of 1967. Although the Minister of Justice has refused to reveal the number of detainees under section 6 of the Terrorism Act, it is unlikely that there have been enough to alter the general pattern of decreasing political criminality rates.[7]

7. Thirty-six persons are known to have been detained up to June in 1969. It can be assumed—I have been told—that no more than 45 to 50 individuals are being detained, most for only a few days, under the Terrorism Act in the course of a year (private source).

TABLE 4. SUBCLASS A-1 CONVICTION RATES BY RACE, 1949-1964

	Whites	Nonwhites
1949	5.8	10.1
1950	6.8	8.5
1951	5.9	7.8
1952	7.6	7.4
1953	7.3	6.9
1954	5.4	7.0
1955	5.3	5.5
1956	4.6	6.4
1957	5.7	5.6
1958	6.2	5.9
1959	4.9	5.3
1960	4.6	4.8
1961	6.9	5.1
1962	3.4	3.6
1963-64	2.8	8.5
Annual average	5.5	6.6

NOTES: Rates/10,000. Subclass A-1 offenses are the more specifically political offenses considered to endanger "public safety, order and peace." Data sources are
the statistical reports of the South African Bureau of the Census (see references).

It would be premature, however, to conclude that South Africa
is on the way to solving her legal ordering problem. Rather, the decline
in the prosecution and conviction rates for "offenses," and especially
political offenses, is not the whole story; and it is an achievement won
at great cost. The over-all "crimes reported" rate has been rising
(Table 5) even as the "offenses" rates have been dropping; this
means that "law infringements" are very much on the increase—which
in effect means that violations of nonwhite control laws and regulations
are rising disproportionately. Moreover, the proportion of South
Africa's population in the country's penal institutions has risen steadily since 1949, until the rates for both whites and nonwhites are nearly
twice as high as twenty years ago (Table 6).

It is also indicative of failure to achieve the conditions of legal order that the authorities continue to find it necessary to hang approximately 100 persons each year.

The price of the declining "offenses" rates has been paid and is
being paid in many ways, adding up to the forfeiture of authority by
South Africa's authorities. They have gambled their credibility as
legalists committed to playing by the rules against the prospect of
success for separate development, on the assumption that the policy
will work if alternatives are emphatically ruled out. To this end they

TABLE 5. CRIMES REPORTED TO THE SOUTH AFRICAN POLICE,
1949-1967

	Number (000's)	Rate/1,000
1949	1,397	11.4
1950	1,432	11.5
1951	1,507	11.9
1952	1,597	12.2
1953	1,727	12.9
1954	1,879	13.7
1955	1,989	14.1
1956	2,091	14.5
1957	2,088	14.1
1958	2,156	14.2
1959	2,286	14.7
1960	2,141	13.4
1961	2,194	13.5
1962	2,149	12.9
1963-64	2,153	12.3
1964-65	2,176	12.2
1965-66	2,430	13.3
1966-67	2,706	14.4
Annual average	2,005	13.2

NOTES: Since 1963 detailed statistical reports have been kept only for "the more important economic-sociological offenses," a category that excludes as "law infringements" ("of lesser importance from a sociological point of view") mainly violations of nonwhite control and of traffic laws and regulations. Such law infringements account for over 60 percent of reported crimes. Data sources are the statistical reports of the South African Bureau of the Census and the annual reports of the Commissioner of the South African Police (see references).

have invested heavily in enforcement even while falling short of what it will take by their own estimates to begin solving the ecological problem of South Africa's nonwhites; they have promoted a garrison-state mentality among their supporters that frequently finds xenophobic expression; they have scared or forced many of their most creative people into silence, pedestrianism, or exile; they have made apparent to even the most obtuse how illusory are the protections of law and how unrestrained are the police; and they have belied their stated good intentions by their increasingly coercive legalism—in which the stress is plainly upon the logic of force more than the logic of

TABLE 6.   DAILY AVERAGE PRISONERS IN CUSTODY, RATES FOR
1949-1968

	Total pop.	Whites	Nonwhites
1949	22.0	4.9	26.5
1950	22.7	5.3	27.3
1951	23.0	5.3	27.7
1952	24.5	5.7	29.3
1953	26.4	6.3	31.6
1954	26.3	6.7	31.3
1955-56	26.6	7.2	31.5
1956-57	27.9	7.7	32.9
1957-58	29.3	8.5	34.4
1958-59	32.1	9.4	37.6
1959-60	33.3	7.9	39.3
1960-61	34.2	9.3	40.1
1961-62	37.7	9.5	44.3
1962-63	39.1	9.7	46.0
1963-64	40.3	9.0	47.7
1964-65	40.6	9.0	48.1
1965-66	40.5	8.3	48.0
1966-67	39.1	8.1	46.4
1967-68	42.0	8.7	49.8
Annual average	32.0	7.7	37.9

NOTES: Rates/10,000. Data sources are the statistical reports of the South African Bureau of the Census and Horrell's annual surveys of race relations in South Africa for the years 1965-69 (see references).

political persuasion, itself no gentle art but yet one less demoralizing than police-state repression and less bloody than open war. None of this helps to make South Africa's professions and disclaimers more plausible as the authorities try to win understanding and tolerance by the outward movement. South Africa has a bad record that dogs her, regardless of what happens, and will continue to do so at least until the most blatant expressions of coercive legalism are eliminated. Even though the South African polity will be threatened for the foreseeable future, defense will be easier to justify and international support more readily and reliably available when the South African authorities demonstrate that they are again distinguishing between protecting polity boundaries and beating people into submission. I am not sanguine regarding the ability of the authorities to reverse their course; they themselves may well be in the situation, in the words of Matthews and Albino (1966), "in which it is no longer possible to distinguish between the preservation of order and the preservation of the power of the ruling party and between opposition and subversion." It should be no cause for rejoicing if the South African polity fails, for its disintegration will mark another failure to find a way out of the horrors of racism and to achieve a viable social order.

REFERENCES

Annual Survey of South African Law.
    1947-1968   Johannesburg: The School of Law, University of the Witwatersrand.
Bandura, Albert, and Richard H. Walters.
    1964   Social Learning and Personality Development. New York: Holt, Rinehart & Winston.
Barratt, John.
    1970   "South Africa's Outward Movement." Modern Age 14 (2):129-139.
Brookes, Edgar H., and J. B. Macaulay.
    1958   Civil Liberty in South Africa. Cape Town: Oxford University Press.
Burgess, Robert L., and Ronald L. Akers.
    1966   "A Differential Association-Reinforcement Theory of Criminal Behavior." Social Problems 14:128-147.
Carter, Gwendolen M., Thomas Karis, Newell M. Stulty.
    1967   South Africa's Transkei: The Politics of Domestic Colonialism. London: Heinemann.
Ehrlich, Eugen.
    1936   Fundamental Principles of the Sociology of Law. Reprint edition, 1962, of 1936 translation by Walter L. Moll. New York: Russell and Russell.
Gurr, Ted Robert.
    1970   Why Men Rebel. Princeton: Princeton University Press.
Horell, Muriel.
    1970   A Survey of Race Relations in South Africa, 1969. Johannesburg: South African Institute of Race Relations. Also see her annual surveys for the years 1965-1968.
Hudson, William, Gideon F. Jacobs, and Simon Biesheuvel.
    1966   Anatomy of South Africa: A Scientific Study of Present Day Attitudes. Cape Town: Purnell and Sons.

International Commission of Jurists.
    1961   The Rule of Law in South Africa. Geneva.
    1968   Erosion of the Rule of Law in South Africa. Geneva.
Jaarsveld, F. A. van.
    1964   The Afrikaner's Interpretation of South African History. Cape Town: Simondium Publishers.
London, Perry.
    1969   Behavior Control. New York: Harper & Row.
Louw, Eric H.
    1963   The Case for South Africa. New York: Macfadden Books.
Matthews, Anthony S., and R. C. Albino.
    1966   "The Permanence of the Temporary—An Examination of the 90- and 180-day Detention Laws." South African Law Journal 83: 16-43.
Merryman, John Henry.
    1969   The Civil Law Tradition: An Introduction to the Legal Systems of Western Europe and Latin America. Stanford: Stanford University Press.
Munger, Edwin S.
    1967   Afrikaner and African Nationalism. London: Oxford University Press.
Ngubane, Jordan K.
    1963   An African Explains Apartheid. London: Pall Mall Press.
Pienaar, S., and Anthony Sampson.
    1960   South Africa: Two Views of Separate Development. London: Institute of Race Relations.
Republic of South Africa.
    1967   Annual Report of the Commissioner of the South African Police (for July 1, 1965, to June 30, 1966). Pretoria: R.P. 39/1967.
    1966   Annual Report of the Commissioner of the South African Police (for July 1, 1963, to June 30, 1965). Pretoria: R.P. 68/1966.
Republic of South Africa.
    Statutes of the Republic of South Africa: Classified and Annotated from 1910 (Butterworths).
Republic of South Africa, Bureau of Statistics.
    Statistics of Offences and of Penal Institutions, 1949 to 1962. Pretoria: Special Report No. 272.
    Statistics of Offences and of Penal Institutions, 1963-64. Pretoria: Report No. 08-01-01.
    1968   South African Statistics. Pretoria.
Republic of South Africa, Department of Foreign Affairs.
    1968   South Africa and the Rule of Law. Pretoria.
Republic of South Africa, Department of Information.
    Ethiopia and Liberia versus South Africa. Pretoria.

Rhoodie, Eschel.
    1968   The Third Africa. Cape Town: Nasionale Boekhandel.
Rhoodie, N. J.
    1969   Apartheid and Racial Partnership in Southern Africa. Pretoria: Academica.
Roux, Edward.
    1964   Time Longer than Rope. Second edition. Madison: University of Wisconsin Press.
Scheepers Strydom, C. J.
    1967   Black and White Africans: A Factual Account of South African Race Policies in the Verwoerd Era. Cape Town: Tafelberg-Uitgewers.
Selznick, Philip.
    1961   "Sociology and Natural Law." Natural Law Forum 6:84-108.
    1968   "Sociology of Law." International Encyclopedia of the Social Sciences.
    1969   Law, Society, and Industrial Justice. New York: Russell Sage Foundation.
Shklar, Judith N.
    1964   Legalism. Cambridge: Harvard University Press.
Spooner, F. P.
    1960   South African Predicament. London: Jonathan Cape.
Stone, Julius.
    1965   Human Law and Human Justice. London: Stevens and Sons, Ltd.
Turk, Austin T.
    1967   "The Futures of South Africa." Social Forces 45:402-412.
    1969   Criminality and Legal Order. Chicago: Rand McNally.
    1970   "Legal Control in South Africa: The Present Significance of the Past." Unpublished paper given at the annual meetings of the Rural Sociological Society, Washington, D.C., August 29, 1970.
United Nations.
    1966   Text of the 1966 statement from the dock made during his trial by Abram Fischer (then head of South Africa's outlawed Communist party, sentenced to life imprisonment). United Nations, General Assembly Special Committee on Apartheid. New York: United Nations, A/AC.115/L.175/Rev.1, July 7.
Walker, Eric A.
    1957   A History of Southern Africa. Third edition. London: Longmans, Green.
Wilson, Monica, and Leonard Thompson, editors.
    1969   The Oxford History of South Africa, I. South Africa to 1870. London: Oxford University Press.

❖ *Comment* JOHN B. MARSHALL

Three Ingredients for
Understanding Social Processes

PROFESSOR TURK'S paper makes a significant contribution to the understanding of social processes and engenders an inclination to rejoice over what it offers rather than to challenge it for shortcomings.

It contains three ingredients: first, a definition of legal order and a model for the development of this order; second, a discussion of reasons for the failure of any society to reach the ultimate stage of this order; and third, factual information about South Africa, some of which is fitted to the theoretical material.

The initial definition and model are the basic, controlling theoretical components of the paper. They seem unnecessarily narrow. Consequently the observation later in the paper, that observed facts do not fit the theory, is hardly surprising. But instead of seeking to reconstruct the basic definition and model to arrive at a more useful foundation, the paper in its second part seeks additional insights to explain the problem of fit, in an effort to preserve the basic elements by adding to them. While this approach may have been worth a try, and indeed it produced some of the most valuable material in the paper, the ultimate results indicate that the theory does not explain the facts of history or of societies around the world, and consequently the basic definition and model should be reconstructed.

To stop with the foregoing comment would view the theoretical content of the paper as merely a hypothesis that was not confirmed. But the paper obviously treats its theoretical components as having a more durable status, and consequently a fair assessment requires closer review.

The basic definition and model are not extensively derived in the paper, but the general basis is indicated. The discussion points out that many writers attempt to eliminate or minimize the factor of coercion in the concept of legal order, arbitrarily attempting to limit the term *legal* to those systems that possess a substantial degree of moral justification. This appears to be another round in the battle between *legal positivism* and its critics, with the present paper tending to reject the moralist view, if not actually siding with the positivists. In part, of course, it is an argument over the use of the word *legal*, but more substantial questions are also involved in the controversy, as regards the kind of social order that can, in fact, be established in a world of human beings and the role that must or should be played therein by concepts of values and morals. Professor Turk takes the position that coercion cannot be arbitrarily disregarded, if a realistic understanding is to be achieved. This point is well taken, but it appears to be overworked in the subsequent construction of a theory of *legal order* which is limited to order based on class domination. Such a narrow conception is not supported, and its narrowness appears to be the cause of later inadequacies in the theoretical content of the paper. Legal order is regarded as "an established distribution of power" based on "domination and deference." This hardly explains any society based on democratic ideology. It restricts the definition of *legal order* as arbitrarily as those who attempt to exclude coercion from the definition.

Further narrowing the theoretical framework, Professor Turk postulates a model that *legal order* is achieved through a process of military struggle followed by a period of cultural conditioning which still needs some supplement of coercion in order to persist as a stable society based on class domination. It is not clear whether cultural conditioning factors are to be regarded as components of legal order, as the term is used in the paper, but at this point the definition seems unimportant. This model of historical development does not appear to be a description of fact, but rather a formula to be followed by groups who seek to achieve class domination. The evidence later in the paper that this formula does not work comes as a welcome relief rather than a disturbing inadequacy in scientific understanding.

The second phase of the paper inquires into the reasons why the definition and model are not fully achieved anywhere at any time, and this discussion in substance constitutes an inquiry into the factors that will prevent the achievement of the ambitions of a group that attempts class domination. Here, the paper speaks for itself in pointing to the limitations in the processes of cultural conditioning, environmental variability, the factor of hope, and other topics. This material offers a number of insights, many of which seem to result from the fact that the concept of legal order appears to presume a closed system in which the only variables are the acts of the parties; in reality no social system is sufficiently closed to correspond to this precondition, so it is not surprising that variables can be identified that will prevent the legal order from being fully achieved. Although the paper never manages to escape its tendency to force understanding of social phenomena into narrow stereotyped concepts of class analysis, this discussion of the impediments to class domination offers much interesting material. Further development of such factors as hope and fear, feedback, propaganda, elitism, economic circumstances, and other influences on the processes would be most enlightening and useful.

Considering the theoretical material in the first and second parts of the paper, it seems regrettable that Professor Turk did not take a broader view of the concept of legal order. A functioning society may be achieved by means which can be included within a concept of legal institutions broad enough to cover much more than rules, coercion, struggle for class domination, and the characteristics of criminal law (which are too often regarded as the only components of a legal system). A broader view would of course be much more complex, but it would open the way for a more adequate understanding. Indeed, the very attempt to separate law out of the context of all influences on behavior (the totality of such influences being traditionally regarded as the province of the social scientist rather than the lawyer) means that the subject of law is studied apart from the context with which it interacts. This isolation has not been characteristic of every society, and it appears to be largely the result of occupational specialization. But even accepting the need in modern society for the identification of law as a separate subject, a strong point must be made in favor of adequate scope so that the concepts of law, the legal system or legal order will have some realistic correlation with the operation of the society. A suitable scope for the concept of legal order in the paper would have led to a more adequate inquiry into the components in the over-all system and would surely have produced a more useful model.

It remains to be asked whether the narrow theoretical concepts may nevertheless be useful for understanding of the factual material about South Africa contained in the third part of the paper. To the extent that the class domination model describes the intended plan of the South African authorities, it is of course relevant and helpful. The model is simplified, as any model must be, and should not be devalued merely because it does not account for all varieties of facts. The strength of a model lies in its ability to identify significant factors, and in this respect the paper indicates the nature of class domination and coercion as elements in South Africa, and it provides analysis by way of application of theoretical concepts to the reported facts. The paper demonstrates convincingly that the "conflict moves" on the part of South African authorities indicate a misunderstanding of the nature and province of law and that such a heavy reliance on law and the ordinary sanctions of criminal law (fines, imprisonment and capital punishment, and a variety of other measures) constitute an unrealistic attempt to make those aspects of social governance accomplish more than they are able to accomplish. In this regard, the discussion of South Africa indicates that any group which seeks to achieve class domination must employ methods that lawyers do not use. Viewed from a framework of democratic values, this may be regarded as a compliment to the legal profession. At any rate, few lawyers would be disturbed by the observation that their profession is not equipped to impose class domination. At this point, the inadequacy of the original definition of legal order demands a reformulation, for the term *legal* must be used with more faithful relation to the facts of society. The paper demonstrates that what is normally regarded as law, although involving some coercion, is inadequate to achieve class domination. Accordingly, the paper is inaccurate in its use of the term *legal order* to refer to a state of class domination, which law is not suited to achieve.

The further message, to the effect that complete class domination appears to be unattainable by any methods, is also encouraging. But Professor Turk indicates, both theoretically and factually, that a substantial degree of class domination may be achieved by suitably ruthless measures. This message is not new, but it continues to be worrisome, and his analysis of methods and processes offers valuable insights for people who deal with such matters. Regrettably, no solution is offered to the complex problems of South Africa, but since no one else has found such a solution, the lack thereof can hardly be a criticism of this valuable and scholarly paper.

❧ *Comment* THOMAS E. NYQUIST

A Theoretical Framework for
South African Realities?

I APPROACH Dr. Turk's paper rather gingerly. It is obvious that he has put a good deal of thought into it and I respect his effort. At the same time, I find his attempt to set the realities of the South African situation into a theoretical framework rather forced. In my view, the framework does little to facilitate our understanding of coercion in South Africa, though his subsequent discussion does. I must admit from the outset, however, that I have little patience with much of the jargon of the social sciences, which all too often obscures rather than enlightens.

To recap Dr. Turk's paper, he has distinguished between *conditionals* of legal order and *conditions* of legal order. He has spoken of the conditionals being: (1) solving of ecological problems (which he seems to be using largely as a synonym for economic problems); and (2) problems of asserting and maintaining the polity's boundaries, i.e., the problem of foreign relations.

Further, he has spoken of the conditions being: (1) demonstrating military supremacy of one party (group) over others; (2) asserting the territorial and social boundaries of the polity, which I presume means that one is establishing a country; (3) crime control; (4) stable power structure; and (5) acceptance of the distribution of power.

He then asks to what extent the five conditions have been reached, suggesting that number four (stable power structure) has only been partly reached in South Africa, and number five (acceptance of the distribution of power) not at all.

He asks further to what extent these last two phenomena have been caused by a failure to solve ecological and foreign relations problems, which he has referred to as his conditionals of legal order. He notes that in South Africa the conditionals have not been satisfied— South Africa is a developing nation which has not fully achieved ecological goals. Further, its foreign policy problems are serious, with its boundaries continually threatened to a serious degree. Once having said this, Dr. Turk fails to demonstrate satisfactorily the extent to which his conditionals have contributed to the inability of South Africa to achieve a stable power structure and the acceptance of the distribution of power.

Dr. Turk also asks to what extent the failure to achieve the political conditionals can be said to result from the feedback of coercive legalism. Yet he fails really to answer the question. He convincingly sketches examples of coercive legislation, but does not delineate how these lead to the inadequate achievement of the political conditionals of ecological and international goals.

It is not totally clear how all of this ties into one of the principal objectives which he has indicated in the preface of his paper—which is to spell out the incompatibility between the goals of the South African authorities and their means as indicated by "the use and limits of coercive legalism in regulating social conflict." This is not to say that the topic is ignored, but the discussion—useful in itself—does not seem to fit wholly within the theoretical concept to which he has devoted considerable time.

One of the more attractive aspects of Dr. Turk's paper, and an aspect to which I wish he had given more time, was the degree of effectiveness of coercive legalism in South Africa. He implies that South Africa has got itself caught in a malaise where coercion leads to further coercion and the situation grows ever more tense. This may well be the case, and it is a most interesting hypothesis. In part, however, his evaluation seems to have its roots in an earlier assumption of his that deprivation in society, when coupled with hopelessness, necessarily leads to greater intractability among people, creating the impetus for more coercion. If this is the case, why is it that black people in the United States chose a period in American history when coercion had somewhat eased to resort to violence? Why, in 1967, for example, did we have serious riots in the black slums when opportunities—though limited—were greater than in the past, and when the United States had begun to take some hesitant steps toward a more equal society? And why did the riots occur in the North, when the conditions of servitude were more severe in the South?

I would suggest that there is not necessarily a causal relationship between the twin factors of deprivation and hopelessness and the existence of a so-called dangerous class, but that there is a very significant relationship between *expectations* and problems of disorder. I am not a disciple of Eric Hoffer, but I think there is some truth in his assertion that:

> Where people toil from sunrise to sunset for a bare living, they nurse no grievances and dream no dreams. . . . The intensified struggle for existence "is a static rather than a dynamic influence" . . . . The poor on the borderline of starvation live purposeful lives. . . . Every meal is a fulfilment; to go to sleep with a full stomach is a triumph; and every windfall a miracle. . . . Discontent is likely to be highest . . . when conditions have so improved that an ideal state seems almost within reach.[1]

Indeed, it seems to me that situations of extreme deprivation can be accepted in a society, either because nothing else is known, or because the coercion necessary for acceptance has endured for so long that the oppressed have lost faith in their ability to bring about change.

In summary, I disagree with what appear to be some of Dr. Turk's assumptions—not an unusual phenomenon in the scholarly world. But more seriously, I question his basic formulations, though they are stated in a very scholarly fashion. I do not find that they help us in the search for clearer ways of organizing and understanding phenomena.

Couldn't one, for instance, evaluate the limits and effectiveness of coercion more simply with such factors as the following in mind:

1. The strength of those doing the coercing—numbers, kinds of military equipment, organization, etc.
2. The attitudes of those doing the coercing—which would be a result of their moral and ethical values, sense of fear, and so on
3. Strength of those being coerced
4. Attitudes of those being coerced—value system
5. Danger of outside intervention—extent and kind

---

1. Eric Hoffer, *The True Believer: Thoughts on the Nature of Mass Movements* (New York: Harper and Row, 1951), pp. 32-33.

Applying this, one might have the following scenario where the apparent increase in coercion in South Africa does not necessarily imply the demise of the present structure of power in the foreseeable future.

1. The strength of those committing coercion increases, permitting the application of even further coercion.
2. The coercers have the will to apply further coercion, when deemed necessary.
3. Those being coerced lack adequate strength to oppose effectively.
4. The sense of hopelessness among those being coerced increases, with the helpless acceptance of coercion which previously would have seemed unbearable.
5. The level of danger of outside intervention fails to increase perceptibly due to changes in policies of Communist China; unwillingness of the Soviet Union, the United States, and other large powers to become actively involved in efforts to oppose the regime; preoccupation of African countries with internal problems of integration and economic development.

Or one might have other less gloomy scenarios where the limits of coercion are less and/or the effectiveness less. But whatever the scenario, the prime concern of a schema ought to be how it facilitates the ordering and understanding of phenomena—rather than how it exemplifies the ability of scholars to work at a high level of abstraction.

To conclude, I find Dr. Turk's choice of a topic germane and his statistical material highly useful, but his presentation unnecessarily complex, and the linkage between theory and application weak.

7 IMMANUEL WALLERSTEIN

Social Conflict in Post-Independence
Black Africa: The Concepts
of Race and Status-Group Reconsidered

The Theoretical Confusion

Everyone "knows" that something called "racial tensions" exists in South Africa, in the United States, in Great Britain. Some people think it exists in parts of Latin America, in the Caribbean, in various countries of South and Southeast Asia. But is there such a thing as "racial tension" to be found in the independent states of Black Africa? Conversely, everyone "knows" that "tribalism" exists in Black Africa. Is "tribalism" a phenomenon only of Africa or is it also known in industrialized, capitalist states?

The problem arises from some conceptual difficulties. The categories of social strata or social groupings in everyday scientific use are many, overlapping, and unclear. One can find such terms as class, caste, nationality, citizenship, ethnic group, tribe, religion, party, generation, estate, and race. There are no standard definitions—quite the contrary. Few authors even try to put the terms into relation with each other.

Our famous attempt was that of Max Weber who distinguished three basic categories: class, status-group (*stand*), and party (see Weber, 1968:302-307, 385-398, 926-940). One trouble with Weber's categorization is that it is not logically rigorous, but is in many ways constructed out of examples. And he draws these examples largely from 19th century Europe, the European Middle Ages, and classical

A French translation of this paper appears in *Cahiers du CEDAF* 8 (1971): 1-19. The journal is a publication of the Centre d'études et de documentation africaines (CEDAF), Brussels, Belgium.

antiquity. Fair enough for Weber, but for those who deal with the empirical reality of the 20th century non-European world, it may be difficult to find an appropriate reflection in Weber's distinctions. Weber defines class more or less in the Marxist tradition, as a group of persons who relate in similar ways to the economic system. He defines party as a group who are associated together within a corporate group to affect the allocation and exercise of power. Status-group, however, is in many ways a residual category. There seem to be positive criteria, to be sure. Status-groups are primordial[1] groups into which persons are born, fictitious families presumably tied together by loyalties which are not based on calculated goal-oriented associations, groups encrusted with traditional privileges or lack of them, groups which share honor, prestige-rank, and, above all, style of life (often including a common occupation) but which do not necessarily share a common income level or class membership.[2]

Does not the nation, the nation towards which we have "nationalist" sentiments, fit this definition very closely? It would seem so. Yet it is not national affiliation which is usually first thought of when use is made of the concept of status-group. Weber's concept was inspired primarily by medieval estates, a category of rather limited applicability to contemporary Africa. Much of the literature of modern Africa, rather, talks of a "tribe" and/or "ethnic group." Most writers would take "ethnic group" as the most meaningful empirical referent of status-group, and there is no doubt it fits the spirit of Weber's concept. The term *race* is often used, though its relation, in the spirit of

---

1. To use the term added by Shils (cf. Shils, 1957, 130-145). For Shils, primordial qualities are "significant relational" ones, more than just a "function of interaction." Their significance (p. 142) is "ineffable" (cf. Geertz, 1963).

2. Weber's (1968:932) definition emphasizes honor:

> In contrast to classes, *Stände (status-groups)* are normally groups. They are, however, often of an amorphous kind. In contrast to the purely economically determined "class situation," we wish to designate as *status situation* every typical component of the life of man that is determined by a specific, positive or negative, social estimation of *honor*. . . .

> Both propertied and propertyless people can belong to the same status-group, and frequently they do with very tangible consequences. . . .

> In content, status honor is normally expressed by the fact that above all else a specific *style of life* is expected from all those who wish to belong to the circle.

most authors, to status-group is left inexplicit. *Race* is used in studies of Africa primarily with reference to conflicts between white persons of European descent and black persons indigenous to the continent (a third category in some areas being persons coming from or descended from immigrants from the Indian sub-continent). But the term is seldom used to distinguish varieties among the indigenous black population.

Are *race* and *ethnic group* then two different phenomena, or two variations of the same theme? Given the terminological confusion,[3] it might be best to describe first the empirical reality and see what might follow theoretically rather than to lay out in advance a theoretical framework within which to explain the empirical reality.

The Empirical Data: How Many Kinds of Status-Groups?

Precolonial Africa included many societies that were complex and hierarchical. No one has ever estimated what percentage of Africa's land area or population was in such groups, as opposed to segmentary societies, but surely at least two thirds of it was. Some of these states had "estates"—that is, categories of people with hereditary status: nobles, commoners, artisans, slaves, etc. Some of these states had "ethnic groups"—categories of people with separate designations indicating presumed separate ancestry. These were usually the outcome of conquest situations.[4] Many states had, in addition, a recognized category of "noncitizens" or "strangers" (see Skinner, 1963).

3. The French-language literature is even more confusing, since the French word *race* is used by many writers where English writers would use *tribe*.

4. Jean Suret-Canale (1969:112) argues that both phenomena derive from conquest situations, but that for some unexplained reason assimilation proceeds faster in some areas than in others:

> As long as class antagonisms remained almost non-existent within a tribe ... no state superstructure emerged. ... Where class antagonisms developed with the extension of slavery and the creation of a tribal aristocracy, various kinds of states ... emerged ...
>
> When the creation of these states involved the domination and incorporation of other tribal groups, and the creation within the framework of the state of a new cultural and linguistic unity, the vestiges of tribal organization more or less disappeared ... for example, in Zululand. ... It could happen that the division into classes retained the appearance of a tribal conflict: this was the case in the monarchies of the interlacustrian zone of eastern Africa (Rwanda, Burundi, etc.) where the conquerors, the pastoral Tutsi, constituted the aristocracy, dominating the indigenous peasants, the Hutu.

Finally, even the nonhierarchical societies usually had a division of persons according to some specified principle of classification which created a fictitious descent group, often called a "clan" by anthropologists, or according to generation, that is, an "age-set."[5]

The establishment of colonial rule changed none of these categorizations immediately. It did, however, impose at least one new one— that of colonial nationality, which was double or even triple (for example, Nigerian, British West African, British imperial).

In addition, in many instances, religious categories took on a new salience under colonial rule. Christians emerged as a significant subgroup, both within the "tribe"[6] and within the "territory."[7] Although Islam predates European colonial rule almost everywhere, it is probable that Moslems became in many areas a more self-conscious category in counterpoise to Christians. The sudden spread of Islam in some areas seems to indicate this (see Hodgkin, 1962; also Froelich, 1962:chap. III). And everywhere, new "ethnic groups" came into existence.[8] Finally, *race* was a primary category of the colonial world, accounting for political rights, occupational allocation, and income.[9]

The rise of the nationalist movements and the coming of independence created still more categories. Territorial identification—that is, nationalism—became widespread and important. Along with such territorial identification came a new devotion to ethnic identification, often called tribalism. As Elizabeth Colson (1967:205) said,

Probably many youths found their explicit allegiance to particular ethnic traditions at the same time that they made their commitment to African independence. . . . [I]n Africa it has been the school man, the intellectual, who has been most eager to advance his own language and culture and who has seen himself as vulnerable to any advantages given to the language and culture of any other groups within the country.

The economic dilemmas of the educated classes in the postindependence era exacerbated this tendency to "tribalism" (see Wallerstein,

---

5. See the excellent discussion of the social organization of such nonhierarchical societies in Horton (1971).

6. See Busia (1951). Busia describes in some detail the causes and consequences of a Christian-non-Christian split among the Ashanti.

7. Uganda is a prime case, where politics crystallized to some extent along a religious trichotomy: Protestants, Catholics, and Moslems.

8. I have argued this in Wallerstein (1960).

9. This point is argued throughout the works of Georges Balandier and Frantz Fanon.

1971). Finally, nationalism also involved pan-Africanism. That is, there came to be a category of "Africans" corresponding to its opposite, the "Europeans." At first, this dichotomy seemed to correlate with skin color. However, beginning with 1958, Africa as a concept began to include, for many, northern (Arab) Africa (but still did not include white settlers in North, East, or southern Africa).[10]

Independence also intruded one other significant variable: a rather rigid juridical definition of first-class membership in the larger moral community, that of citizenship. The lines drawn by this concept were different not only from those of precolonial Africa but also from those of the colonial era. During the colonial era, for example, a Nigerian could vote in a Gold Coast election, if he had transferred residence, since both territories were part of British West Africa, and the individual was a British subject. After independence, however, although colonial-era federal administrative units often survived as units of national aspiration, membership in them no longer conferred rights of equal participation in each territorial sub-unit, now a sovereign nation-state, as many a politician and civil servant came to learn in the early postindependence years.

It is clear from even the briefest glance at the literature that there is no independent country in Africa in which the indigenous population is not divided into sub-groups which emerge as significant elements in the political divisions of the country. That is to say, "tribal" or ethnic affiliations are linked to political groupings or factions or positions, are often linked to occupational categories, and are surely linked to job allocation. When foreign journalists comment on this, African politicians often deny the truth of such analysis. Such denials, however, as well as the contradictory assertions by outside observers, serve ideological rather than analytic ends. Thus, there are a long list of well-known ethno-political rivalries in African states (for example, Kikuyu versus Luo in Kenya; Bemba versus Lozi in Zambia; Sab versus Samaale in Somalia). In each of these cases, often despite presumed efforts of the government or a nationalist political movement to prevent it, individuals have been aligned and/or mobilized on "tribal" lines for political ends (cf. Rothschild, 1969; Rotberg, 1967; Lewis, 1958).

In some countries, these so-called tribal divisions have been reinforced by some additional factors. In Ethiopia, for example, the divi-

10. Why this came to be so, and what were the consequences of this nonskin-color definition of "African-ness," I have discussed in Wallerstein (1967).

sions between the Amhara or Amhara-Tigre and the Eritreans coincides more or less with a religious division between Christians and Moslems, of which the participants are fully conscious, all the more since such a conflict has a long historical tradition behind it (see Jesman, 1963).

Along the West African coast and into central Africa, there are seven contiguous states (the Ivory Coast, Ghana, Togo, Dahomey, Nigeria, Cameroun, and Central African Republic) through which a continuous horizontal line could be drawn. The peoples to the north and south of this line tend to be opposite in a series of features: savannah versus forest in soil conditions and corresponding large culture-family; Moslem/animist versus Christian/animist in religion; less modern education versus more modern education (largely the result of more Christian missionaries in the southern halves during the colonial era (see Milcent, 1967; also Schwarz, 1968). A similar line might be drawn in Uganda between the non-Bantu, less educated north and the Bantu, more educated (and more Christianized) south (see Hopkins, 1967; also Edel, 1965.)

Further to the north, in the so-called Sudanic belt, an analogous line might be drawn through Mauritania, Mali, Niger, Chad, and Sudan. In the north of Mauritania, Chad, and Sudan, the people are lighter-skinned, Arabized, and Moslem. To the south, they are darker-skinned and Christian/animist. In Mali and Niger, however, those to the south are Moslem, as well. In all these states except the Sudan, those to the north are more likely to be nomadic and less educated. In Mauritania and the Sudan, those to the north are in the majority and in power. In Mali, Niger, and Chad, the reverse is true (see Watson, 1963; Paques, 1967; Shepherd, 1966). Because these cultural distinctions in the Sudanic belt countries correlate with skin-color differences, these divisions are sometimes spoken of as "racial."

There is a further group of countries interesting to note. These are states which existed as political entities in precolonial times and have survived as such through the colonial and postindependence era, and in which there were clear precolonial "tribal" stratification. These are Zanzibar (Arabs and Afro-Shirazis), Rwanda (Tutsi and Hutu), Burundi (Tutsi and Hutu), Madagascar (Merina and others). In all of these cases (except Burundi) the precolonial majoritarian lower stratum has now achieved political top status (see Lofchie, 1963; Kuper, 1970; Ziegler, 1967; Kent, 1962). Where similar precolonial stratification systems existed within larger colonial and postcolonial units, the polit-

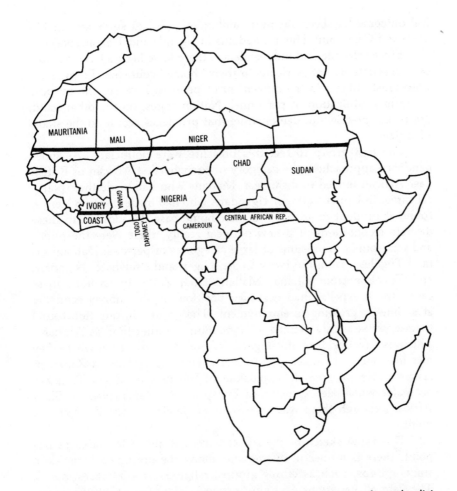

DIVIDING POINTS. Several factors in addition to tribal insularity reinforce the division of Africa's indigenous population into subgroups. A continuous imaginary line drawn through Mauritania, Mali, Niger, Chad, and Sudan indicates for the Sudanic belt a general dividing point. Peoples to the north of the line are lighter-skinned, Arabized, and Moslem; peoples to the south are generally darker-skinned and Christian/animist. A similar line, running from the West Coast into Central Africa through the Ivory Coast, Ghana, Togo, Dahomey, Nigeria, Cameroun, and the Central African Republic, indicates the same sort of division: peoples to the north and south of the line tend toward the opposite in mode of life, culture-family, religion, and education.

ical outcome has been far more ambiguous (Fulani sultanates in Nigeria and Cameroun, Hima kingdoms in Uganda and Tanganyika).

Since self-rule and independence, there have been a large number of "repatriations" of Africans to their "home" countries. Empires are notoriously liberal in the movement of peoples. It serves the purpose of optimal utilization of personnel. Nation-states, on the other hand, are trying precisely to demonstrate that privileges accrue to the status of citizen.

The first group to feel this pressure were politicians. As independence approached, the category of French West African or British East African tended to disappear. Malians who had made their political career in Upper Volta, or Ugandans who had made theirs in Kenya, found it prudent to go back to their home base. In addition to these discrete recognitions of a new political reality, there were the public and semi-public expulsions of large categories of persons: Dahomeans (and Togolese) from the Ivory Coast, Niger, and elsewhere; Nigerians and Togolese from Ghana; Malians from Zaire. In each of these cases, those expelled had occupied positions in the money economy at a time of growing unemployment. The groups in question found themselves suddenly defined as nonnationals rather than as Africans. This was a fortiori true of categories of non-Africans, even where they had in some cases taken out formal citizenship: Arabs in Zanzibar, Asians in Kenya, sporadic expulsions of Lebanese in Ghana. Thus far, no major wholesale expulsion of Europeans has taken place in Black Africa, although there was an exodus of Belgians from Zaire at one point.

This rapid sketch of the African scene is meant to underline one point: there is no useful distinction among the presumed varieties of status-groups, such as ethnic groups, religious groups, races, castes. They are all variations of a single theme: grouping people by an affinity that mythically predates the current economic and political scene and which is a claim to a solidarity overriding those defined in class or ideological terms. As such, they appear, as Akiwowo (1964: 162) says of tribalism, as "a set of patterned responses, adaptive adjustments if you will, to the unanticipated consequences of the processes of nation-building." Or, in the more blunt words of Skinner (1967:173), their central function is "to permit people to organize into social, cultural or political entities able to compete with others for whatever goods and services [are] viewed as valuable in their environment."

Insofar as this function is inherent to the concept, then by definition status-groups cannot exist prior to some larger society of which they are a part, even when groups claim to be organized or to exist in more than one societal system.[11] What Fried (1967:15) states cautiously of "tribes" is true of all status-groups:

"[M]ost tribes seem to be secondary phenomena in a very specific sense: they may well be the product of processes stimulated by the appearance of relatively highly organized societies amidst other societies which are organized much more simply. If this can be demonstrated, tribalism can be viewed as a reaction to the creation of complex political structure rather than as a necessary preliminary stage in its evolution."

In the modern world situation, a status-group is a collective claim to power and allocation of goods and services within a nation-state on grounds that are formally illegitimate.

The Relationship of Class and Status-Group

How then do such claims stand in relation to the claims of class solidarity? Marx, in using the concept of class, distinguished between classes *an sich* and *für sich*. Weber (1968:930) repeated this distinction when he said: "Thus every class may be the carrier of any one of the innumerable possible forms of class action, but this is not necessarily so. In any case, a class does not in itself constitute a group *(Gemeinschaft)*."

Why is it that classes are not always *für sich*? Indeed, why is it they are so seldom *für sich*? Or to put the question another way, how do we explain that status-group consciousness is so pervasive and powerful a political force, in Africa and throughout the world, today and throughout history? To answer that it is false consciousness is simply to push the question one step logically back, for then we

11. Cf. Weber (1968:939):
    [W]e should add one more general observation about classes, status groups and parties: the fact that they presuppose a larger association, especially the framework of a polity, does not mean that they are confined to it. On the contrary, at all times it has been the order of the day that such association . . . reaches beyond the state boundaries. . . . But their aim is not necessarily the establishment of a new territorial dominion. In the main they aim to influence the existing polity.
Except, I should add, insofar as one considers loyalty to a nation-state in a world-system as an expression of status-group consciousness.

should have to ask how it is that most people most of the time exhibit
false consciousness?

Weber (1968:938) has a theory to account for this. He states:

As to the general economic conditions making for the predominance of
stratification by status, only the following can be said. When the bases of the
acquisition and distribution of goods are relatively stable, stratification by
status is favored. Every technological repercussion and economic
transformation threatens stratification by status and pushes the class situation
into the foreground. Epochs and countries in which the naked class situation
is of predominant significance are regularly the periods of technical
and economic transformations. And every slowing down of the change
in economic stratification leads, in due course, to the growth of status
structure and makes for a resuscitation of the important role of social honor.

Weber's explanation seems very simple and makes class consciousness
the correlate of progress and social change, stratification by status the
expression of retrograde forces—a sort of vulgar Marxism. While one
may agree with the moral thrust of the theorem, it is not very predic-
tive of the smaller shifts in historical reality nor does it explain why
one can find modern economic thrusts in status-group garb (see Favret,
1967), as well as mechanisms of the preservation of traditional privilege in class consciousness (see Geertz, 1967).

Favret (1967:73) gives us a clue in her discussion of a Berber
rebellion in Algeria:

[In Algeria] primordial groups do not exist substantively, unaware of their
archaism, but reactively. The anthropologist tempted by collecting
traditional political phenomena is in danger therefore of a colossal
misunderstanding in interpreting them naively, for their context is today
inverted. The choice for the descendants of the segmentary tribes of the
nineteenth century is no longer among ends—to co-operate with the central
government or to institutionalize dissidence—for only the former choice is
henceforth possible. The choice—or the fate—of the peasants of the
underdeveloped agricultural sector is in the means of attaining this end;
among which, paradoxically, is dissidence.

Favret pushes us to look at claims based on status-group affiliation not
in the intellectual terms of the actors in the situation, but in terms of
the actual functions such claims perform in the social system. Moerman makes a similar appeal in an analysis of the Lue, a tribe in
Thailand, about whom he asks three trenchant questions: What are
the Lue? Why are the Lue? When are the Lue? He concludes (1967:
167):

Ethnic identification devices—with their important potential of making each ethnic set of living persons a joint enterprise with countless generations of unexamined history—seem to be universal. Social scientists should therefore describe and analyze the ways in which they are used, and not merely—as natives do—use them as explanations. . . . It is quite possible that ethnic categories are rarely appropriate subjects for the interesting human predicates.

Perhaps then we could reconceive the Weberian trinity of class, status-group, and party not as three different and cross-cutting groups but as three different existential forms of the same essential reality. In which case, the question shifts from Weber's one of the conditions under which stratification by status takes precedence over class consciousness to the conditions under which a stratum embodies itself as a class, as a status-group, or as a party. For such a conceptualization, it would not be necessary to argue that the boundary lines of the group in its successive embodiments would be identical—quite the contrary, or there would be no function to having different outer clothing—but rather that there exist a limited set of groups in any social structure at any given time in relation to, in conflict with, each other.

One approach, suggested by Rodolfo Stavenhagen, is to see status-groups as "fossils" of social classes. He argues (1962:99-101) that:

Stratifications [i.e., status-groups] represent, in the majority of cases, what we call social *fixations*, frequently by juridical means, certainly subjectively, of specific social relations of production, represented by class relations. Into these social *fixations* intrude other secondary, accessory factors (for example, religious, ethnic) which reinforce the stratification and which have, at the same time, the function of "liberating" it of its links with its economic base; in other words, of maintaining its strength even if its economic base changes. Consequently, stratifications can be thought of as justifications or rationalizations of the established economic system, that is to say, as ideologies. Like all phenomena of the social superstructure, stratification has a quality of inertia which maintains it even when the conditions which gave it birth have changed. As the relations between classes are modified . . . stratifications turn themselves into *fossils* of the class relations on which they were originally based . . . [Furthermore], it seems that the two types of groupings (dominant class and higher stratum) can coexist for some time and be encrusted in the social structure, according to the particular historical circumstances. But sooner or later a new stratification system arises which corresponds more exactly to the current class system.

In a later analysis, using Central American data, Stavenhagen spells out how, in a colonial situation, two castelike lower status-groups (in that case, *indios* and *ladinos*) could emerge, become encrusted, and survive the various pressures at what he called class clarification. He argues that two forms of dependence (a colonial form, based on ethnic discrimination and political subordination) and a class form (based on work relations) grew up side by side and reflected a parallel ranking system. After independence, and despite economic development, the dichotomy between *indios* and *ladinos*, "profoundly ensconced in the values of the members of society" remained, as "an essentially conservative force" in the social structure. "Reflecting a situation of the past . . . [this dichotomy] acts as a constraint on the development of the new class relations" (1963:94). In this version, present stratification is still a fossil of the past, but it is not so simply a fossil of class relations per se.

Another approach would be to see class or status-affiliation as options open to various members of the society. This is the approach of Peter Carstens. In two recent papers, one by Carstens (1970) and one by Allen (1970), there is agreement that Africans working on the land in the rural areas should be thought of as "peasants" who are members of the "working class," that is who sell their labor power even when they are technically self-employed cash-crop farmers. But while Allen is concerned with emphasizing the pattern of tied alternation between cash-crop farming and wage-earning,[12] Carstens is more concerned with explaining the status-group apparatus of peasant class organization, or what he calls "peasant status systems."

Carstens (1970:9) starts with the argument that "the retention or revival of tenuous tribal loyalties are resources available to persons to establish prestige or esteem." He reminds us (1970:10) that "the same institutions that effected the hidden force that produced a peasant *class*, also created peasant *status* systems. For example . . . the

---

12. "Wage-earners experience fluctuations in their living standards and employment whereas the peasant producers experience fluctuations in their living standards and the intensity of work. A depression in the living standards of wage-earners or in increase in unemployment, however, produces a movement of labour back to peasant production or is borne because the resources of peasant production exist as an insurance cover" (Allen, 1970). Cf. a similar argument made by Arrighi (1969). An English version under the title "Labour Supplies in Historical Perspective: A Study of the Proletarianization of the African Peasantry in Rhodesia" will appear in a forthcoming volume: Giovanni Arrighi and John S. Saul, Ideology and Development: Essays on the Political Economy of Africa (Nairobi: East African Publishing House).

surest way to achieve recognition, prestige, and esteem in the eyes of the ruling class as well as from the local peasants is to participate in the externally imposed educational and religious institutions." It therefore follows that "it is only by the manipulation of their internal status systems that they are able to gain access to other status systems which are located in the higher class. The strategy of status manipulation is best seen then as a means for crossing class boundaries" (1970:8).

The strength of stratification by status can be seen in this light. Status honor is not only a mechanism for the achievers of yore to maintain their advantages in the contemporary market, the retrograde force described by Weber; it is also the mechanism whereby the upward-strivers obtain their ends within the system (hence the correlation of high ethnic consciousness and education, to which Colson called attention). With support from two such important groups, the ideological primacy of status-group is easy to understand. It takes an unusual organizational situation to break through this combination of elements interested in preserving this veil (or this reality—it makes no difference).

Weber was wrong. Class consciousness does not come to the fore when technological change or social transformation is occurring. All of modern history gives this the lie. Class consciousness only comes to the fore in a far rarer circumstance, in a "revolutionary" situation, of which class consciousness is both the ideological expression and the ideological pillar. In this sense, the basic Marxian conceptual instinct was correct.

The African Data Reanalyzed

Let us now return to the empirical reality of contemporary independent Africa in the light of this theoretical excursus. Independent Black Africa is today composed of a series of nation-states, members of the United Nations, almost none of which can be considered a national society, in the sense of having a relatively autonomous and centralized polity, economy, and culture. All of these states are part of the world social system and most are well integrated into particular imperial economic networks. Their economic outlines are basically similar. The majority of the population works on the land, producing both crops for a world market and food for their subsistence. Most are workers, either in the sense of receiving wages from the owner of the land or in the sense of being self-employed in a situation in which they are obliged to earn cash (and see farming as an economic alternative to other kinds of wage employment). There are others who work as laborers in urban areas, often as part of a pattern of circulatory migration.

In each country, working for the most part for the government, there is a bureaucratic class which is educated and seeking to transform some of their wealth into property. In every case, there are certain groups (one or several) who are disproportionately represented in the bureaucratic class, as there are other groups disproportionately represented among urban laborers. Almost everywhere, a group of whites lives, holding high status and filling technical positions. Their prestige-rank has scarcely changed since colonial rule. The local high rank of whites reflects the position of these countries in the world economic system where they are "proletarian" nations, suffering the effects of "unequal exchange."[13]

The degree of political autonomy represented by formal sovereignty enabled the local elites or elite groups to seek their upward mobility in the world-system by a rapid expansion of the educational system of their countries. What is individually functional in terms of the world-system is collectively dysfunctional. The workings of the world-system do not provide sufficient job outlets at the national level. This forces elite groups to find criteria by which to reward parts of themselves and to reject others. The particular lines of division are arbitrary and changeable in details. In some places, the division is along ethnic lines; in others, along religious; in others, along racial lines; in most, in some implicit combination of all of these.

These status-group tensions are the inefficacious and self-defeating expression of class frustrations. They are the daily stuff of contemporary African politics and social life. The journalists, who are usually closer to popular perceptions than the social scientists, tend to call this phenomenon "tribalism" when they write of Black Africa. Tribal, or ethnic, conflicts are very real things, as the civil wars in the Sudan and Nigeria attest most eloquently. They are ethnic conflicts in the sense that persons involved in these conflicts are commonly motivated by analyses which use ethnic (or comparable status-group) categories; furthermore, they usually exhibit strong ethnic loyalties. Nonetheless, behind the ethnic "reality" lies a class conflict, not very far from the surface. By this I mean the following straightforward and

13. For an elaboration of the concept and an explanation of its social consequences, see Emanuel (1969).

empirically testable proposition (not one, however, that has been definitively so tested): were the class differences that correlate (or coincide) with the status-group differences to disappear, as a result of changing social circumstances, the status-group conflicts would eventually disappear (no doubt to be replaced by others). The status-group loyalties are binding and affective, in a way that it seems difficult for class loyalties to be other than in moments of crisis, but they are also more transient from the perspective of the analyst. If the society were to become ethnically "integrated," class antagonisms would not abate; the opposite in fact is true. One of the functions of the network of status-group affiliations is to conceal the realities of class differentials. To the extent, however, that particular class antagonisms or differentials abate or disappear, status-group antagonisms (if not differentials, but even differentials) also abate and disappear.

The Usefulness of the Concept of Race

In Black Africa, one speaks of "ethnic" conflict. In the United States or in South Africa, one speaks of "racial" conflict. Is there any point in having a special word, *race*, to describe status-groupings that are the most salient in some countries but not in others (like Black African states)? If we were to regard each national case as discrete and logically separate, there would not be, since stratification by status serves the same purpose in each.

But the national cases are not discrete and logically separate. They are part of a world-system. Status and prestige in the national system cannot be divorced from status and rank in the world-system, as we have already mentioned in discussing the role of expatriate white Europeans in Black Africa today. There are international status-groups as well as national ones. What we mean by race is essentially such an international status-group. There is a basic division between whites and nonwhites. (Of course, there are varieties of nonwhites, and the categorization differs according to time and place. One grouping is by skin color but it is not in fact very prevalent. Another more common one is by continent, although the Arabs often lay claim to being counted separately.)

In terms of this international dichotomy, skin color is irrelevant. "White" and "nonwhite" have very little to do with skin color. "What is a black? And first of all, what color is he?" asked Jean Genêt. When Africans deny, as most do deny, that the conflict between the lighter-skinned Arabs of northern Sudan and the dark-skinned Nilotes of southern Sudan is a racial conflict, they are not being hypocritical. They are reserving the term *race* for a particular international social tension. It is not that the conflict in the Sudan is not real and is not expressed in status-group terms. It is. But it is a conflict which, though formally similar to, is politically different from, that between blacks and whites in the United States, or Africans and Europeans in South Africa. The political difference lies in its meaning in and for the world-system.

Race is, in the contemporary world, the only international status-group category. It has replaced religion, which played that role since at least the eighth century A.D. Rank in this system, rather than color, determines membership in the status-group. Thus, in Trinidad, there can be a "Black Power" movement, directed against an all-black government, on the grounds that this government functions as an ally of North American imperialism. Thus, Quebec separatists can call themselves the "white Niggers" of North America. Thus, pan-Africanism can include white-skinned Arabs of North Africa, but exclude white-skinned Afrikaners of South Africa. Thus, Cyprus and Yugoslavia can be invited to tri-continental conferences (Asia, Africa, and Latin America) but Israel and Japan are excluded. As a status-group category, race is a blurred collective representation for an international class category, that of the proletarian nations. Racism, therefore, is simply the act of maintaining the existing international social structure, and is not a neologism for racial discrimination. It is not that they are separate phenomena. Racism obviously utilizes discrimination as part of its armory of tactics, a central weapon, to be sure. But there are many possible situations in which there can be racism without discrimination, in any immediate sense. Perhaps there can even be discrimination without racism, though this seems harder. What is important to see is that these concepts refer to actions at different levels of social organization: racism refers to action within the world arena; discrimination refers to actions within relatively small-scale social organizations.

Summary

In summary, my main point is that status-groups (as well as parties) are blurred collective representation of classes. The blurred (and hence incorrect) lines serve the interests of many different elements in most social situations. As social conflict becomes more acute, status-group lines approach class lines asymptotically, at which point we may see the phenomenon of "class consciousness." But the asymptote is never reached. Indeed, it is almost as though there were a magnetic field around the asymptote which pushed the approaching curve away. Race, finally, is a particular form of status-group in the contemporary world, the one which indicates rank in the world social system. In this sense, there are no racial tensions today within independent Black African states. One of the expressions of national identity, however, as it will be achieved, will be increasing international status-group consciousness, or racial identification, which would then only be overcome or surpassed as one approached the asymptote of international class consciousness.

REFERENCES

Akiwowo, Akinsola A.
    1964   "The Sociology of Nigerian Tribalism. Phylon XXV, 2 (Summer): 155-163.
Allen, V. L.
    1970   "The Meaning and Differentiation of the Working Class in Tropical Africa. Presented at the Seventh World Congress of Sociology, Varna, Bulgaria, September 13-19.
Arrighi, Giovanni.
    1969   "L'offertà di lavoro in una perspettiva storica." In Sviluppo economico e sovrastrutture in Africa, pp. 89-162. Torino: Einaudi.
Arrighi, Giovanni, and John S. Saul.
    Forthcoming   Ideology and Development: Essays on the Political Economy of Africa. Nairobi: East African Publishing House.
Busia, K. A.
    1951   The Position of the Chief in the Modern Political System of Ashanti. London: Oxford University Press.
Carstens, Peter.
    1970   "Problems of Peasantry and Social Class in Southern Africa." Presented at the Seventh World Congress of Sociology, Varna, Bulgaria, September 13-19.
Colson, Elizabeth.
    1967   "Contemporary Tribes and the Development of Nationalism." In Essays on the Problem of Tribe, edited by June Helm, pp. 201-206. Proceedings of 1967 Annual Spring Meeting of the American Ethnological Society.

Edel, May.
    1965   "African Tribalism: Some Reflections on Uganda" Political
            Science Quarterly LXXX, 3 (September):357-372.
Emanuel, Arghiri.
    1969   L'échange inégal. Paris: Maspéro.
Favret, Jeanne.
    1967   "Le traditionalisme par excès de modernité." Archives europé-
            ennes de sociologie VIII, 1:71-93.
Fried, Morton H.
    1967   "On the Concept of 'Tribe' and 'Tribal Society'." In Essays on
            the Problem of Tribe, edited by June Helm, pp. 3-20. Proceedings
            of 1967 Annual Spring Meeting of the American Ethnological So-
            ciety.
Froelich, J.-C.
    1962   Les musulmans d'Afrique Noire. Paris: Ed. de l'Orante.
Geertz, Clifford.
    1963   "The Integrative Revolution, Primordial Sentiments and Civil Pol-
            itics in the New States." In Old Societies and New States, edited
            by C. Geertz, pp. 105-157. Glencoe: Free Press.
    1967   "Politics Past, Politics Present." Archives européennes de socio-
            logie VIII, 1:1-14.
Hodgkin, Thomas.
    1962   "Islam and National Movements in West Africa." Journal of Afri-
            can History III, 1:323-327.
Hopkins, Terence K.
    1967   "Politics in Uganda: the Buganda Question." In Boston Univer-
            sity Papers on Africa: Transition in African Politics, edited by
            J. Butler and A. A. Castagno, Jr., pp. 251-290. New York: Praeger.
Horton, Robin.
    1971   "Stateless Societies in the History of West Africa." In A History
            of West Africa, vol. I, edited by J. F. A. Ajayi and M. Crowder.
            London: Longmans.
Jesman, Czeslaw.
    1963   The Ethiopian Paradox. London: Oxford University Press.
Kent, Raymond K.
    1962   From Madagascar to the Malagasy Republic. New York: Praeger.
Kuper, Leo.
    1970   "Continuities and Discontinuities in Race Relations: Evolutionary
            or Revolutionary Change." Cahiers d'études africaines X, 3, no.
            39:361-383.
Lewis, I. M.
    1958   "Modern Political Movements in Somaliland." Africa XXVIII, 3
            (July 1958):244-261; XXVIII, 4 (October):344-363.
Lofchie, Michael.
    1963   "Party Conflict in Zanzibar." Journal of Modern African Studies
            I, 2:185-207.

Milcent, Ernest.
 1967 "Tribalisme et vie politique dans les Etats du Bénin." Revue française d'études politiques africaines, No. 18 (Juin):37-53.
Moerman, Michael.
 1967 "Being Lue: Uses and Abuses of Ethnic Identification." In Essays on the Problem of Tribe, edited by June Helm, 153-169. Proceedings of 1967 Annual Spring Meeting of the American Ethnological Society.
Paques, Viviana.
 1967 "Alcuni problemi umani posti dallo sviluppo economico e sociale: Il case della Repubblica del Ciad." Il Nuovo Osservatore, n.s. VIII, 63 (giugno):580-584.
Rotberg, Robert I.
 1967 "Tribalism and Politics in Zambia." Africa Report 12, 9 (December):29-35.
Rothschild, Donald.
 1969 "Ethnic Inequalities in Kenya." Journal of Modern African Studies VII, 4:689-711.
Schwarz, Walter.
 1968 Nigeria. London: Pall Mall Press.
Shepherd, George W., Jr.
 1966 "National Integration and the Southern Sudan." Journal of Modern African Studies. IV, 2:193-212.
Shils, Edward.
 1957 "Primordial, Personal, Sacred and Civil Ties." British Journal of Sociology VIII, 2 (June):130-145.
Skinner, Elliott P.
 1963 "Strangers in West African Societies." Africa XXXIII, 4, (October):307-320.
 1967 "Group Dynamics in the Politics of Changing Societies: The Problem of 'Tribal' Politics in Africa." In Essays on the Problem of Tribe, edited by June Helm, pp. 170-185. Proceedings of 1967 Annual Spring Meeting of the American Ethnological Society.
Stavenhagen, Rodolfo.
 1962 "Estratificación social y estructura de clases (un ensayo de interpretación)." Ciencias políticas y sociales VIII, 27 (enero-marzo): 173-102.
 1963 "Clases, colonialismo y aculturación: ensayo sobre un sistema de relaciones interétnicas en Mesoamérica." América Latina VI, 4 (outubro-dezembro):63-103.
Suret-Canale, Jean.
 1969 "Tribus, classes, nations." La Nouvelle revue internationale, No. 130 (juin):110-124.
Wallerstein, Immanuel.
 1960 "Ethnicity and National Integration in West Africa." Cahiers d'études africaines, No. 3 (October):129-139.

1967   Africa: The Politics of Unity. New York: Random House.
1971   "The Range of Choice: Constraints on the Policies of Governments of Contemporary African Independent States." In The State of the Nations, edited by Michael F. Lofchie, pp. 19-33. Berkeley: the University of California Press.
Watson, J. H. A.
1963   "Mauritania: Problems and Prospects." Africa Report 8, 2 (February):3-6.
Weber, Max.
1968   Economy and Society. 3 vols. New York: Bedminster Press.
Ziegler, Jean.
1967   "Structures ethniques et partis politiques au Burundi." Revue française d'études politiques africaines, No. 18 (juin):54-68.

8 MILTON J. ESMAN

Malaysia: Communal Coexistence and Mutual Deterrence

MALAYSIA IS a polycommunal state. By "communal," we refer to solidary groups based on such primordial attachments as race, religion, ethnicity, or language. Malaysia's diverse communal composition by geographic distribution is indicated on Table 1. The most salient cleavage, especially in West Malaysia, is between Malays (50 percent of the total) and Chinese (36 percent).[1] The achievement and maintenance of peaceful coexistence among these improbable partners is the key problem in Malaysia's politics.

The major societal structures in Malaysia are communally organized:

Identity. People identify themselves and are identified by others according to communal categories. Malays identify themselves by the re-enforcing properties of race, religion (Muslim), language, and a distinctive life style. Chinese maintain a strong racial identity linked to a proud and enduring cultural tradition. The pride of each community in its own institutions and traditions is more than matched by unflattering and suspicious views of the other. Malays caricature Chinese as avaricious and materialistic, morally unscrupulous, ritually (pork-eating) and physically unclean, crude in their manners, and of dubious loyalty to Malaysia, while according them grudging respect

---

1. Throughout Malaysia, Malay-Muslims are 46%, Chinese 36%.

for hard work and business skills. Chinese regard Malays as lazy, superstitious, backward, and prone to subsist on government hand-outs. Aside from formal economic and administrative exchanges, there is little communication or social interaction among members of these two communities. A high degree of civility accompanies these ex-

TABLE I
MALAYSIAN POPULATION STATISTICS
ESTIMATED POPULATION BY STATE AND RACE AT 31 DECEMBER 1967

State	ALL RACES	MALAYS	CHINESE	INDIANS AND PAKISTANIS	OTHERS[b]
Johore	1,316,772	654,936	532,083	98,434	31,319
Kedah	936,825	635,287	139,007	88,888	23,643
Kelantan	684,554	626,640	38,033	8,171	11,710
Malacca	416,795	210,639	164,213	33,745	8,198
Negri Sembilan	517,451	219,598	206,989	78,120	12,744
Pahang	431,747	246,069	148,398	31,823	5,457
Penang	761,194	219,937	433,925	90,871	16,461
Perak	1,656,985	666,285	721,944	242,510	26,246
Perlis	118,987	91,606	21,395	2,167	3,819
Selangor	1,431,707	426,889	678,311	278,476	48,031
Trengganu	382,282	353,135	23,125	4,739	1,283
West Malaysia	8,655,299	4,351,021	3,157,423	957,944	188,911
Sabah	590,660	145,000[a]	145,000[a]	—	300,660
Sarawak	902,841	163,022	296,977	—	442,842
ALL MALAYSIA	10,148,800	4,659,043	3,599,400	957,944	932,413

SOURCE: Malaysian Government Statistics Bulletin. 6 November 1968.
a: Crude estimate by author
b: Others include Eurasians, Kadazans, Melanaus, Ibans, Land Dayaks, but not aborigines, who are listed with Malays.

changes and interactions, but the underlying social distance approaches infinity. Except for a small group of intellectuals and government officials, they maintain distinctive lifestyles in separate residential en-claves. The perceptions of difference which pervade both communities are re-enforced by suspicion and distrust which achieve a visceral quality. Seldom have two peoples with so little in common been fated to share the same territory and participate in the same political system.

The development of a synthetic "Malaysian" national identity would be a dubious prospect, even over an extended period of time, so long as mutually hostile communal identities maintain their salience.

Malaya, the predecessor of Malaysia, became an independent state only in 1957. The national identity is thus unfamiliar, shallow, and somewhat artificial to members of both communities except in their relations with foreigners. It is emotionally empty to Chinese and other non-Malays because all the official symbols of the state—the Malay king, the Malay language, the Islamic religion—draw exclusively from Malay culture. They contain not a single symbol drawn from the traditions of any of the non-Malay peoples which could grip them emotionally.

Economy. The urban areas are predominantly Chinese. The modern sectors of the economy are owned, controlled, and staffed by expatriate (mostly British) firms or by Chinese. Locally owned rubber and palm oil plantations, mines, banks, factories, construction and transportation firms, large and petty commerce, rural shopkeeping, money-lending, processing, marketing, professions, and skilled labor are overwhelmingly Chinese. Very few Malays work in Chinese-owned enterprises, which are Chinese social systems. Because of their superior skills and business experience, most of the local managerial, professional, clerical, technical, and other skilled employees in foreign-owned enterprises are also Chinese. Except for public employment which will be discussed below, Malays work primarily in subsistence agriculture and fishing and in less skilled urban occupations. While there are vast disparities in income distribution within both communities, it has been estimated that average per capita income for Chinese is two and a half times that of Malays (Silcock, 1963:276-281). This is a classical symptom of urban-rural dualism, compounded by the entrepreneurial, managerial, and technological gaps between the two communities.

Education and Technology. The educational system reflects and re-enforces the prevailing communal pluralism. Elementary education is provided in four separate streams, all governmentally financed and operated, according to the language of instruction—Malay, Chinese, Tamil, and English. At the secondary level, these are collapsed into two governmentally supported streams, Malay and English, but there are a few Chinese language "nonconforming" secondary schools operating without government assistance. Higher education has been entirely in English. In fulfillment of its national (Malay) language policy, the government has initiated the gradual elimination of instruction in non-Malay languages and has founded a new national university, teaching exclusively in the Malay language, while refusing to establish a Chinese medium university.

Educationally and technologically, Chinese are far ahead of Malays, and the gap appears to be widening. In 1967, Malays comprised only 2, 7, and 14 percent respectively of students in the faculties of engineering, science, and medicine in the University of Malaya (University of Malaya, 1966-67). In the College of Technology at Kuala Lumpur, they were less than 10 percent. This imbalance reflects the neglect of Malay education during the colonial period, the greater urbanization of the Chinese, and the differential value systems and socialization processes in the two communities. While the government is making strenuous efforts to overcome this imbalance, it cannot be a rapid process.

Political. Political parties are communally organized. The dominant Malay group is the United Malay National Organization (UMNO). It faces significant opposition from the Pan-Malayan Islamic party (PMIP) which espouses religious orthodoxy, favors closer association with Indonesia, purports to speak for Malay "have nots," and rejects the present role of Chinese in Malaysian society. There is also a very small Malay Marxist party, the Parti Rakyat. Until recently, the leading Chinese party has been the conservative Malayan Chinese Association (MCA), which accepts Malay political hegemony in exchange for the protection of basic Chinese political and cultural rights and continued economic opportunity. There are three parties led by middle-class intellectuals which espouse noncommunalism, but their leadership, cadres, and popular support are almost entirely non-Malay and predominantly Chinese.[2] The Labor party (LP) is the legal expression of the underground Malayan Communist party which carried out the costly and extended 1948-1960 insurrection. While its ideology is Marxian, there is a strong element of Chinese chauvinism in its appeal, and its support is almost entirely Chinese.

After a few abortive attempts to organize politics along noncommunal lines in the early 1950s, the Malayan elites evolved the "Alliance" formula. This was a political coalition of three communal parties —the aforementioned United Malay National Organization, Malayan Chinese Association, and the smaller Malayan Indian Congress. Each of these organizations was dominated by its "natural" leaders or notables

2. These are the Democratic Action Party (DAP), the peninsular offshoot of the dominant Singapore People's Action Party; the Peoples Progressive Party (PPP) regionally based in the West Coast state of Perak; and the Garakan Raayat Malaysia (The Malaysian Peoples Movement) which controls the government of Penang. The Garakan has a few Malays among its leadership and draws some Malay electoral support.

—Malay aristocrats, Chinese capitalists, and Indian merchants.[3] According to the implicit formula that governed this coalition, political demands were to move through these communal channels into the Alliance decision-making structure where they would be broken down and bargained out quietly *in camera*. This would mitigate the tensions and the possible violence inherent in the overt expression and escalation of communal differences. Each party would be sensitive to the legitimate needs of its partners; after apportioning the benefits and costs of government on specific issues through quiet negotiation, the leaders of each party would be required to sell the outcomes to its backbenchers and its constituents and thus to maintain discipline within the Alliance. They would also, of course, be expected to deliver the vote at election time.

The explicit premise of the Alliance system is that Malays control the structures and symbols of government. The king is a Malay sultan, Islam the state religion, Malay the national language. Through the drawing of constituency boundaries in favor of rural areas, Malays would predominate in the Federal Parliament and in the state assemblies and thus hold the key ministerial positions. Malays would be dominant in the military establishment and would be recruited to the administrative class of the civil service at the ratio of four to one. Certain lands would be reserved exclusively for Malays; there would be Malay preferences for scholarships and various licenses for minor business activities. Government would engage in deliberate and special efforts to improve the economic lot of Malay. In return, Chinese would be eligible for citizenship, voting, office holdings and public honors, have full access to the courts, enjoy religious and cultural freedom, participate in continued educational and economic opportunities and, above all, their existing economic stakes would not be abridged by the action of government. To overseas Chinese in Southeast Asia, this was an unprecedentedly attractive package. In effect, the Alliance system confirmed the political and governmental hegemony of the Malays and the economic superiority of the Chinese.

Despite severe strains, this system governed Malaya and later Malaysia peacefully and reasonably effectively from 1955 to 1969. The goodwill, spirit of accommodation, and mutual loyalty of the senior leaders of the three components of the Alliance sufficed to overcome the incompatible demands that frequently agitated their

---

3. For an analysis of these organizations, see Roff (1967); Arasaratnam (1970); and Wang (1970).

rank and file and junior politicians. The Alliance broke down in the
1969 elections because (1) the established parties failed to produce
fresh personalities which could compensate for the accumulated
grievances of nearly fifteen years in office; (2) the opposition parties
formed an effective working agreement; and (3) above all, their constituencies were increasingly convinced that the senior Alliance politicians had become too accommodating to the other community and
were not vigorous enough in promoting the interests of their own
group.

   Other Cleavages.   There are, of course, important cleavages of a
noncommunal character in Malaysian society. There are class tensions
between Malay tenants and landlords, between English-speaking,
westernized Malay officials and ordinary citizens, between Chinese
employers and workers, and between Chinese middle-class intellectuals and the Chinese capitalist "establishment." The severe income
differentials and status stratification in both communities provide
ample opportunities for resentment and class conflict, particularly
among Chinese who are economically more differentiated and retain
little of the traditional deference toward persons of higher status
which still prevails in Malay society. There is increasing criticism
among Malay intellectuals of the behavior of the Malay sultans and
princes. There are regional rivalries and urban-rural tensions among
Malays and frictions among the subethnic and linguistically differentiated Chinese—the Hokkienese, Hainanese, Cantonese, Hakka,
etc. No student of Malaysian politics can disregard these intraethnic
tensions which occasionally explode into political controversy. Yet
these lines of cleavage quickly dissolve and lose their saliency in the
face of intercommunal threats to the perceived common interest of
either group. Repeated efforts to reformulate and redefine the issues
of Malaysian politics in class terms—"haves" versus "have-nots"—
have in every case failed, even though it is widely recognized that
the upper-class personalities who dominate the components of the
Alliance tend frequently to interpret the interests of their community
in terms of their class interests. There are no cross-cutting occupational, economic, or ideological solidary interests or structures that
are important enough to displace or even seriously attentuate these
fundamental communal cleavages and no likelihood that such cross-
cutting interest groups can emerge in the foreseeable future.

   Rhetoric and Doctrine.   The rhetoric and doctrine of politics
tend to re-enforce, rather than mitigate communal cleavages. The
need for understanding, harmony, forbearance, and mutual respect is

the formal doctrine of the Alliance and of all men of good will in Malaysian society. Yet the politically significant slogans which define and enunciate the aspirations of the two communities are extremely abrasive to the other. The "bumiputera" (sons of the soil) doctrine which is articulated by all Malay politicians justifies the Malay claim for political hegemony, a Malay-style political system, special rights and special treatment by government on the premise that Malays are the indigenous people with a superior moral claim on government. To Chinese and other non-Malays, the nativist "bumiputera" slogan condemns them symbolically and materially to discriminatory treatment and to second-class citizenship. It is thus deeply resented, particularly among members of the younger generation born and raised in Malaysia.

Chinese intellectuals and politicians counter with another slogan: "a Malaysian Malaysia," meaning full political equality, equal treatment, and equal competitive opportunities in all spheres of activity for all Malaysians, regardless of race. Malays construe this slogan as a threat to their special position and their political dominance, a means by which the Chinese, invoking the appealing doctrine of equal citizenship and free competition, would use their superior economic and educational resources to encroach further on the few areas of control left to Malays, thus reducing Malays to the level of "red Indians" in their own country.[4] The rhetoric of Malaysian politics contributes far more to communal cleavage than to integration.

Modernization and Communal Cleavages. Social modernization and political independence have intensified communal tensions in Malaysia.[5] With improved communications and the legitimation of political action, Malays have become increasingly aware of a common situation that transcends their kinship and traditional local loyalties and have imputed to the boundary relationships between Malays and Chinese a set of important political meanings. Chinese

4. That this slogan was first popularized by Lee Kwan Yew, Prime Minister of Singapore, during the brief period of Singapore's membership in Malaysia does not contribute to its popularity among Malays. Under the recently enacted Sedition Act intended to diminish communal conflict by placing certain Constitutional provisions that establish Malay hegemony and special rights "out of bounds" for political debate, the "Malaysian Malaysia" slogan may be criminally proscribed. There is no likelihood, however, that the bumiputera slogan will be similarly treated.

5. The relationship between modernization and communal conflict is developed in Eric Nordlinger's forthcoming study, *Conflict Regulation in Divided Societies.* See also Melson and Wolpe (1970).

had been politicized during the harsh period under Japanese rule in World War II and the ensuing insurrection. As Malays mobilized politically under national leadership, it became necessary for Chinese to mobilize responsively under elites who could deal at the emergent national level with the politically dominant Malays. As independence approached, it became clear to the politically aware that government could be a mighty allocator of important values and that the unorganized could expect little in the way of consideration or benefits.

Even more basically in the Malaysian context, members of the two communities began to compete for the same values. So long as groups do not compete for the same values, they can coexist peaceably for an indefinite period of time. So long as the Chinese looked upon themselves as "sojourners" in Malaya, they had only limited and defensive political interests; so long as Malays were satisfied with a traditional subsistence way of life, they had few aspirations to participate in the modern economy. As Chinese became committed to permanent residence in Malaysia, they began to develop and to articulate political needs and interests; with enhanced communications, Malays became increasingly aware of their economic and educational backwardness and interested in participating in and enjoying the material benefits of an exchange economy and modern technology. Thus, political mobilization and modernization brought the two communities into a single arena competing for the same values.[6]

Both groups demand the right to influence and participate in government at the *political* level. The premise of all Malays is secure political hegemony at federal and state levels. Consistent with that premise, the UMNO has been prepared to admit Chinese as junior partners. Their Alliance partners, the MCA, negotiate the number of constituencies in which Chinese can run with Malay support and the number of cabinet-level posts which Chinese can fill. Chinese outside the MCA reject this junior-partner status, claiming on democratic and majoritarian premises full equality of political opportunity for non-Malays who comprise half the population. At the symbolic level Malays insist on full control of the symbols of the polity. While Chinese parties have not openly challenged the existing monopoly of these symbols they are clearly not consistent with the notion of a "Malaysian Malaysia" and are the source of continuous grumbling and occasional demonstrations.

Civil service positions are a major source of employment for the

6. This point was first developed by Kennelm Burridge (1956).

educated middle class and thus an area of intense competition. Government jobs, including school teaching, employ 10 percent of the labor force and 47 percent of the high-level professional and managerial manpower. Chinese complain bitterly of the established four Malays to one non-Malay ratio for recruitment to the administrative class of the civil service which Malays consider a necessary adjunct to their control of government and compensation for Chinese control of the modern economy. This is re-enforced by the difficulties facing Malays in finding employment in foreign-owned and particularly in Chinese-owned enterprises. Because of their educational superiority, however, non-Malays still hold about two thirds of the professional and managerial (Division I) positions in the civil service and similar proportions seem to prevail at the technical and clerical levels. Malays thus claim that the civil service does not perform the same employment function for them that the private sector performs for Chinese. Informal efforts on the part of government to achieve a measure of Malay preference in appointments and promotions are bitterly resented by non-Malays. Malays argue that, in government employment, ratios should not be skewed against them and should at least reflect the racial division of the population.

The communities are competing for scarce and valuable educational opportunities which are the key to individual mobility and to communal economic power. If there are 100 places in the Faculty of Medicine at the University of Malaya, shall these be awarded according to free competition on objective examinations, as they are at present (which benefits the Chinese), or by racial quotas (which would benefit the Malays)? Why should Malays enjoy preference, Chinese ask, for scholarships? But were it not for such preferences, Malays reply, the existing racial gap in educational and technological achievement would widen, not narrow. Is it fair to exclude Chinese from the Malaysian Institute of Technology (MIT), which trains Malays for roles in modern industry and commerce, when there are many poor but deserving Chinese who could benefit from similar training? Pressures from more militant Malays to make Malay the sole medium of instruction at all levels of education is intended not only to ensure a Malay-style polity, but also to benefit Malays in educational and civil service competition. This is so perceived and resented by Chinese. The chronic tensions over the implementation of language policy reflect the differential interests of the two communities.

Malays are no longer willing to be excluded from the modern sectors of the economy and believe they cannot participate in significant numbers without vigorous governmental assistance. Thus, the government presses foreign firms, especially those that benefit from pioneer industry tax benefits, to employ Malays in nonmenial positions, particularly those who are being trained for that purpose in government educational programs. But such governmental initiatives on behalf of Malays tend to be construed by Chinese as a denial of opportunities to them. The most emotional demand from Malay intellectual circles involves the displacement of "exploiting" Chinese middlemen from rural areas. Since there are few Malays with the capital or experience required to perform these intermediary services, they would be replaced by government-supported co-operatives. Thus government would be using its power to destroy existing Chinese economic stakes, a policy which government has, to date, resisted, despite strong demands from more militant Malays, including members of UMNO. The government intends to initiate public sector manufacturing and commercial enterprises, some on a joint-venture basis with foreign companies, to give Malays opportunities and experience in modern management. Demands from the Bumiputera Economic Congress that minimum quotas of import licenses be reserved for Malay firms or that preferences be given to Malay contractors appear to Chinese, both employers and workers, as unfair governmental encroachment on their economic opportunities. Malays argue that they cannot achieve economic parity through individualistic competition, as Chinese advocate, but only through group advancement with government initiative and support—which Chinese consider both discriminatory treatment and a threat to their economic interests.

One resource for which both groups are competing is land, particularly agricultural land. This applies both to small holders and commercial estates. Land, constitutionally, is reserved to state governments controlled by Malays. It has been virtually impossible for Chinese small holders, though they are starved for land as their numbers increase, to acquire land from state governments even where it is still available in the public domain. The federal land development schemes which provide supervised plots on a modified plantation pattern are not open to Chinese. Despite a federal policy to open up land for commercial estate development to the private sector for export crops in order to increase employment, tax revenues, and export earnings, the private sector, which happens to be primarily Chinese, has been largely unsuccessful in getting land. Malay politicians do not see enough benefit to Malays in long-term leases to Chinese and, in

effect, prefer to maintain this land unused as part of the Malay patrimony than to release it to Chinese for economic development. As
one Malay politician observed: "When the Chinese share their factories and banks with us, we will share our land with them." Some
Chinese groups succeed in avoiding this impasse by "Ali-Baba" arrangements, in which the land is released to a Malay who for a fee
or a percentage of earnings turns it over to Chinese for management.
Members of state royal families and leading politicians often participate in these profitable arrangements.

Polarization. The polarization of the two communities as they
mobilize socially and politically and compete for the same values has
raised political tensions to the breaking point. It has made Malaysia,
one of the most affluent of the Third World countries, a conflict-prone
society. Any public problem or policy choice, however innocuous on
the surface, may have communal implications, some quite obvious,
others nearly impossible to predict. There have been serious riots: in
Singapore (1964), which contributed to the separation of Singapore
from Malaysia a year later; in Penang (1967), ostensibly over an issue
of monetary policy which no politician could have anticipated would
result in a communal outbreak; and most seriously of all, in Kuala
Lumpur (1969), resulting in the suspension of parliamentary government.[7] The violence usually occurs in urban areas where density
of settlement, the breakdown of traditional social controls, and overt
competition for similar values create a propensity for conflict. While
conflict might erupt from the frustration of expectations—stagnant
rural incomes, urban unemployment, failure of Malays to break into
the modern economy or of Chinese to achieve equal political participation—the manifest basis of conflict seems to inhere in fears that
existing stakes are being threatened by the actions of the other community. Malay anxieties that the outcome of the 1969 elections was
threatening Malay control of two important state governments and
of the federal government as well were an important precipitator of
the May 1969 riots. Chinese would be inclined to fight if they believed
their existing economic, educational, or cultural positions were being
seriously jeopardized by the action of government. In an atmosphere
of pervasive scarcity re-enforced by mutual distrust, the more fundamental motivations of both groups seem to be defensive. Groups are

7. For two Malay-oriented accounts of the May 1969 riots, see Rahman (1969) and
The National Operations Council (1969). For an opposite interpretation, see Slimming
(1969).

more inclined to react defensively to perceived threats to their existing stakes than to frustrated aspirations. In a culture of poverty,
they are least likely to look for ways to expand available values and
solve problems by an equitable distribution of the increments.[8]

The prevailing distrust and defensive psychology is exacerbated
by the rhetoric and styles of the emergent generation of politicians in
both communities. The patrician political leaders of both wings of the
Alliance who negotiated the terms of independence with the British
and guided the Alliance for its first decade and a half in office were
moderate in speech and in action, inclined to mutual accommodation,
and skilled in the arts of compromise and give and take. This very
moderation contributed to the Alliance's electoral setback in 1969,
senior UMNO and MCA politicians both being vulnerable to charges
from within their own communities of being insufficiently vigorous
in the pursuit of communal interests and too solicitous of the interests
of the other group. The more articulate younger politicians in both
camps demonstrate, at least in their rhetoric, a much more strident
and uncompromising assertion of communal claims and are mobil-
izing support and building their political reputations along these lines.
As political leadership in each community is increasingly drawn from
less patrician strata and becomes more representative of its constituency, it is likely to become more militant in its definition of communal
interests, less autonomous, less able to resist communal pressures,
and less inclined to intercommunal accommodation and compromise.
This is likely to re-enforce other factors contributing to polarization
and to intensifying an already dangerous propensity for conflict.

The Future is Plural. From this description of the structures and
dynamics of communal relations in contemporary Malaysia, it is
clear that integration in identities, values, interests, institutions, and
behavior is likely to proceed only very slowly over the next decade
or more. The symbols of common nationality offer insufficient psychic
satisfactions to displace more primordial loyalties. There are not
enough mutually rewarding cross-communal interactions or structures to provide credible substitutes for existing communal loyalties.
Communal pluralism is and will remain the essential reality in Malaysian society and politics. Because of their relative parity in numbers
and in power—Chinese techno-economic strength balancing Malay
political and governmental hegemony—the communities *coexist* in a

---

8. The prevalence of zero-sum game thinking among senior Malaysian administrators is documented by Scott (1968).

condition of precarious *mutual deterrence* or unstable equilibrium. Since each community is in a position both to defend itself and to inflict unacceptable damage on· the other, there are strong incentives, particularly among leadership elements, to pursue policies of peaceful, if competitive, coexistence and mutual, if competitive, accommodation. Neither community, notwithstanding the fantasies of their more chauvinistic members, is strong enough to expel or to destroy the other without risking heavy punishment to itself, nor do the patterns of settlement make geographic partition a possibility. Thus, Malaysia seems fated to a process of competitive communal coexistence.

The governance of this delicately balanced structure provides few degrees of freedom for policy makers. Since members of each community are inordinately sensitive to threats to their existing positions, structural changes are hard to achieve, for they are likely to generate conflict along communal lines, precisely what responsible rulers are attempting to avoid. Thus, any move to displace Chinese middlemen from rural areas would be perceived by all Chinese, including ideological anticapitalists, as a hostile act, the beginning of uncompensated and unpredictable encroachments on Chinese economic positions. Any movement to redraw constituency boundaries in order to equalize urban and rural representation would cause enormous fears among Malays as an attack on their political hegemony.

The same would apply to reforms that disturb existing intracommunal social and class relations. Many Malays, especially among the educated youth, would like to reform or eliminate the Sultans and their retinues on the ground that they are retarding the social and economic development of Malays. While a revolutionary measure of this kind would be conceivable in a purely Malay political system, it is unthinkable in contemporary Malaysia because any move against the Sultans would be construed by a vast majority of politically sensitive Malays as a threat to one of the pillars of Malay hegemony, a gratuitous victory for the Chinese. Similarly, any move by Chinese workers to weaken or undermine the position of Chinese capitalists would be construed by most Chinese, including those with no special affection for the rich, as a blow at the economic position of the Chinese as a community—for, without these capitalists, who would provide jobs for Chinese and who would finance their institutions? Certainly not the Malay-controlled government.

Since structural reforms are so threatening, government must innovate on the margin or within existing structures. One improves the lot of the Malay subsistence farmer by resettlement schemes, by improved technologies, by better public services, by public works and welfare measures. One helps Chinese by promoting and subsidizing industrial expansion, which will produce the necessary employment, by public welfare services, housing, and other measures that do not impair existing structures. This does not mean that government cannot initiate structural changes—it has begun to eliminate non-Malay medium public schools and may soon undertake significant moves in public enterprise manufacturing—but that any such measures bear a load of communal consequences that may be politically destabilizing and thus require extremely careful political and administrative handling. The awareness of these conflict potentials tends to discourage political leadership in this delicately balanced coexistence-deterrence situation from embarking on major structural reforms.[9]

Political management under these conditions has an inevitably conservative bias. Political elites are confronted with the nearly incompatible tasks of aggregating and maintaining support in their own community—which implies a vigorous prosecution and defense of communally defined interests—and regulating conflict so that the polity may survive in peace—which implies the bargaining away of some of these demands in the process of compromise and accommodation. The moderation and disciplining of communal demands cannot be accomplished within a populistic framework.[10] It requires political elites who either enjoy sufficient legitimacy to discipline communal demands in the interest of the collectivity or have sufficient autonomy because of the institutional arrangements within which they work to survive and function politically even in the face of decisions which

9. The Alliance government, prior to the May 1969 riots, had followed the policy of avoiding the public discussion of communal issues, on the premise that public discussion could only be inflammatory in the Malaysian context. After the riots, this policy was changed. The government adopted the alternative premise that structured intercommunal dialogue might contribute to ventilating communal grievances and to the emergence of accommodative policies and programs. The beginnings of this dialogue are underway at the macro-governmental level in a National Consultative Council (NCC) made up of 55 leading figures from communally based organizations. A new Department of National Unity has been established in the Prime Minister's Department to study the implications of alternative policies and governmental programs for communal relations. At present this limited dialogue occurs only at the national level in a highly formal atmosphere at the infrequent meetings of the NCC.

10. Note a similar finding in the Dutch context by Lijphart (1968). He suggests that "overarching co-operation at the elite level can be a substitute for cross-cutting affiliations at the mass level."

distribute dissatisfactions among their own constituents on communally sensitive issues. It is important for politicians working under these constraints to have the support of strong and effective administrative resources which can participate in the search for accommodative policies, implement the resulting programs of action effectively, and maintain the credible capacity to enforce order.

In Malaysia the leaders of the Alliance enjoyed sufficient legitimacy and autonomy from 1955 to 1967 to function effectively in these conflicting roles. Their last important achievement was piloting into law the highly sensitive National Language Act of 1967 despite bitter opposition among both constituencies and making this delicate compromise stick. With its setback in the 1969 elections, including the collapse of the Chinese wing of the Alliance and the subsequent communal rioting, the government was compelled to restore its autonomy by superseding political with administrative structures while it searched for new patterns of legitimacy which would both guarantee Malay political hegemony and assure the Chinese that their vital interests would be protected and respected.[11]

Communal Pluralism and National Politics. Malaysia's situation epitomizes the salience of communal identities, structures, and cleavages in many modernizing societies and its importance as a variable for public policy. Although distinctive, Malaysia is in no way unique. Indeed, though the patterns vary, racial, religious, ethnic, linguistic, and tribal pluralism and tension are more the norm than the exception in developing countries. As the recent experience of the United States, Canada, Belgium, Yugoslavia, and the Soviet Union demonstrate, this phenomenon is not confined to less industrialized countries. Contrary to a long tradition in Western political theory, these primordial identities and solidary structures are not readily homogenized as nation states become mature. They are not necessarily eclipsed into irrelevance or vestigial significance by class, occupational, or ideological changes and conflicts which are supposed to be the normal and respectable issues of modern political controversy. These identities have an unexpected persistence and may even surface into political prominence after they have been long dormant: note Scottish and Breton nationalism in the United Kingdom and France.

11. Parliamentary government was restored in February 1971 with the Alliance dominated by UMNO firmly in control. Public discussion of communally sensitive issues has been limited by a sedition act designed to curb inflammatory speech or writing that might provoke communal violence.

One of the major tasks of contemporary political science is to cease regarding communal pluralism and its politics as transient, abnormal, or taboo and to study them intensively in their many manifestations. One important concern would be the implications of communal pluralism for political development; another would be the search for alternative strategies to regulate and manage this dangerous form of internal societal conflict.

REFERENCES

Arasaratnam, Sinnappah.
    1970   Indians in Malaysia and Singapore. London: Oxford University Press.
Burridge, Kennelm.
    1956   Report on Field Work in Batu Pahat, Johore. Mimeographed. University of Malaya.
Esman, Milton J.
    Forthcoming   Administration and Development in Malaysia: Institution Building and Reform in a Plural Society. Ithaca: Cornell University Press.
Lijphart, Arend.
    1968   The Politics of Accommodation. Berkeley: University of California Press.
Malaya, University of.
    1966-1967.   Eighteenth Annual Report.
Melson, Robert, and Howard Wolpe.
    1970   "Modernization and the Politics of Communalism: A Theoretical Perspective." In American Political Science Review, vol. LXIV, no. 4 (December).
The National Operations Council.
    1969   The May 13 Tragedy, a Report of the National Operations Council. Kuala Lumpur: JCK Press.
Rahman, Tunku Abdul.
    1969   May 13—Before and After. Kuala Lumpur: Utusan Melayu Press.
Roff, William.
    1967   The Origins of Malay Nationalism. University of Malaya Press.
Scott, James.
    1968   Political Ideology in Malaya. New Haven: Yale University Press.
Silcock, T. H.
    1963   "Approximate Racial Division of National Income." In The Politi-

cal Economy of Independent Malaya, by T. H. Silcock and E. K. Fisk. Berkeley: University of California Press.

Wang, Gung-wu.
1970 "Chinese Politics in Malaya." Mimeographed.

Malaysia: A Beginning at Nation-Building

PROFESSOR ESMAN has given us an impressively detailed account of the great schism in Malaysian society, of the multitudinous ways in which the Malay and Chinese communities are divided from each other. All that he says is unhappily true; and yet, such an account must surely make us wonder not why there have been sporadic outbreaks of violence in the past few years, but why there have been so few. While in no way questioning Professor Esman's facts, nor indeed his argument, I think that it is possible to look for some more positive components in the equation. "Nation building" may not have proceeded far in Malaysia, but a beginning has been made.

To only two matters do I have time to draw your attention. First, the matter of citizenship, and second, the establishment of a national education system.

During Malaya's colonial period, the British maintained intact the fiction that although the Malays were the subjects of their sultans, the immigrant Chinese and Indians were merely temporary intrusions upon the scene. It was not until after the second World War that any attempt at all was made to regularize their status and to acknowledge them as permanent residents; and in the period immediately preceding independence, the question of citizenship was the one most hotly debated by all parties. That the principle of *jus soli*—citizenship by right of birth—was written into the constitution with which Malaya became independent was an enormously important determinant of the components with which a Malayan nation would have to be built. In all the talk of cleavages between the communities, and the divisive consequences of Malay "special privileges," it is important to remember that the Chinese do share the privilege of citizenship and its responsibilities.

When the British left Malaya, their educational record there was as bad as in any British colony in the world. Few children were in government-supported schools, and those who were were irrevocably divided into quite separate language systems. Within five years of independence, most of the children of all the communities of Malaya were in schools wherein a Malayan-centered curriculum was in force, and where at least some of the Malay language was taught to children, whatever their mother tongue. While it would be naive to suppose that a national education system might be able to turn out homogenized nationals bereft of communal indicators, it seems needlessly gloomy to think that slow change cannot occur. The children of Malaya today are different from their parents, and certainly from their grandparents; and at its best, the education system can contribute something to the process of fitting them for the realities of a multiracial nation.

The final point I should wish to make briefly is that, although Professor Esman's paper purports to be about Malaysia, it is in fact confined entirely to West Malaysia—that is, to the Malay peninsula. The addition of the Bornean states of Sabah and Sarawak to the discussion greatly complicates the picture, for there the important indicator of communal distinctiveness is not so much ethnicity as religion. Granted that there are Chinese and Indian minorities present in both states, it is the line between Muslim and non-Muslim indigenes that is politically and otherwise the most significant. Building a nation to span the South China Sea is an even more formidable task than the one to which Professor Esman has addressed his paper.

❖ *Comment* JAMES L. PEACOCK

Malaysia: Cultural and Racial Meanings

I HAVE no strong criticism of Professor Esman's balanced and lucid paper, but I do wish to suggest a refinement: that he distinguish explicitly between the cultural and the racial meanings of *Malay*.

The term *Malay (orang melayu)* denotes in many contexts persons not ordinarily considered racially Malay but who practice the Muslim religion *(to masuk Melayu means both to become Malay and to enter Islam)* and who speak the Malay language. Muslim Arabs, Indians, and Pakistanis are in many contexts termed *Malays*. For example, in Singapore the so-called Malay Chamber of Commerce has an Arab as its president and a Pakistani as its vice-president. Similar instances could be found in Malaysia. And certain of the early twentieth-century Malay nationalist movements (and related Muslim movements) were led by cultural Malays who were of immediate Arab, Indian, or Pakistani ancestry. (I use the term *racial* not in the strict anthropological or genetic sense but in the sense used by Malaysians themselves when they speak of a man as being of the Arab, Indian, Pakistani, or Malay race—that is, born of a mother and father or perhaps only of a father descended from one of these groups.)

To see the analytical advantages of distinguishing between the cultural and racial meanings of *Malay*, consider the situation in Indonesia. In Indonesia, the racial Malays (whom I shall henceforth call Indonesians) are not so neatly divided from the Chinese by cultural factors as are the racial Malays in Malaya. Instead, cultural divisions cross-cut racial divisions in Indonesia. As a result, racial tensions are not so dominant a problem in Indonesia as in Malaya.[1]

Consider first religious divisions. Virtually all Malays are Muslim, but this is by no means true of all Indonesians. There are reportedly eleven million Christians in Indonesia, but only some three million Chinese. Obviously, many non-Chinese Indonesians are Christian. And of course the strongly Christian regions of Indonesia—Menado, the Toba Batak area, Ambon—are well known. No such Christian regions exist in Malaya among the Malays. In fact, in Malaya, Christians are forbidden by law to proselytize Muslims. Hence, virtually no Malays and Chinese share Christianity. Numerous Indonesians and Chinese do.

Many Indonesians and Chinese also share Buddhism; at least a trend in this direction can be observed. For example, when I attended the 1970 celebration of the Buddhist holiday of Wesak at the Buddhist monument, Borobodur, I observed ten thousand or so participants, of whom perhaps a third were Indonesian and the rest Chinese. In the Jogjakarta area, entire rural villages, wholly Indonesian, have recently converted to a certain brand of Buddhism. The Javanese have featured Hindu-Buddhist symbols for fifteen hundred years, and their "conversion" to Buddhism essentially means that their affection for these symbols is given official status by the Hindu-Buddhism department of the Indonesian Ministry of Religion. The Buddhist Chinese can participate in this system of symbols with some success, as at Wesak, where their "Buddhist" dances were simply the *srimpi* and *wajang wong* dances of traditional Javanese Hindu-Buddhism.

Just as the Indonesians are not monolithically Muslim, so is the dominant Indonesian political party, the Indonesian Nationalist party, not monolithically Muslim as is the PMIP of Malaysia or the PKM of Singapore. In fact, the symbols and ideology of the Indonesian Na-

---

1. Professor Esman's paper refers only to West Malaysia, i.e., Malaya, and so do my comments. Professor Peter Goethals, whose critical reading of my commentary I greatly appreciate, notes that the situation in East Malaysia, i.e., Borneo, more closely resembles that of Indonesia than does the situation in West Malaysia. Urbanized members of Bornean groups, such as the Dusun, Iban, and Melanau, closely resemble the Chinese physically, and they are frequently Christians. Goethals also notes that there are no Malay and Indonesian terms for *race* in the strictly biological sense; their terms (e.g., *bangsa*) always distinguish groups at least partially according to cultural features. The distinction between race and culture is thus an analytical rather than a native distinction but useful for comparison.

tionalist party are of Hindu-Buddhist inspiration.

Indonesia lacks the Muslim sultans who sustain Islam as the state religion in each of their states in Malaya. The Indonesian sultans have either abandoned their sultanates—as in Ternate or Bima—or retain only token power—as in Jogja and Solo. In any case, they embrace Hindu-Buddhism as much as Islam. They support a culture potentially more penetrable by the Chinese than the Malay-Muslim monolith bolstered by the Malay sultans.

Indonesian occupations are not divided along racial lines so much as in Malaya. Stroll around Singapore or Malacca in Malaysia and you see virtually no Malay businessmen; Chinese overwhelmingly dominate commerce and industry. Sight-see in Surabaja, Jogja, or Solo in Indonesia and you certainly see more Chinese than Indonesian enterprises, but there is a sizable number of Muslim entrepreneurs. And should you travel to Padang Pandjang, Bima, or Pekadjangan, you see a dominance of Indonesian over Chinese tradesmen.

Even skin color is more ambiguous in Indonesia than in Malaysia. For example, the pale Menadonese are regarded by their fellow Indonesians as looking like Chinese. The brown-yellow distinction is not so definitive as between the Malays and Chinese of Malaya.

A final cross-cutting pattern is kinship. Malays, with some exceptions (e.g., the Minangkabau of Negeri Sembilan), pattern their social relations and ideologies in terms of the image of the nuclear, bilateral family (consisting of parents and children). Chinese tend to pattern their lives and thoughts in terms of the model of the extended, unilineal clan (consisting of parents, children, cousins, uncles, aunts, nieces, nephews, and grandparents). The distinction in kinship patterning reflects and reinforces a general contrast in life style. That contrast is not so marked in Indonesia, where not only the Chinese live in extended, unilineal groups, but also the Batak, Minangkabau, Balinese, and others.

Primordial cultural and economic divisions thus reinforce the division between Malays and Chinese, but cross-cut the division between Indonesians and Chinese.

What are the implications of this difference? The Malaysian pattern, coupled with other conditions (e.g., the numerical balance of Chinese and Malays), encourages the Malay/Chinese conflict to assume a prominent position in the list of Malaysian tensions. The Indonesian pattern, coupled with other conditions (e.g., the numerical imbalance of Chinese and Indonesians), encourages the Indonesian/Chinese conflict to assume a lower position on the list of Indonesian tensions.

Compare the riots of May 13, 1969, in Malaya with the Gestapu affair in Indonesia of 1965—the most recent important events of violence in Malaysian and Indonesian history, respectively. The central conflict of May 13 was that between Malays and Chinese. The central conflict of Gestapu was not that between Indonesians and Chinese, though this conflict became involved, but between such groups as the army and the Communists or the Muslims and the Communists.

Thus, a comparison between Indonesia and Malaysia suggests that the relation between the cultural and racial components of the Malay group must be understood in order to understand the reasons behind racial tensions in Malaysia.

Index

The Authors

WERNER BAER
> Professor of Economics, Department of Economics and Business Administration, Vanderbilt University, Nashville, Tennessee

ERNST BORINSKI
> Chairman, Social Science Division, Tougaloo College, Tougaloo, Mississippi

ERNEST Q. CAMPBELL
> Professor of Sociology, Department of Sociology and Anthropology, Vanderbilt University, Nashville, Tennessee

MILTON J. ESMAN
> Professor of Government and Director, Center for International Studies, Cornell University, Ithaca, New York

GERRY E. HENDERSHOT
> Assistant Professor of Sociology, Vanderbilt University, Nashville, Tennessee

HARMANNUS HOETINK
> Director, Institute of Caribbean Studies, and Professor of Sociology, University of Puerto Rico, Rio Piedras, Puerto Rico

IRA KATZNELSON
> Assistant Professor of Political Science, Columbia University, New York, New York

MARTIN KILSON
> Professor of Government, Harvard University, Cambridge, Massachusetts

JOHN B. MARSHALL
> Associate Professor of Law, Vanderbilt University, Nashville, Tennessee

THOMAS E. NYQUIST
> Assistant Professor of Political Science, Department of African Studies, State University College, New Paltz, New York

JAMES L. PEACOCK
> Associate Professor of Anthropology, University of North Carolina, Chapel Hill, North Carolina

RICHARD A. PETERSON

Associate Professor of Sociology, Vanderbilt University, Nashville, Tennessee

ANSELME REMY

Associate Professor of Anthropology, Fisk University, Nashville, Tennessee

MARGARET ROFF

Southern Asia Institute, Columbia University, New York, New York

STANLAKE SAMKANGE

Professor of African History, Department of History, Harvard University, Cambridge, Massachusetts (Professor of History, Fisk University, Nashville, Tennessee, until September 1971)

JOHN SAUNDERS

Professor of Sociology, University of Florida, Gainesville, Florida

STANLEY H. SMITH

Chairman, Department of Sociology, and Dean of the College, Fisk University, Nashville, Tennessee

AUSTIN T. TURK

Professor of Sociology, Indiana University, Bloomington, Indiana

IMMANUEL WALLERSTEIN

Professor of Sociology, Department of Sociology, McGill University, Montreal, Canada (Associate Professor of Sociology, Columbia University, New York, New York, until July 1971)